IT'S ALL ABOUT
AUSTRALIA mate

IT'S ALL ABOUT

AUSTRALIA
mate

DENIS GREGORY

EXISLE
PUBLISHING

First published 2004

Exisle Publishing Limited,
PO Box 60-490, Titirangi, Auckland 1230
www.exisle.co.nz

The National Library of Australia Cataloguing-in-Publication data:
Gregory, Denis, 1938- .
It's all about Australia, mate.

ISBN 0 908988 29 X.

1. National characteristics, Australian. 2. Australia - Social life and customs.
3. Australia - Description and travel. 4. Australia - History - Anecdotes. I. Title.

994

Text design and production by *Book*NZ (www.booknz.co.nz)
Cartoons by Bruce Potter
Cover design by Dexter Fry
Printed in China through Colorcraft Ltd., Hong Kong

Contents

Introduction

A British general touring the Somme battlefront in France in World War I sees an Australian slouch hat sitting on top of an ocean of thick, sticky mud. Standing safely on a line of duckboards, he orders one of his soldiers to retrieve it, but the hat is stuck rock solid. It won't budge an inch.

Then, to their amazement, they hear a muffled Aussie voice coming from underneath the goo: 'For gawd's sake go easy, mate, I've still got the strap under me chin.'

Working feverishly to try to rescue the buried soldier, the general's men strain and pull and tug for several minutes before the muffled voice again comes through the mud: 'It's no flamin' good, mate. You'll have to leave me here. I can't get me bloody feet out of the stirrups ...'

There's nothing funny about war, of course, but from the first time the gung-ho young Aussie volunteers sailed overseas to the Sudan in 1885 to help fight for the king's empire, they had a totally different outlook on life from that of their British allies. And they were pretty special people. They had left their farms and their homes and their families to tramp hundreds of miles along dusty roads to join the army and go to war, knowing there was a better than even chance they wouldn't come back.

In fact, in the wars Australia has been involved in – all of them belonging to another country – 97,688 men and women didn't come back. Another 222,908 were wounded. In the Iraq war in 2003, more than 2000 Australians served. No troops in combat lost their lives and most came home.

The early Aussie Diggers accepted that strict army discipline was necessary, but they were never convinced that they had to continually toe the line and spend every day shackled by rules.

They were accustomed to making their own decisions, often wrong ones, and were always ready to stand by their mates, even if it meant sticking their necks out. Like the soldier struggling to carry a wounded comrade on his back to the safety of the trenches. Rifle and machine-gun fire was everywhere. 'Hey,' says the wounded man. 'How about turning around and goin' backwards for a bit? You're gettin' the medal but I'm gettin' all the bloody bullets.'

The unique Aussie sense of humour was inherited from a melting pot of previous generations – convicts, farmers, stockmen, shearers and miners from nations around the world who had pioneered the new Land Down Under. They were the ones who blazed the tracks into the inland, cleared the bush to grow the crops, mustered the stock, built the towns, performed marriages, baptised babies, wrote poetry and dreamt of riches (which most of them never saw).

Some shot and robbed each other. Others died in bushfires and floods, and some were speared by the country's traditional owners. The Australian character is a product of all those experiences. It's what makes Aussies firm believers in the principle of a 'fair go'.

Australia is a nation built on adversity but balanced by a unique sense of humour, which has so many times been confused with so-called ockerism. Australian society has changed considerably since the late 1960s, when our image was as a nation of chauvinistic beer swillers, bigots and loudmouths.

We've come a long way since then. Some might even describe us as sophisticated now, even though we're still unsure whether to scrap the ocker image altogether or keep it alive.

But who cares? We're what we are. We're what other people think of us. If visitors are confused by our lifestyle and diversity, so be it.

We're proud of the way we live, our sporting prowess, our icons, our movie stars and our characters. This book is all about that.

1 A snapshot

The 'fair go' philosophy Australians love to promote led to a bitter battle at the Eureka gold diggings, near the Victorian town of Ballarat, on 3 December 1854, when around 300 miners stood up for their rights against 275 armed soldiers and police.

The miners, led by a bloke named Peter Lalor, were a mixture of Australians, American adventurers, Irish patriots, European exiles and supporters of English Chartism (a democratic reform movement). And although they were protected only by a log stockade and armed with long wooden sticks with pointed metal heads, they were prepared – having sworn an oath to their mates – to die for their cause in what turned out to be a brief skirmish, later described as 'the death knell of tyranny'.

A month earlier the miners, their Southern Cross flag fluttering proudly overhead, had set up the Ballarat Reform League as a forum for their grievances, which included (among other things) being ripped off by authorities who forced them to pay 30 shillings a month for a mining licence regardless of whether or not they struck it rich, the very strict policing of the goldfields and continual harassment by troopers. The miners included a group of American revolutionaries who wanted to scrap the British connection and form the five-star Republic of Victoria.

The battle of Eureka was short-lived, but 34 miners and five soldiers lost their lives in it. Lalor was wounded, and later had an arm amputated, but went on to become a Member of the Victorian Parliament. He also refused a knighthood.

But the miners' stand sped up the introduction of the political reforms they wanted and helped the campaign for nationhood. The vision of a republic faded, but

Eureka is still a symbol of unity and its message is seen as the heart of the Australian tradition: the willingness to fight for freedom and democratic rights.

The first representative government in Australia came with the Australian Colonies Act. But by then, the States, or colonies as they were known, were already rivals and intensely jealous of each other. They had their independence, and weren't about to give it up, so they simply carried on as usual, putting their own interests first. This resulted in separate postal systems and different policies on immigration, transport, communications, trade and tariff, which obviously confused every bugger. Even the trains had to stop at State borders because the rail lines were all of a different gauge. It was not until January 2004 that the first goods train running on a new $1.2 billion railway line between Alice Springs and Darwin completed the national rail network. The Ghan tourist train now carries passengers between Adelaide and Darwin, taking about 48 hours for the 2979 kilometre trip. The other trans-continental train, the Indian Pacific, runs between Sydney and Perth.

The working classes, people of all nationalities who had come to Australia to try their luck on the goldfields or raise a few cattle or sheep, were not satisfied with the slow growth of the colonial self-government, which was dominated by the rich and influential squatters. They wanted more, like the right to vote and secret ballots.

But it was the annoying problems of inter-colonial tariffs, as well as the need to have an army for protection and a common immigration policy that finally led to more unity. At one stage, for example, Victoria imposed a bounty on ships bringing in Chinese immigrants. The shipping companies responded by dropping them off at Robe, in South Australia, and they had to walk to the Victorian goldfields.

At this time, NSW believed in free trade. The Premier in 1888, John Robertson, referred to his southern neighbour as the 'cabbage garden' and once commented that 'those bloody people across the Murray River grow the same as us but all they can do is send us bloody cabbages'.

Victoria, on the other hand, wanted to use protection to develop its own local industries, so it set up Customs houses along the Murray, the boundary between the two colonies, to collect a few bob in taxes from NSW farmers who wanted to take their produce to Victorian markets. They didn't appreciate having to kick the tin every time they crossed the river, so they too began to push for a federation.

NSW Premier Henry Parkes, on a visit to Tenterfield, in northern NSW – this town has some claim to being the birthplace of federation – campaigned for governments to co-operate more with each other. He eventually talked the colonial premiers into getting together at a meeting, at which they agreed to hold a conference to frame a constitution for a federation. But although this was done, an economic depression in 1891 put the skids under the plan and nothing happened.

Edmund Barton, who went on to become Australia's first Prime Minister, was another champion of federation, and in late 1892 he went to the NSW border towns of Corowa and Albury to promote the formation of federation leagues, organisations that would work towards creating a federation. One was formed at Corowa in January 1893. Its aim was to use free trade to promote the need for federation; other towns followed suit.

The Berrigan league suggested that a conference be held at Corowa of 'citizens eager for action', so the courthouse was booked for the day and shopkeepers and businesspeople, federation leagues, the Australian Natives Association and NSW and Victorian governments were invited. Special trains ran from Sydney and Melbourne and people arriving in Corowa were welcomed by banners declaring 'Advance Australia'.

Victorian Premier JB Patterson made the comment: 'When a man from Victoria is regarded [as] a foreigner in Corowa and a woman who goes to Wahgunyah on the other side of the river is treated like a smuggler, it is time some change is made …'

After a few more meetings and a lot of talk, a draft constitution was drawn up and approved by the people in referendums in 1898 and 1899. The Commonwealth of Australia was constituted by an Act of the British Parliament in July 1900, and on 17 September 1900, Queen Victoria signed a proclamation to inaugurate the Federation of Australia, which took effect from 1 January 1901.

Under the Australian Constitution, the State Governments didn't lose their identities, and the powers the Founding Fathers took from them and gave to the new Federal Government were a compromise. Trade and commerce among the States took pride of place, and only two of the new Commonwealth's powers – assistance to some industries by tariff or bounty and the provision of social services – went against the concept of a free-market economy. So things were up and running. Australia at last was fair dinkum about becoming a nation.

Social advances in the first few years after Federation included women getting the vote, the introduction of workers' compensation and invalid and old-age pensions, the selection of Canberra as the site for the national capital, the installation of electric street lighting in Sydney (16 years after the country towns of Young and Tamworth had installed it), the demonstration of the first life-saving reel at Bondi Beach, and the making of Australia's, perhaps the world's, first full-length feature film, *The Story of the Kelly Gang*.

Life rolled along nicely as the nation developed, but it took one of Australia's biggest and most tragic military losses – in 1915 at Gallipoli, a little-known peninsula on Turkey's southern coast – to really create a national spirit. Soldiers of the Australian and New Zealand Army Corps, now referred to as the Anzacs, were mowed down in their hundreds as they stormed the beaches to try to drive the Turks out of their strongholds on the hilltops.

The Australian commanders, seeing how hopeless the situation was, wanted to get out of there as fast as they could, but the British ordered them to stay put. The Anzacs fought on courageously for eight months, losing more than 10,000 soldiers, before they were finally told to pack up and leave. Some people still believe the British deliberately sent them to their maker to keep the Turks occupied while an attack was launched elsewhere, but it was more likely just another tactical stuff-up.

Anzac Day, 25 April, is now a national holiday to honour all Australians who died in wars. Street marches are held in every town and city throughout the nation, followed by services of remembrance, official luncheons and the traditional coin-tossing gambling game of two-up. There's talk of Anzac Day becoming Australia's national day but nothing has come of it yet. People are probably too obsessed with sport to bother.

Surveys have shown that two-fifths of Australians play some sort of sport and three-quarters of the population watch it, with the major interests being football, cricket, swimming, golf, netball, basketball and athletics. A few million punters spend their Saturdays betting on the gallopers, the harness races or the dogs. And the Melbourne Cup is the only horse race in the world that can bring a nation to a standstill.

But as well as a good deal of passive participation, Aussies have also built up an international reputation for their sporting prowess, which started with the bare-knuckled boxers of the convict days, an attraction for huge crowds on the outskirts of Sydney. Boxing was legalised in the 1870s and gloves were then required to be worn, under the Marquess of Queensberry's rules.

The first real taste of big-time boxing didn't come until 1908, when more than 30,000 people in Sydney watched a world heavyweight title fight between Canadian Tommy Burns and American challenger Jack Johnson. The much taller and heavier Johnson belted the ears off Burns and police were forced to stop the one-sided contest.

Les Darcy was thought by many to be the greatest fighter Australia has produced, but he copped lots of unkind criticism when he went to America in 1917 to have a crack at the world heavyweight title rather than enlist in the Army. World War I was in full swing, and thousands of young Australians were dying on the western front. Darcy, labelled a deserter at home, was also shunned by American promoters. He later died in hospital in Memphis, from infections from a mouth wound.

Denver Post journalist Otto Floto wrote that Darcy's physical self could not repel the charge that he ran away when his country called him, and then fell victim to a sickness that would have caused him no concern had he been himself. Back in Sydney, thousands turned out at Darcy's funeral to pay their last respects to the legend who had knocked up 46 wins from 50 bouts.

Tennis player Norman Brookes, who dominated the game for nearly 20 years, was the first Aussie to win Wimbledon, and helped take the Davis Cup off the United

States in 1907. Jack Crawford was the darling of the 1930s, along with Harry Hopman, who coached 14 Davis Cup teams and fired up stars like Ken Rosewall and Lew Hoad.

Other stars of Australian tennis, Rod Laver, John Newcombe, Neale Fraser, Rod Emerson, Pat Cash and Lleyton Hewitt (in 2002) were Wimbledon winners, some of them three times. In the women's game, Margaret Court and Evonne Goolagong (later Cawley) were the queens of Australian tennis.

Our swimmers also have an enviable reputation. Fred Lane in Paris in 1900 was the first Australian to win an Olympic gold medal, and superfish Kieren Perkins turned in one of the greatest performances seen in the pool when he stormed home to take gold in the 1500 metre freestyle event at the 1996 Atlanta Olympics after the critics had written him off. He followed that up with silver in the same event at the Sydney 2000 Olympics, and then retired. His world record lasted 7 years, until it was smashed by an amazing 7 seconds by Grant Hackett at the 2001 World Championships in Japan.

Perkins, one of the greatest distance swimmers in history, was in Japan as a TV reporter for the championships, and as he was about to board a media boat to take him to the women's open water event, a concerned Japanese official told him to put on a lifejacket – he could fall out of the boat and drown!

Ian Thorpe is well on the way to becoming one of the greatest swimmers of all time. As a 15-year-old, he was the youngest male world record holder. At 18 he had chalked up 8 world titles and a string of records. He won a record 6 gold medals at the 2001 World Championships.

At the 2003 Australian championships, Thorpe won the 100, 200 and 400 metre freestyle events, the 200 metre individual medley, and then backed up as a member of the 4 x 200 metre relay to win that event as well. Little wonder they call him Thorpedo.

Being constantly compared with other great Australian swimmers like Dawn Fraser, Thorpe says his judgement day will come at the end of his career. That's when people can make comparisons. But thank goodness he didn't go ahead with his childhood plans to be a fireman or an astronaut.

Speedway, or dirt track racing, is an Australian invention. It began in NSW at the Maitland Agricultural Show in 1925, and 3 years later was introduced to England. In 1930 the first Australia versus England Test match took place.

Boomerang throwing and woodchopping are another two sports that originated in Australia. Boomerang throwing was an ancient Aboriginal way of killing game but is now a sport run under rules set down by the Boomerang Association of Australia. The first organised woodchopping event took place in Tasmania in 1891.

Australia's most offbeat athlete was William King, known as The Flying Pieman. King was a schoolteacher at Sutton Forest, in the NSW southern highlands, and then a barman in Sydney before he turned his hand to making pies, which he sold on the streets, while elegantly dressed in knee-breeches and stockings, white shirt and top hat.

In September 1847 King walked 192 miles (307 km) non-stop around the racecourse in the Hunter Valley town of Maitland, in 46 hours 30 minutes. Two months later, at the back of Maitland's Fitzroy pub, he had no difficulty in walking 1000 quarter-miles in 1000 quarter-hours.

In December 1847 The Flying Pieman set himself 1 hour 30 seconds to run a mile (1.6 km), walk a mile, wheel a barrow half a mile, pull a trotting gig with a woman in it for half a mile, walk half a mile backwards, pick up 50 stones and perform 50 leaps. He allowed himself 5 minutes 15 seconds rest, and did all the tasks with 45 seconds to spare.

The following month, at Dungog in northern NSW, he carried a live goat weighing 80 pounds (32 kg) a mile and a half in 12 minutes. And while on a trip to Queensland, he walked from Brisbane to Ipswich, a distance of about 25 miles (40 km), carrying a pole weighing 100 pounds (40 kg) – and beat the mail coach by an hour. Twice he beat the mail coach from Sydney to Windsor, a distance of about 36 miles (58 km).

While most of our modern-day athletes restrict themselves to the more traditional endeavours, Australians still dream up dozens of offbeat challenges. Tom Hayllar, of Sydney, walked 12,000 km around Australia, starting on 1 March 1975 and finishing on 25 January 1976. He also walked from Cape Byron, on the NSW north coast, to Steep Point, in Western Australia, a distance of 5672 km, in less than four months.

Marathon runner Pat Farmer completed a 14,500 km run around Australia on 1 January 2000. The 191 day run, designed to draw attention to Australia's Centenary of Federation in 2001, broke 13 world records.

Farmer had earlier run 379 km non-stop across more than 1000 towering sand dunes in the Simpson Desert in blistering 55°C (130°F) heat from Alka Seltzer Bore to the Birdsville pub in three days, 17 hours and 38 minutes. Each day he ate 10 tins of fruit, a couple of dozen bananas and drank 30 litres of water.

Farmer describes himself as an ordinary Australian doing extraordinary things. His run was inspired by Donald Mackay, who in 1900 completed a 240 day bicycle ride around Australia to mark the coming Federation. Farmer is now a federal Member of Parliament.

In April 1983, Cliff Young, who was then 61, won the ultra-marathon 870 km run from Melbourne to Sydney, covering the distance in five days, 15 hours and four minutes. Potato farmer and bachelor, Young shuffled rather than ran; his training was chasing the cows around his paddocks in gumboots. Young died in 2003.

In the small township of Mirrool, in southwest NSW, only three footballers have been able to kick a ball over the top of a wheat silo 29.8 metres high from a circle 10 metres from the base. Many others have tried, but all have failed. The first to do it was Geelong Australian Rules player Bill Brownless, who stopped there on the way to a wedding and punted the ball over the silo in bare feet.

Golfers Billy Dunk and Ted Ball planned to play the world's longest golf hole, 1,460,800 metres. They intended to tee off at Ceduna Golf Club, in South Australia, and play across the Nullarbor Plain, finishing at the 18th at Kalgoorlie Golf Club, in Western Australia, 1461 kilometres away.

Dunk, five times Australian PGA champion, and fellow World Cup player Ball, were to hit alternate shots in the attempt to beat the par, which was 7173. The Great Australian Bight, police stations, hotels, homesteads and Aboriginal burial grounds were to be out of bounds.

A ball landing near a sleeping kangaroo, dingo, emu or snake could be lifted and dropped no nearer Kalgoorlie without penalty. The feat attracted widespread interest but never went ahead because a sponsor couldn't be found.

Australians also love doing other strange things, like seeing how far they can push a bathtub on wheels (497 km in 24 hours, as it turns out), carry a brick in one hand or throw a custard pie or rabbit trap. They've walked 82.9 km under water, raced over 1.6 km carrying a bag of potatoes, and pushed a wheelbarrow 14,500 km, all in the name of achievement.

In fact, Australians have been on top of the world heap in more than 60 sporting events. Among them have been high-profile performers like Greg Norman and Karrie Webb in golf, Jack Brabham and Alan Jones in Formula One motor racing and Wayne Gardner and Mick Doohan in motorcycling, but few people know that Aussies have been world champions in many lower profile events as well – woodchopping, saddle bronc riding, windsurfing, yachting, water skiing, triathlon, ten pin bowling, squash, shooting, trampolining and underwater hockey.

Australia's wealthiest households are typically DINKS (double income, no kids). They pay nearly four times as much tax as the average and have private health insurance although they are generally healthy. They take overseas holidays every 2 years, and when they do have kids, they send them to private schools. They eat in restaurants at least once a week and like new cars and motorbikes.

The national median weekly income is between $700 and $799 for households. A typical family in the top income range is a two-income couple with no children, both working fulltime and pulling in a combined post-tax income of around $1815 a week.

The median monthly housing loan repayment is between $800 and $999 nationally, but Sydneysiders are paying between $1200 and $1399.

Australians in the top income range spend around $170 a week on recreation and entertainment, another $170 on food and soft drinks, including $70 for restaurants and takeaways, and $30 on alcohol.

They have several credit cards, but pay off their bills in full each month to avoid having to pay interest on them. They spend about $3000 a year on a holiday, employ a cleaner who comes in once a fortnight, and hire someone to mow the lawns in summer.

The average family doesn't do quite so well. They earn $785 a week, spend $120 on food and soft drinks, which includes $31 on restaurant and takeaway meals.

The most popular names Australians in 2003 called their girls were Emily, Jessica, Chloe, Isabella, Sarah, Sophie, Olivia, Georgia, Grace, Hannah, Ella and Emma. The most popular boys' names were Joshua, Lachlan, Jack, Thomas, Ethan, James, Daniel, Nicholas, William, Benjamin, Matthew and Liam.

So that's it in a nutshell. Australians, once called Cornstalks because they were generally taller and thinner than the immigrants, are a unique lot. Some of the crazy things they do are probably a sort of relief from the contrasts of everyday life: drought one day, floods the next, and bushfires the day after that.

And although today's Aussie might be a bit rough around the edges, still a little rebellious and often wary of authority, the offbeat humour and sense of fair play and achievement are still well and truly there.

2   Aussie talk

Australians hopelessly misuse, maltreat, debase, distort and stuff up the English language every day. But to get the message across, whether it's rhyming slang like having a 'pig's ear' (beer) at the 'rubbidy', (rub-a-dub, pub), or being gobsmacked or going ballistic, you've got to conform. And each generation of Australians speaks and writes differently, so keeping up with the latest lingo is a never-ending challenge.

But struth, the future's looking crook for true Aussie English. Blokes once chased sheilas, sausages were snags, and if you went somewhere on shank's pony, you were walking. A town was 'the smoke', and your mate was a cobber.

The native tongue is now giving in to foreign imports, and words creeping into our vocabulary include woo hoo (bewdy), outta here (skedaddle), wuss (sook) and flake (ratbag). 'Cool' and 'awesome' can be used for almost anything by young 'uns.

Other new buzz words brought on by fashion and technology include cargo pants, body art, dot coms, chat rooms and provider numbers. All those have now made it into the dictionary. A mouse potato is an internet junkie, and a cyberchondriac haunts internet medical sites.

But everyday Aussie talk is still infectious and will survive, because with only a few words – like g'day, owyagoin', orright? hotenuforyer? (or, in winter, colenuforyer?), fair dinkum, she'll be right, give it a go, bewdy, goodonya, no worries, fairenuf, absolutely, seeya and catch ya – Australians can hold a sensible conversation. In fact, the way we love to twist, make up, join and shorten words and phrases has almost reached the stage where people who 'talk proper' would be totally misunderstood.

Once you get out of the big cities and the trendy subcultures, people can still be up the creek without a paddle, flat out like a lizard drinking, game as Ned Kelly, bald as a bandicoot, as dry as a dead dingo's donger, mad as a cut snake, silly as a square wheel, pissed as a parrot, touchy as a mallee bull in a bog, lower than a snake's belly, and dressed up like a pox doctor's clerk. We still love to crack a few coldies while watching the footy on the telly, and we'll be back in a flash, in like Flynn, out like a light, or done like a dinner.

Busier than a one-armed paper hanger, right as rain or round the twist, we work as pen pushers, fat cats, shiny bums, wharfies, cockies, brickies, posties, coppers, chalkies, truckies and garbos. We're bugged by mozzies and blowies, especially if we're having a barbie in the backyard.

We eat cornies for brekky, take sangers to work for smoko and have a cuppa for crib in the arvo. We bet big bickies on the nags, the pan lickers and the red hots (trots) and like a flutter on the pokies.

When things are OK, Bob's yer uncle, she'll be right, we've got the game by the throat or we're rolling in clover. When our nose is out of joint, we're likely to bung on a blue, do the lolly, spit the dummy or chuck a spas.

When something happens that brings tears to the eyes, we wouldn't have missed it for quids. That's if we haven't shot through, taken a powder, done a runner or a moonlight flit.

Several generations of Aussie kids have now grown up not knowing the meaning of good old ocker words like drongo (a slow-witted person, named after a racehorse that never won), lair (a flashily dressed young man of brash behaviour), ridgy-didge (true), yakka (work) and geezer (an odd character).

And worse, men now are more likely to be guys instead of blokes, because of the American influence on our lives. But 'bloke' is hanging on, and still appears in Australia's *Macquarie Dictionary*. There is a difference between them, though: while a young guy might be attractive to girls, a good bloke is more likely to be strong, and someone who stands by his mates.

Macquarie has also retained 'sheila' after its publisher and executive editor, Susan Butler, read a piece in a newspaper column about gender signs on toilet doors that included: 'A little bloke wearing strides and a sheila in a frock …' She had thought sheila had become obsolete, but decided it should keep its place in the dictionary – along with dunny, dinky-di and dinkum.

The *Australian Concise Oxford Dictionary* has added a string of new words teenagers use, like mosh (dancing in a violent manner involving colliding with others and head banging), himbo (a sexually attractive but unintelligent young man), babelicious (sexually attractive) and bodacious (remarkable, excellent). Dictionary editor Dr Bruce Moore says the new words give an interesting insight into changes taking place in Australian society. He says that while people often think that new words come from advances in science and technology, societal changes and teenage culture also play a big part. Teen terms from the entertainment scene, like grunge and rave, are now officially recognised.

What's more odd is the influence of our colloquialism on Americans. Common Aussie terms like 'no worries', 'walkabout' and 'aggro' are being regularly used by the Yanks; they are probably copying Australian movies and TV shows like Steve Irwin's *Crocodile Hunter* series.

Older Aussies were masters at making up colloquialisms, or rhyming slang, although neither is distinctively Australian. Both these forms of language use words and phrases that are simple substitutions for the normal word, in order to create more effect, attract more attention, be more personal, more blunt or more amusing: she had a great pair of bacon and eggs (legs), talking on the dog and bone (phone), it's time to hit the frog and toad (road), he's a blinky bill (dill) or having hols in steak and kidney (Sydney) on your Pat Malone (own).

One chooses not to use the word shark – it's a Noah's ark. Then that's shortened to Noah's. So Noah's becomes the word for shark. Doing a Harold is another. It comes from drowned Prime Minister Harold Holt (bolt), and means to run away.

There's eighteen, from eighteen pence (fence), giving someone the Murray, from Murray cod (the nod), drawing money from the J Arthur, from J Arthur Rank (bank), or meeting your China, from China plate (mate) at the airs and graces (races). Newer colloquialisms now added to the *Macquarie Dictionary* include Stuart Diver (survivor) and full monty (taking all your clothes off, originally a British term made popular by a movie, and now widely used in Australia.)

The Aussie crooner who sang the *Neighbours* TV soap theme song, Barry Crocker, has also worked his way into the dictionary, thanks to TV football commentator Paul 'Fatty' Vautin. A 'barry' is defined as a mistake or error in judgement, especially in sport, or an act of bad play. Also, there is the Barry Crocker (shocker): 'What a terrible kick. He's having a Barry Crocker …'

Aussies use other types of substitutions, too, particularly metaphors – names or terms that are not applicable. An old car is called a bomb or a rust bucket, an off-road vehicle a paddock basher, a pushbike a treadley and a poker machine a one-armed bandit. Too much of something is a welter, a sentimental novel or film is a tear-jerker, a mess is a dog's breakfast and an appeal for a fair go is a fair suck of the sausage, saveloy or sauce bottle.

Painter and author Alistair Morrison, who died in 1998, observed that Australians spoke not English but a language called Strine, which is made up of comic transliterations of speech. A terrace house becomes a 'terror souse' and a sandwich becomes a 'semmitch'. Better known as the scholarly Professor Afferbeck Lauder (say it aloud and you'll get it!), of Strine Studies at the University of Sinny, his first book, *Let Stalk Strine*, presented his language theory to the world.

Some examples of Strine include the popular breakfast dishes of baked necks, emma necks, scremblex and fright shops. Garment is an invitation to 'garment seamy anile seward icon do'.

Jess tefter means it is necessary to, as in: 'She'll jess tefter get chews twit.' Spin-ear mitch means much alike or closely resembling one another as in: 'He's the spin-ear mitch of his father.'

The device keeping the house cool in summer is an egg nisher, while laura norder is something maintained by police. You can live in a gloria soame and be interested in the yarts. A sly drool is used for calculations.

Professor Afferbeck Lauder recalled the day English author Monica Dickens was autographing copies of one of her books in a Sydney store. A woman handed her a copy and said, 'Emma chissit.' Thinking it was her name, Ms Dickens wrote it in the dedication. It could only happen in Ostraya!

Voice-recognition technology backs up Strine. An editorial in the *Canberra Times* quoted the Prime Minister as saying: 'One Nation supporters are average astray aliens.' What the paper meant to say was 'One Nation supporters are average Australians', but its subeditors missed the blue.

A columnist in Sydney's *Daily Telegraph* was caught hook line and sinker when he published a letter from a reader about the Canberra Press Gallery's infamous practice of 'ottering', which he claimed was sliding head first on the stomach down a flight of stairs. He signed the letter Alexander Farr-Carnell. (Think about that.)

'Mate' is probably one of the best-known Aussie words. It first meant a partner in an enterprise, but as a republican mood emerged on the goldfields, more emphasis was put on equality. Then in World War I mates became Diggers, giving the word a national overtone.

Mate still has plenty of flavour. It's used to describe an associate or friend, but is also a popular form of address among men as in 'How are you going, mate?' It's also handy when you can't remember someone's name – you simply call them mate. Sometimes it's also used in an unfriendly sense, like 'Watch it, mate ...'

Women never used to be mates. They were the missus, the better half, the girlfriend, the sheila or the old boiler, but never a mate. That's changing now, as the traditional Australian notion of mateship – doing favours for each other and making sure you buy the beers when it's your shout – is gradually being broken down. Women now can be mates. In fact, according to research, an Aussie bloke's best friend is a woman.

It's interesting to note that some men don't like being called mate. Paul Harvey-Greene wrote to the Sydney *Sun Herald* newspaper to protest about its increasing use in shops and other retail outlets. He said he didn't want servility, just a little civility. What upset him was male shop assistants asking, 'Waddaya want, mate?' The reply 'I am not your mate' provoked outrage, he said.

'You old bastard' and 'you old bugger' are still affectionate terms of greeting. Then there's the more international 'fuck'. The NSW Supreme Court ruled that the language of a police sergeant who repeatedly used 'fuck' while at work at Sydney's Blacktown police station was not legally offensive. The judge said there was no evidence that people in the public area were ever offended, 'not that the public area was frequented by gentle old ladies or convent girls …'

The decision upset the then Police Minister Paul Whelan, who said that if the judge's decision went unchallenged it would make police stations unacceptable workplaces. 'Bullies, harassers and incompetents will rule in an environment where obscenities are acceptable management tools,' he said. 'Such behaviour may be acceptable in the Court of Appeal, but it will no longer be tolerated in the NSW Police Service.'

A Sydney magistrate also dismissed an offensive language charge against a man who told police to 'fuck off', saying that because he had used a non-threatening tone, it was not offensive in this day and age. A magistrate from the NSW regional centre of Dubbo also let off a man on the same charge – he said the word had to be judged on community standards.

Magistrate Robert Abood, in Sydney's Downing Centre Local Court, said a day didn't go by when the word was not used, either as a noun, a verb or an adjective. People used it without second thought and it was part and parcel of everyday conversations, he said.

The Supreme Court set out to determine the meaning of the word 'tart' as it was allegedly used by Australian Olympic cycling coach Charlie Walsh when describing Barcelona gold medallist Kathy Watt. Watt sued for defamation, claiming that Walsh had tried to 'disgrace, discredit and belittle' her when he supposedly called her 'a little tart' in an address to the Adelaide Press Club. The matter was settled.

Former deputy president of the Senate Sue West pulled up Senator Ron Boswell after he called Senator Chris Schacht a 'drop kick'. Was it unparliamentary language? Boswell didn't think so, but it was left to the then Senate President Margaret Reid to decide.

Senator Reid later confirmed the ruling. She consulted the *Macquarie Dictionary* definition of 'drop kick', which is rhyming slang for 'prick' when used to describe someone, and said that it equated to being 'obnoxious', which would be clearly offensive and unparliamentary when applied to a senator.

Senator Schacht was in trouble himself a few weeks later when he remarked that 'life's a bitch' for Treasury staff. Senator Ian Campbell asked for a ruling on whether use of the word 'bitch' was parliamentary language and after a short argument, Senator Schacht agreed to withdraw it. Nearing the end of his term in 2002, Senator Schacht used 'fuck' in debate. He used the English translation for the name of the banned film *Baise-Moi* in a speech criticising the government's handling of film censorship. 'If I said the translation is now *Fuck Me*, is that in order?' he asked. Senator Reid asked him to withdraw the word, which he did.

In the Queensland Parliament, Premier Peter Beattie got the thumbs up from the Speaker after he said: 'Is it my fault the bloody clerk's office lost it?' A Liberal MP objected, but the Speaker found there was no case to answer. Beattie said use of the word 'was in the Anzac tradition ...'

Pizza Hut caused a stir when it told all its customers to get stuffed. And the company spent $6 million doing it. A plane towing a giant 'Get Stuffed' flag flew over Sydney and its beaches, and huge billboards were put up around the city. Travellers arriving at Sydney Airport were greeted by outdoor ads that said 'Welcome to Sydney, now you can get stuffed.'

The cheeky promotion was to launch a new stuffed-crust pizza, and the company said it was aimed at injecting some excitement into a pizza market that had become boring and price-focused. Pizza Hut didn't think the campaign was offensive, just 'very Australian ...'

Australians are mad on making up acronyms, words formed from the initial letters of other words. A lot of them come from the public service, university academics, and newspapers whose editors like to shorten words to make them fit in headings.

Some examples of the awful results are CHOGM (Commonwealth Heads of Government meeting), ABARE (Australian Bureau of Agricultural and Resource Economics), AUSLIG (Australian Surveying and Land Information Group), RIBES (Rural Industries Business Extension Service), LEAP (Land and Environment Action Plan), WAMP (water allocation management plan) and EPIRB (emergency position indicating radio beacon). In 2003 we were introduced to SARS, the deadly flu called severe acute respiratory syndrome.

Wowser, used to describe a prudish teetotaller or killjoy, is popularly believed to have originated as an acronym for the slogan, 'We Only Want Social Evils Remedied', first used in the *Sydney Truth* in October 1899 by the paper's owner and politician John Norton. It was used in the heading 'Willoughby Wowsers Worried'.

Two organisations with apt acronyms are the Far North Regional Obstetrics and Gynaecological Service (FROGS) and the South Pacific Regional Obstetrical and Gynaecological Society (SPROGS). A wine and food group from Cowra, Orange and Mudgee called itself COME. Even good old Kentucky Fried Chicken is now known as KFC.

Politicians, bureaucrats, businesspeople and human resources managers are experts on gobbledegook. They use words like 'downsizing' when they mean sack, 'at this point of time' when they mean now, 'gainful employment' when they mean work, 'outsourcing' when they mean giving their employees' jobs to someone else and 'down the track' when they mean soon.

They run things by you, talk about windows of opportunity, use ballpark figures, make benchmark decisions, ratchet up rafts of overviews, aim for the cutting edge and sign off on contracts. Waffle like that is enough to send you round the bend.

Then there are the so-called politically correct words. In George Orwell's novel, *1984*, Winston Smith's job in the Ministry of Truth was to get rid of words and phrases in books and newspapers that were unacceptable to Big Brother (or should we say 'Big Person'?) and replace them with Newspeak. He was a member of the word police.

Well, George can roll over. The year of Newspeak is well and truly here. In the public service we now have access holes instead of manholes, letter carriers instead of postmen, adulthood instead of manhood, milk deliverers instead of milkmen and bushpersons instead of bushmen.

Fishermen have gone – they're fisherpersons – and no-man's land has become wilderness. Non-expert is another Newspeak replacement for the ideologically dangerous layman.

And if you can't master (whoops, sorry, 'become skilled at') Newspeak, look out. Advertising for an employee or tenant of a specific sex carries a $5000 fine for a newspaper or company and $1000 for a 'person'.

Strangely, it's OK to advertise for a 'female stripper', but not OK to ask for a 'storeman'. Advertising for a waitress is also out.

Notwithstanding all that nonsense, some pretty famous Aussies have said some bloody silly things. Former Prime Ministers Bob Hawke and Paul Keating often put their foot in their mouths. Bob Hawke's fabled affinity with people took a dive when he told a 74-year-old pensioner: 'I don't know what you're talking about, you silly old bugger.'

But Michael Patkin, a retired surgeon in the South Australia city of Whyalla, where the infamous one-liner was delivered, suggested that a statue be put up to commemorate the quote. He said the 'silly old bugger statue' could become as well known as Gundagai's Dog on the Tucker Box and Sydney's Opera House.

Paul Keating's comment to Bob Hawke that Australia was 'the arse-end of the world' still haunts him. But few can match former Australian Labor Party (ALP) leader Arthur 'Cocky' Calwell, who told the Federal Parliament in 1947, when debating immigration policy, that 'two wongs don't make a white'. He also described Larry Anthony, father of former National Party leader Doug Anthony and a long-time National Party MP, who looked vaguely Chinese, as 'the chink in the Government's armour'.

To be fair, Calwell explained (in his memoirs) that the 'wong' quip was not intended as a racial slur, but was a play on the name of the then federal Member for Balaclava, Thomas White.

Former boxer and Liberal candidate Rocky Gattellari stood against Labor's Reba Meagher in the Sydney seat of Cabramatta in the NSW elections and told millions of viewers on national TV that he was going to 'kick the shit out of her'. But Reba Meagher romped in and Gattellari's political career didn't get off the ground.

And what about Sir Les Patterson, Australia's cultural attaché to the Court of St James and honorary Minister for the Yarts, explaining royal protocol after Prime Minister Paul Keating touched the Queen during her Australian tour (in 1992): 'You've got to have a bit of a chat with the Queen before you stick your hand up her frock. It's called foreplay ...'

Former Queensland Premier Joh Bjelke-Petersen, who once described himself as a bushfire out of control, was an excellent mincer of the language. As he said himself: 'The secret of my success is that I don't beat about the bush and say exactly what I mean.' Some of his memorable quotes include: 'If you fly with the crows, squawk like a crow and look like a crow, you can't yell out if you get shot at.' Or 'I would like to thank the men and women all over Queensland who have been working together with their husbands.'

And when he was on the campaign trail in a failed attempt to become Prime Minister: 'It's been said the wheels are coming off. Well, I said you want to watch out because you'll get run over. The wheels are still on and it's going to keep going and anyone who gets in the way and tries to stop us, we'll just run them over.'

What about this gem: 'Who wants to stick together with them and get your stick feet? You know, if you get, stick foot on sticky paper, you get both of them on, you fall over and Mr Hawke asks us to stick with him. You put your foot on sticky with him, his and Keating, his government's got their feet on sticky paper, my word they have.'

Chewie-stretching Kylie Mole, the TV schoolgirl alter ego of actress Maryanne Fahey, thought everyone was a bogan, which is her description of a dag, an untidy person or a person who lacks style, and that's 'roolly spac'.

The Victorian *Footy Show* compere Sam Newman decided to sell one of his Melbourne homes at West St Kilda because of attacks by vandals who often pelted it and its Pamela Anderson mural with eggs and rocks. Newman told a newspaper: 'Bogans and pisspots, the people who generally frequent the community, are making it hard for those who live here.'

Aussies excel in making up nicknames. What about the wharfie who was called Judge because he was always sitting on a case? Then there was his mate Perry Mason. He handled only one case a week. A drover called Eighty Mile Mick got Seventy-nine Mile Mick for short.

A tall, thin girl whose initials were HB is likely to be called Pencil; all big blokes are Tiny; and people with red hair are Bluey. Two boys from a country family in the small town of Lyndhurst were called Dingbat and Wombat. When a third brother came along, they called him Cricket Bat.

Autumn Leaves is the nickname for a motorcyclist who keeps falling off, and tall, lanky people are called beanpoles. Our first Prime Minister, Edmund Barton, was called Tosspot Toby because he liked fine food and wine. Bob Hawke was the Silver Bodgie, and Alfred Deakin, another former Prime Minister, was Affable Alf.

Rugby league players get the oddest nicknames, for no apparent reason. Newcastle's Andrew Johns is Joey, Sydney Roosters' Brad Fittler is Freddie, and NSW State of Origin coach Phil Gould is Gus.

People in the Northern Territory call their orange overall-wearing Emergency Services members the Bionic Carrots. Important people get Bigwig, and Freemasons are called Billygoat Riders. A grovelling person is an Earthworm.

But thenk hivvens Aussies don't talk like Kiwis. Macquarie University linguist David Blair had often heard Sydney people say 'yis' rather than 'yes' and 'pin' rather than 'pen', not to mention 'fush and chups' and 'sux' for 'six'. A research project put everyone's fears to rest: a study of the speech of young people in Sydney's northern beaches didn't find the New Zealand pattern at all.

Blair says comparisons with tapes of teenagers' voices made back in the 1950s show that the Australian accent has altered little in that time. But he believes there could be regional differences in accents, and that people get rid of them a few years later. There is also a theory that there are so many Kiwis in Australia that the locals are unknowingly copying them.

A change in accent has been noticed with Melbourne people. They've done away with the difference between 'el' and 'al', and are likely to call themselves Malburnians. Queenslanders also have their little quirks of speech. They finish their sentences with 'eh'. 'How are you going, eh?' 'It's good weather, eh.' 'Close game, eh.' So you can pick someone from Queensland when you're talking to them. It's easy, eh.

People who live in the bush have the reputation of talking slowly. A farmer is sitting in his local country pub when a city slicker walks in and asks how he's going.

'Not ... too ... bad ... thanks,' the farmer says.

'You from round here?' the city bloke asks.

'Yeah ... I've got ... a place ... just down ... the road ... a bit,' the farmer says.

'I don't want to seem disrespectful, but you speak very, very, slowly.'

'They reckon ... that,' the farmer says. 'But I'm the ... fastest speaker ... in the ... family. My brother ... Jack speaks ... very ... very slowly ... and my sister ... Mary speaks ... slower than ... him. A bloke ... put the ... hard word on ... her one night ... and before she ... could tell ... him she ... wasn't ... that kind ... of girl ... she bloody well ... was.'

A kind of public conversation was held for 12 years between the publican of Sydney's Broadway Hotel, Arthur Elliott, and the rector of an Anglican church across the road, Canon Robert Forsyth. The church had been posting signs outside its doors since the 1920s; the conversation began when Arthur, a former mayor of Goulburn, in southwestern NSW, decided to reply to one, in 1985.

The church had put out a sign saying 'Hear John Smith this Sunday, 7.15 pm'. Canon Forsyth was telling his flock that the Reverend John Smith, a preacher who rode a Harley-Davidson motorbike, would be speaking at the service. Arthur Elliott had a regular drinker named Jack Smith, so up went his reply: 'Hear Jack Smith here every day.'

Arthur answered all Canon Forsyth's signs from then on. 'Jesus bowled over death' was countered with, 'And Lillee bowled overarm' (a reference to Dennis Lillee, one of Australian cricket's most successful and beloved fast bowlers). 'This church is only for sinners' was answered by, 'This pub is only for drinkers.' 'Money does not make you happy' received the reply, 'I'd rather be rich and happy than poor and happy.' And 'He'll be back' was met by, 'When?'

A truce was called when Arthur pulled up stumps and sold the hotel. He was invited to address the church's congregation, and afterwards shouted them all a beer. Canon Forsyth put out a sign: 'God bless you and farewell, Arthur. Now who will we have to argue with?' Arthur responded with: 'To the Rev. It's been nice know'n yer!'

3   Our clobber

People at the time wondered whether he was a dentist, a barber, a hospital orderly or a mixture of all three. But no. It was Australia's colourful Minister for Immigration, Al Grassby, showing off what he called the Riverina Rig Mark 1, his idea of Australian national dress. This was January 1974.

He looked on the grey suits worn by generations of politicians and businesspeople with total distaste, so with help from his wife, he produced a virgin white shirt suit he hoped would start a sartorial revolution among Australian men.

It didn't. But it certainly raised some eyebrows. The ultra-light outfit was made from gaberdine. The shirt had long crepe sleeves and two side vents, and hung outside the slightly flared pants. It was buttoned at the collar, and had no pockets. There was no tie. The pants had the only pockets – two in hipster style at the front. Mr Grassby wore cufflinks made from large Australian opals, set in gold.

He described his Riverina Rig as a reflection of a colourful, vigorous, young country, and said it was the type of gear the Australian male might feel much happier in – the usual office wear for men at the time was a traditional suit and tie. He was sick and tired of the lookalike mentality and had decided to do something about it.

The mind boggles. An Australian national dress? If there were such a thing it would be more likely to be an ensemble of blue jeans, T-shirt and joggers for casual wear, the traditional dark suit for the white-collar worker, and an Akubra hat, RM Williams moleskin trousers and Baxter elastic-sided boots for people in the country.

Young males are inclined to get around in baggy tracksuit pants, sloppy joes emblazoned with American slogans and baseball caps. Some add a skinhead haircut.

Akubra hats are probably the best known item in the limited range of classic Aussie clobber. And they've earned the respect they get. They have to be tough enough to stand up to the sun, rain, wind and dust, and be a suitable container for feed and water for the horse and dog. They must be able to fan a fire, survive going through a sheep dip, and retain their shape when jumped on, kicked, talked through or thrown into the ring.

For more than 100 years Akubras have been worn by farmers and squatters, jackeroos and jillaroos, trappers and shooters, stock and station agents, railway fettlers and fencers. They've also become the accepted fashion for police and ambulance officers.

Prime Ministers have an Akubra. John Howard has one. Former Deputy Prime Minister Tim Fischer wears one most of the time, and on a visit to Italy, he had it blessed by the Pope. Top international sportsmen and women consider them national dress.

Former US President Bill Clinton bought an Akubra on his visit Down Under. Ronald Reagan had one and so does Nancy. So does Hollywood actress Linda Evans, no doubt inspired by Paul Hogan in *Crocodile Dundee*, which is still one of Australia's most profitable international movies.

The Australian Olympic team has worn Akubra hats, and when Bob Hawke was Prime Minister, he gave them away to visiting VIPs, especially Americans, who also reckon they're swell. The Three Tenors, Luciano Pavarotti, Placido Domingo and José Carreras, wore Akubras when they sang 'Waltzing Matilda' at a concert in Melbourne as part of their world tour.

And there are not many make-believe farmers and outdoors people who haven't got some kind of Akubra – a Down Under, Snowy River, Pilbara, Bushman or Cattleman – in their wardrobe.

Akubra attribute their popularity to national pride. 'Australians want to be proud of being Australian,' the company says. 'And wearing an Akubra is one way of doing that.' The factory at Kempsey, on the north coast of NSW, employs around 120 people and churns out 1200 hats a day, or around 300,000 a year, using an average of 12 rabbit pelts for each one. That's an awful lot of bunnies, especially now that they're as scarce as hen's teeth because of the control method called rabbit calcivirus disease, which has almost wiped them out in the wild.

The ubiquitous little pests, Australia's most damaging animal enemy, were costing the farming economy more than $120 million a year, stripping the land bare, especially during droughts, destroying some grasses and herbs and causing major soil erosion.

Domesticated rabbits were among Australia's first colonists: they were brought here in the First Fleet, in 1788. More were brought here over the next 30 or 40 years. They flourished for a while but eventually perished. Things changed dramatically in 1859, when Victorian farmer Thomas Austin set free 24 much hardier English rabbits he had imported to give him something to hunt.

The poor fellow had no idea what he'd done. By the turn of the century the furry pests had spread to most parts of Australia. This is now recognised by scientists as the fastest recorded invasion by a mammal in the world – so far! They spread up to 100 square kilometres a year.

Thousands of kilometres of expensive fencing between the States failed to stop their grass-munching advance. Bounty hunters, although turning in nearly 30 million annually, made little impression on rabbit numbers. Farmers trapped, shot, poisoned, fumigated and dug up rabbits for years, but it was a losing battle until the 1950s, when myxomatosis, a mosquito-borne virus from Brazil, was introduced. The virus spread rapidly and hundreds of millions of rabbits died within 2 years, reducing their population to less than 100 million.

But the rabbits fought back. They developed a resistance to 'myxy'. Estimates in 1997 put their population at around 250 million, so new control measures were introduced – this happened accidentally at first, when the calcivirus 'escaped' from an island where it was being tested. All that aside, thousands of Australians would have starved in poor economic times if they had not eaten rabbits, once dubbed 'poor man's chicken'.

Akubra has tried using lots of other fur, including kangaroo and possum, but it just doesn't work. The Australian wild rabbit comes out on top every time. Because of the shortage of rabbits brought on by calcivirus – which has all the graziers smiling – Akubra now import rabbit fur from England and Hungary to blend with its own.

Making an Akubra hat is slow and tedious compared with modern automation: there are 162 different hand movements required before each hat goes into its box. Some of the plant used by Akubra is more than 60 years old – one piece was made in 1905 – and finishing off is still done by hand on sewing machines.

Akubra, which comes from an Aboriginal word meaning head covering, had modest beginnings. An English engineer named Benjamin Dunkerley set up a fur-cutting business in Tasmania in 1872. At the turn of the century he moved to Crown Street in Sydney, where he opened a small manufacturing plant.

There he met young English hatter Stephen Keir, who had arrived in NSW in 1901 to work for a Sydney hat-maker named Anderson. Keir joined Dunkerley and managed the hats side of the business, later marrying Dunkerley's daughter Ada. In 1972 Stephen Keir II moved the business from the expensive Sydney premises to Kempsey, which was then closer to the company's biggest market – Queensland, where 40 per cent of the total annual production was sold.

Five generations have steered this Aussie institution through the whims of fashion and economic fluctuations of boom and bust, competition and war. Stephen Keir V is now running the show. The company has never had a strike, something else that may well be unique in Australia.

Akubras are recognised all around the world, and they've even been known to save lives. Sydney accountant Richard Sevier was backpacking through Africa, and in eastern Zaire, near the Rwandan border, he was arrested by Tutsi militia, apparently because they thought he was a journalist.

Nearby was a Care Australia camp, and one of the Aussies there saw Richard being marched off down a road. The battered Akubra he was wearing had been through Indonesia, India and Africa, but was still recognisable by the Care Australia people, who ran after the Tutsi and persuaded them that Richard was an innocent dinki-di tourist taking in the sights. They let him go.

It's fine to have an Akubra hat, but to be properly decked out you need a pair of RM Williams moleskin trousers, a Clancy's or Gloster shirt, a Driza-Bone jacket and a pair of Baxter elastic-sided boots.

Akubra, RM Williams and Driza-Bone all had the official OK to market their products under the Sydney Olympics banner. An estimated $60 million in royalties from these companies, among others, helped fund the Games.

The Baxter Boot Company has been around for more than 150 years and, like Akubra, is still owned and controlled by the same family. It is based at Goulburn, in southwestern NSW. The company sells its quality products throughout Australia and New Zealand and is looking at expanding into other overseas markets. Baxter's also won a contract in 2002 to supply 20,000 shoes – worth $1 million a year – to the Australian Army, Air Force and Navy. The company beat four other manufacturers to get the contract.

Henry Baxter began the business after working as a shoe repairer for Henry Teece at Goulburn, and then buying him out. He believed Goulburn was the ideal site for a boot factory because of the ready availability of hides from the local abattoir. Henry turned the business into a proprietary company in 1913 when he moved the factory to its present premises.

There were seven brothers in the family, four of whom worked in the business. Company chairman Brian Baxter is the third generation, and his son Marshall is managing director. There are also grandchildren coming along, so the business is likely to stay in the family for a while yet.

Reginald Murray Williams went bush as a camel boy in 1926 with a missionary who wanted to study the Aborigines. He spent three years exploring a huge chunk of outback Australia where few white people had been before, and then worked as a well-driller, stockman, miner, tea-planter and writer before launching into business.

When the Great Depression hit the country in the late 1920s, the value of our money crashed, businesses closed, farms were abandoned and thousands of people lost their jobs. Reg Williams was in the same boat. He wandered along the Murray River sharpening knives so he could buy food. And because he couldn't afford a pair of boots, he made his own.

That's how his enterprise began. For years he ran a mail-order business from a shed in the backyard of his father's home in Prospect, South Australia, specialising in clothes and boots for the battler. RM Williams is now owned by millionaires Ken Cowley and Kerry Stokes (the latter also owns the Seven TV network).

Until his death at 95 in November 2003, Reg Williams grew gum trees, bred horses and helped run the Stockman's Hall of Fame, at Longreach, in central western Queensland. He also had hopes of his rose garden becoming the largest in the world.

Ken Cowley said RM was as comfortable with Prime Ministers as he was under a gidgee tree with a ringer (shearer); his death was a sad day for Australia.

RM Williams boots are still made the same old way, from one piece of leather, and with one seam at the back. This makes the boots strong and helps keep them waterproof.

Driza-Bone, which makes waxed cotton coats with distinctive styling, was sold to British-based James Halstead Group and then bought back a few years later. Its products are a part of Australian country life and an important fashion item. They're modelled on the English Belstaff jackets, first developed for North Sea fishermen and then used for years by motorcyclists.

But Driza-Bone, which exports its coats to fashion outlets in London, Paris, New York and Berlin, has been through tough times because of cheaper copycat versions. Driza-Bone has a factory at Beenleigh, south of Brisbane, and employs about 100 people. It might be a pretty small operation, with an annual turnover of around $14 million, but its products have a big reputation.

The Australian team was outfitted in burnt-terracotta Driza-Bone stockman coats for the 1998 Winter Olympics at Nagano, in Japan. Designed to represent the red Australian earth, Driza-Bone staff matched the colour by collecting red rock samples from the Northern Territory.

The alternative Aussie clobber, favoured by blue-collar workers and truckies, is the classic Chesty Bond blue singlet, Stubbies shorts (not to be confused with a stubby of beer) and boots.

Chesty Bond, the cartoon character launched in 1938 by the *Sydney Sun* newspaper and taken up by advertising agency J Walter Thompson to promote the singlets, represented strength, virility and good health. He was Australia's answer to Popeye the Sailor Man (who spent a good deal of his time selling the virtues of spinach).

Chesty Bond ran as a paid-for comic strip in the *Sun* and other newspapers around Australia until 1964, and was credited with selling more than 130 million singlets. You can still buy them, but they now have a more modern look.

Sydney man Max Whitehead was the model for the original Chesty Bond cartoon character, although he was in some ways not much like the quintessential Aussie bloke the singlets related to – he was a vegetarian who ate mainly fresh fruit, vegetables and whole-grain cereals, never smoked and didn't drink much. He was probably the perfect choice, though, because of his good looks and pale blue eyes. He was fit as a fiddle, bristled with muscles and was strong-jawed, although at public appearances he was fitted with an artificial jaw so that he would match the extreme jaw of the cartoon Chesty.

Max was, at various times, in the police force and the Air Force, captain of the 1947-48 Manly-Warringah rugby league team, a Manly Beach lifesaver, and a professional wrestler. As a wrestler, he was beaten only once – by Killer Kowalski, who Max described as a 'great big bastard ...' Max received only modelling fees for being Chesty, and reckoned he never even got a free singlet.

Ron Reeve, a new Chesty, has since made a series of TV commercials and hosted the character's 60th birthday party at Sydney's Museum of Contemporary Art. His image is considerably more upmarket than the original Chesty.

A Bond's spokesman says Chesty has appeal across the community, and represents more than just the blonde bronzed Aussie. He is liked by all Australians, no matter what race or creed. Women are probably his biggest fans. After all, they buy 80 per cent of the men's underwear sold in Australia.

Stubbies shorts, with their elasticised waist, initially had a poor image – they were seen as clothing for ockers, for beer-swilling, pie-eating, uncultured (and possibly rude and chauvinist to boot) blokes. However, they have become part of our clothing history. Stubbies first hit the market in 1972, with a range of 16 colours, and 750,000 pairs were snapped up – at $1.99 each. Their success peaked in 1980, when 2.9 million pairs were sold. Since then the company has become a bit more fashion conscious, but it hasn't forgotten its roots.

Stubbies say their shorts are the quintessential short shorts, and while they might not be as suitable to work in as they were 20 years ago, there's still a strong market for them. You can now buy a longer-leg Stubbie, in line with latest fashions.

The typical Stubbies wearer is a 35-year-old blue-collar worker who toils hard for his money. He sees clothes as a necessity and doesn't believe in high fashion. He wants something practical to wear to work – and then to a barbecue or the pub. Stubbies have now sold more than 50 million pairs, and have become such a part of the Aussie culture that the *Macquarie Dictionary* put them in the 1980 edition ... and they've been there ever since.

Now for the feet. The ancient Greeks and Romans gave the world sandals, a sole without an upper that was attached to the foot by a leather lace. The thong is Australia's answer to the sandal. Made from rubber, with a strip between the toes to hold them on, thongs, called flip-flops or jandals in other countries, are worn until they're totally buggered. People never throw them away. Thongs teamed with a T-shirt and a pair of Stubbies are standard weekend leisure wear.

At Pomona, near Noosa, in Queensland, the World Thong Throwing Championship is held every year, with competitors coming from America, Japan, New

Zealand and Malaysia. They have to see how far they can throw a size 10 thong, which must be 29cm long and weigh no more than 150g. The record is held by a Queenslander – 42.8 metres.

In Sydney there's a group called the Australian Thong Clappas' Society which meets every month and, thongs in hand, claps along to old favourites like *Thing a Thong of Thixpence*.

The small village of Wattle Flat, near Bathurst, has an annual Bronze Thong race meeting. It isn't as upmarket or glamorous as the Sydney Turf Club's Golden Slipper, but the 500 patrons who go reckon it is every bit as good.

There are no bookies or betting, the trainers and jockeys are mostly people off the land, and the horses have names like Radar, Rambo and Ginger. There are no fancy stands or flower gardens and no high fashion. The bar and food stalls are built from timber and bark from gum trees, and the other facilities are not what you'd expect at Rosehill, but everyone has a top time. The Australian Thong Throwing Championship is held in conjunction with the race meeting.

The Thong race meeting was first run about 1984 by a group of local people who thought something should be done to revive the old racecourse, which was set in the bush, about 5 km out of the small village. Deep erosion gutters were filled, swampy areas were drained and fallen timber was cleared from the track.

The running rails were made from stringybark, and although they mightn't be too straight, they did the job – until a fierce storm hit the racecourse in 2003 and destroyed everything. But you can't keep a keen committee down. Residents got the Thong up and running again.

And while we're talking about small items of clothing, Speedo, established in 1929 by MacRae Knitting Mills in Sydney, dominated the cossie (another of our famous diminutives – for swimming costume) market. In the 1970s, Speedo was the official swimwear supplier to all countries in the Munich and Montreal Olympics.

Berlei bras, now made in Asia, was another Aussie company. It was established in 1927 by corset-maker Fred Burley. He had 6000 women measured so he could design his bras to fit properly. He called his products 'Berlei' because he didn't think the name 'Burley' was suitable when dealing with women's figures.

4 The Aborigines

A whitefella in his four-wheel-drive is lost in the outback. He sees an elderly Aborigine sitting under a tree, screeches to a halt and asks: 'Hey, mate, can I take this road to Sydney?' The Aborigine looks at him and says: 'Might as well, you've taken everything else.'

Eddie Mabo lived on an island off Queensland and reckoned it was pretty poor that his people, most of whom had maintained their traditional way of life and connection with the land, were not recognised as the island's owners. So Eddie spent most of his life trying to do something about it.

With four of his mates from the Meriam tribe, he took the matter to the High Court in 1982, challenging the argument that Australia was 'terra nullius', a land belonging to nobody, when the Europeans first arrived.

The case dragged on for 10 years, but the court eventually ruled in Eddie's favour. The sad part was that he had died in the meantime. But the decision still put the cat among the pigeons, and authorities, farmers and mining companies went into a panic, believing the whole country would be returned to the Aborigines.

In 1993 the Labor Federal Government passed the Native Title Act, which allowed Aborigines who had continually occupied (or maintained a connection with) a piece of land to make an ownership claim or be entitled to compensation from other people who use it. A Native Title Tribunal was set up to rule on the claims.

The result has been a better relationship – though still a rocky one – between non-Aboriginal and Aboriginal Australians. Aboriginal Australians have had few rights for most of their lives. They were written out of the Australian Constitution when it was drawn up in 1900 by being excluded from population counts, and were unable to vote or go into hotels.

That's all changed now, but the lot of Australia's 270,000 indigenous people is still not a happy one. There's a long way to go to rectify the grave injustices they've endured. Their health generally is bad, their housing and living conditions are poor, their education levels are low, and their employment opportunities are far from good. But they've been able to survive all these years, and one would hope things can only get better.

Digby Moran knows what it's like to be down for the count. As well as getting knocked around for a few years in a boxing tent run by showman Jimmy Sharman, and being shot off the back of bucking broncos at rodeos, he became too fond of the grog. His life hit rock bottom.

But Digby, a member of the Bundjalung people, gave up drinking a few days after New Year in 1991 and his life did an about-turn. He began making boomerang brooches, and then took a short arts and media course at a technical and further education college at Ballina, on the far north coast of NSW, because of a wish to paint. That brought out his unique talent.

Now his artwork, done using sticks and sponges, is turning up in all the right places. He has twice had works accepted for entry in the Northern Territory Art Awards, has had successful exhibitions at Lismore Regional Gallery, which bought one of his paintings (he is the first Aboriginal artist to have work bought by this gallery), and hopes to have work shown in the Art Gallery of NSW.

He's painted murals on walls for local businesses and on a regional health care bus. He paints on ceramics, plates and jewel boxes. He has paintings in the Ballina Information Centre and two dozen pieces of his work have gone to America as a trial shipment. He is determined to become a successful Aboriginal artist.

Born on Cabbage Tree Island mission on the Richmond River, just south of Ballina, Digby left school early and joined Jimmy Sharman's boxing tent, touring the show circuit around country towns for three years. He won most of his fights and enjoyed the life.

'It was tough, but I was young and silly. I also did a fair bit of rough riding and got the nickname Cowboy. When I gave that away, I had a go at everything, from cutting cane and chipping cotton to digging trenches and picking grapes around Mildura. But the booze was making a mess of my life so I stopped drinking and started painting and I've never looked back.'

Lewis Burns is another enterprising Aborigine. He spends a lot of time in the mallee scrub, tapping saplings to see whether the white ants have done their job munching through the centre. If they have and the wood is hollow, he cuts it to the right length and takes it home.

There, with some skilful work, he turns it into a rich-sounding didgeridoo, the traditional Aboriginal wind instrument; he has sold didgeridoos all over the world. Lewis, who ran his own business at Dubbo, in western NSW, until the cheap fakes imported from Asia put him out of business in 2001, used to be kept busy filling orders from craft shops and galleries around Australia and from a string of overseas countries. He also paints in the traditional dot style for a Sydney T-shirt manufacturer, and carves emu eggs.

Lewis had been around didgeridoos since he was a boy, and learning to make and decorate them came as easily as learning to speak. After working for a while as a builder's labourer in Sydney, he found himself back in Dubbo without a job in 1999. He made some didgeridoos and they were snapped up, so he decided to do it fulltime. He found a shed, took a business course at the Enterprise Centre to learn how to keep the books, and off he went.

Lewis makes his didgeridoos as instruments, not as artefacts, concentrating on getting a good sound. When he gets the mallee saplings home, he does a lot of poking with a stick and a brush on a chain to break up the ant nests and get all the dirt out of the centre before running glue through it as a sealer. The glue isn't part of the didgeridoo tradition, but as well as giving a better sound, it stops the wood splitting. The bark on the outside is peeled off with a knife and scraper, which leaves a natural look, and then it's coated with vegetable oil or butter to give a golden colour. The Aboriginal decorations are burnt in.

Lewis reckons the didgeridoo is easy to play. He can usually teach someone to do the basic drone, which is the first step, fairly quickly. He says it's like teaching someone to ride a bike. You get them going and then it's up to them.

He worries about the loss of Aboriginal culture – many of the old ways which have disappeared can never be replaced – but he believes he's helped retain some of the traditional art styles and techniques by making his didgeridoos and by visiting schools and talking to kids.

Vince Bulger shares Lewis' concerns for young Aborigines. Vince has a simple philosophy on life: respect your elders regardless of their colour, creed or nationality. He drummed that message into his 11 children, and says he's been blessed with a good family.

Vince, who has been there, done that – as a stockman, footballer and railway ganger – believes the reason there are so many young Aborigines in retention centres and jails is because they've lost that respect. Before they leave school, kids have to be taught, regardless of what ethnic group they belong to, to respect other people, he says. 'We've got to sit down and talk to them so they never lose sight of their culture. I did that with my kids and it worked for me.'

Vince, who lives in the southern NSW timber town of Tumut, now spends most of his time fishing. But life wasn't always easy. Born at Yass on a mission called

Hollywood, his family was booted off when he was 10 because his father died – the Aboriginal Protection Board wouldn't allow widows to stay there. Vince and his family loaded their belongings onto an old horse and cart and moved to Oak Hill reserve, also near Yass.

There they built a humpy from stringybark poles and flattened tar drums and kerosene tins they found at the tip. The walls were lined with old hessian bags and newspapers and the floor was dirt. But the family was happy, and lived there for 12 years before moving to Brundle.

'Mum was the sole provider. She did domestic work and we cut wood and mowed lawns,' Vince says. 'We earned five bob and used it to buy two loaves of bread, a pound of sugar, some broken biscuits and a bit of devon – and there was still enough left to go the pictures.

'I used to ride my bike from Yass to Murrumbateman, collect wool from dead sheep and hide it in a hollow stump until I had enough to fill two sugarbags. Then I'd take it back to Yass and sell it for two shillings, which bought our meat.'

Vince worked as a ganger on the railway for 32 years. After two heart attacks, he retired. All he does now is eat, sleep and fish. And he says that's not a bad life.

Aborigines have made a real name for themselves in the art world. People are now sitting up and taking notice of bark paintings which are fetching world-record prices. A tribal art and Aboriginal bark painting auction held by Sothebys in Sydney netted $900,000 in 1996. A small bark painting by Northern Territory artist Yirawala, a Gunwinggu elder from Arnhem Land, brought $17,250, breaking a previous world record price of $17,000, in 1995. Minutes later, at the same auction, another of his bark paintings went for $18,400.

Yirawala, who died in 1970, received international recognition when Spanish artist Pablo Picasso wrote to him saying that he (Picasso) had always tried to paint with the freedom and purity he saw in Yirawala's work, work that sent mimi spirits, praying mantis men, rainbow serpents and spirit children dancing across bark canvasses.

A Sothebys auction in July 2001 again resulted in record prices for Aboriginal art. A stockman's painting of a waterfall broke a world record for Aboriginal art when the National Gallery of Australia paid nearly $800,000 for it. Called *All That Big Rain Coming Topside*, it was painted by Rover Thomas. An impressive 1.2 metres by 1.8 metres, it takes the number of Rover Thomas paintings held by the gallery to 35.

Thomas, of Kukatja and Wangkajunga parentage, was born around 1926 at Gunawaggi, on the Canning Stock Route in Western Australia. He usually painted the land as a metaphor for the overlaying of ancestral and European history. But with *All That Big Rain Coming Topside* he attempted a more naturalistic approach to the landscape – admirers say you can actually feel the flow of water as it cascades over the cliff edge. Rover died in 1998.

At the same auction, a painting by Mick Namarari Tjapaltjarri called *Hopping*

Mouse Dreaming went for $110,500, and *Yam III*, painted by Emily Kame Kngwarreye, fetched $104,750.

Albert Namatjira, who lived just out of Alice Springs, in central Australia, was probably one of Australia's best artists. He began in the 1940s by carving wood plaques on a mission station, before being tutored by white watercolour painter Rex Battarbee. He was soon making $2000 per exhibition, a sizeable income back then.

But according to tribal law, he had to share his earnings with as many as 500 relations, and although he was not recognised as a full citizen and not allowed to vote or drink, he still had to pay income tax. He wasn't even allowed to buy a house in Alice Springs because Aborigines weren't allowed in the town after dark.

Albert was taken to meet the Queen in 1954. In 1958 he was caught smuggling alcohol and was sentenced to six months' jail. There was a huge outcry against this, so the sentence was reduced to two months, but Albert died soon afterwards, a sad and sorry man.

Aborigines have excelled in a variety of other fields, too. Tribal elder Gnarnayarrahe Waitarie became a modelling star in Sweden for Boomerang International, a Stockholm clothing company. The artist, musician and actor, who is in his mid-50s, modelled a range of clothing for the company's catalogues with fellow Aboriginal actor David Gulpilil.

This overseas assignment came after an agent saw him in the film *Dead Heart*, with Bryan Brown. His tall build, thick beard and distinctive features made him a natural choice for the company with the Aboriginal name. And he's proud of what he does: 'When I do this sort of work, I breathe the culture, I am free of government funding and social security (payments) and I am doing something for my people.'

In outback Queensland, rough rider Buddy McKellar had an enviable record for staying on a wild buckjumper longer than anyone else. Nicknamed The Cunnamulla Kid, Buddy chalked up a string of bruising rodeo wins that included all-round champion cowboy of Queensland and the prestigious Mitchell Rodeo bareback title.

He also rang the bell on crazy broncos with names like The Undertaker, Bobby McGee and Drunken Duncan, broncos which had defied all efforts to ride them until Buddy came along. People wondered why he was so good, but the pint-sized cowboy's secret was simple. He practised on bar stools in Cunnamulla's Billabong Hotel, a notable watering hole in the back-of-buggery town on the banks of the Warrego River.

Patrons used to watch in amazement as Buddy threw himself backwards, forwards and sideways on a stool, legs and arms going in all directions, just as if he was on a Brahman bull or a bucking bareback. Often he was parallel to the bar, balancing precariously on a few square centimetres of twisting and turning stool, but he only crashed a few times. He reckoned the stools were the nearest thing he knew to riding a real buckjumper. He busted the legs off a few but the pub didn't seem to mind because they had their own mini-rodeo when he was there. And it was good practice for him. Almost as good as riding the real thing.

Buddy won the Queensland calf-riding title when he was 12 and then went to Nudgee College in Brisbane for a couple of years. He dropped out and went back to Cunnamulla to work as a ringer and rouseabout. Now his four sons and daughter also love rough riding.

Buddy has a telling story about the relationship between Aborigines and Europeans in this country: a station owner asks his Aboriginal stockman how he liked the bottle of port he (the owner) gave him for Christmas. 'It was just right, boss,' he replies.

'Just right? What do you mean?'

'Well, if it had been any better you wouldn't have given it to me, and if it had been any worse, I couldn't have drunk it. So it was just right.'

Colin Davis, one of the stolen generation, was taken from his mother at Cowra when he was nine and put in a home at Kempsey, on the NSW mid-north coast. There he had to grapple with conflicting influences, most of them bad.

The other boys formed themselves into groups – the runaways, the bullies, the troublemakers, the passives and the smokers – and he was expected to take sides. Staff drummed it into him that black people were inferior, his peers told him that white people were bad, and he wasn't allowed to talk to outsiders. And he had to cope with the bullies.

Three ganged up on him, and often took his meals. One day they asked for his dessert. It was his favourite, rice and custard pudding. 'So I reckoned it was time to make a stand. I said "no" and ate the lot myself, knowing I would have to pay the consequences later,' he said. 'But that's when I found out I could use my dukes. When they confronted me, it turned out I could hit harder than they could. They left me alone after that.'

Colin Davis is resident artist at the Dimbaloo Aboriginal Art and Crafts Workshop and Gallery at Mogo, just out of Batemans Bay, on the south coast of NSW, and spends a lot of his time working with young people, trying to give them the basic grounding in life that he was denied. He teaches art and talks about the importance of good manners, respect and taking responsibility, and how young kids should learn to enjoy their job.

He explains the importance of staying at school and getting an education, something else he missed out on while at Kinchela Boys' Home at Kempsey. He didn't know the first thing about school, so he didn't learn and couldn't do the tests. Instead, he kept his head down and doodled and drew. He loved drawing Captain Cook's ship. To him those old sailing ships were beautiful, and he drew them for the other kids.

When he left the home at 19, Colin was given a job at a Woy Woy nursery seven days a week. He wanted to be a body-builder, though, so he left and worked for a while with weightlifter Don Othaldo on the show circuit, chipping a couple of teeth biting metal as part of the act. Then he went to Redfern and got into trouble with alcohol and gambling.

But along the way he met Mum Shirl, an Aboriginal elder, and a group of nuns doing outreach work in the Redfern community, and his life began to change.

He had had five names at the boys' home, so he really didn't even know who he was. He had been Smith, Perry, Monaghan, Davis and Carmody, and the nuns and Mum Shirl were the only people he could whinge to about it. They listened. He says they sowed the good seeds in him.

Colin married a South Coast woman and moved to Batemans Bay, later giving up his gambling. He took up painting and began working with young people. He said the Lord helped provide for him. When Brian and Mary Daley opened Dimbaloo, they gave Colin the opportunity to exhibit his work and run art workshops. His work sells well, and some of it goes overseas. He also paints on pendants, key rings, refrigerator magnets, greeting cards and crossword puzzles.

Ted Egan is one of Australia's best Aboriginal trackers, and police called him in to help in the hunt for a gunman suspected of killing an English tourist in the outback. The grey-haired Walpira elder learned his skills from his mother 'chasin' goanna and kangaroo and things to eat ...' As is common among desert people, he took the name of a white man he respected – outback poet Ted Egan (who was sworn in as the Northern Territory's 18th Administrator in November 2003).

Ted's skill in tracking criminals and finding lost people is legendary. He went to Germany once to help police track down three dangerous crooks who had escaped from jail and hidden in the German forests. Ted found two of them.

Father and son tracking team Tommy and Thomas George chase marijuana-growing crooks in the Cape York country, in Australia's far north. They use their traditional skills to lead police to illicit plantations worth millions of dollars on the street.

Thomas works from the police station in the tiny Aboriginal community of Laura, 100 km west of Cooktown, and is one of only two official Queensland Police trackers. He can follow faint motorbike and car tracks through dense bushland, an art he learnt from his father.

Magic and traditional healing are still used, and sometimes they are combined with modern medical practices. Cairns Base Hospital in Far North Queensland still calls on the wisdom of Aboriginal elders.

George Musgrave, of the Gugu Taipan people, learnt his traditional healing methods from his father, whom he calls Old Dad. 'He was a witchdoctor,' he says. 'He showed me what to do. With white ants in water and a handkerchief on the chest and back, you can look through the person and see what's bad inside. I've pulled a marble out of a belly.' Musgrave was a tracker and a police officer at Laura in north Queensland.

Ernie Dingo, one of the most popular people on Australian TV, believes Aborigines have for too long been portrayed as stereotypes in white Australian drama. Ernie, host of *The Great Outdoors*, a travel program, and veteran of a string of successful films, has helped change that with some of his productions, such as *Heartland*, a mainstream TV drama series with an Aboriginal storyline and an almost all Aboriginal cast.

The series reflects the fact that both performers and audiences are finished with the limitations that come with Aborigines forever being represented as stockmen and black trackers. Ernie says the series is for those Aboriginal kids and their families who don't see enough Aboriginal influence on TV.

Ernie, with his big grin and fluffy hair, says there is no black or white; there is only saltwater or freshwater. Saltwater if you live on the coast and freshwater if you live inland. 'Doesn't matter if you're black or white or a man or a woman.'

5 | Aussie icons

Australians love things that promote us and show the world what we're all about. Whether it's the Sydney Harbour Bridge, a meat pie and sauce, the Opera House, Chesty Bond singlets or Vegemite, they're all part of life Down Under.

One of the shining symbols of Australian lifestyle is the meat pie and tomato sauce. But it's more than just an Aussie icon. The combination of soft pastry, tender slurpy meat and rich gravy in a good pie is one of life's little pleasures.

So it's little wonder that Australians munch their way through 30 million pies a month. They're made with a range of meats now, including beef, veal, lamb, kangaroo, emu, crocodile tail, camel, buffalo and yabbies, and some have vegetables and herbs added.

The statisticians tell us that men eat an average 3.8 pies a month in winter (we're not sure whether they throw the 0.2 away or not, but number-crunchers always talk in fractions like that), more than twice as many as women, who eat 1.5. The biggest addicts are people between 18 and 24, who eat 4.2 pies a month. On the other end of the scale, people over 50 account for only 1.7 a month.

Personal tastes vary, depending on where you live. People in NSW and Queensland prefer steak and mushroom pies, Victorians steak and onion, and Tasmanians steak and kidney. South Australians and West Australians like their pies to be plain steak without any such fancy additives.

More than half the pies consumed are eaten for lunch, but in colder weather they're more likely to be a snack between meals. Meat pies are also popular for breakfast, but that seems to be an exclusively male habit. Women certainly prefer a more conventional brekky of cereal or toast.

A competition is held every year to find Australia's best meat pie, and hundreds of entries are received. The judges look for consistency and colour of the filling, the meat/gravy ratio, pastry thickness, taste, aroma and the sensations in the mouth. They take off points for soggy or undercooked pastry and shiny bottoms.

Ideally, you should be able to hold a pie in one hand and a beer in the other without spilling the filling down your arm or on the front of your shirt. But above all, it must be enjoyable and have a nice aroma.

One of the competition judges, pastry chef Shayne Bell, believes the meat pie has reclaimed its rightful position as Australia's favourite tucker. He says Big Mac and KFC had better look out, because creativity is taking gourmet pies out of the bakery and onto restaurant tables. And he claims they're healthier than hamburgers and fried chicken.

But a study by BIS Shrapnel in April 2003 found that Australians were eating more Asian takeaway and fewer pies and sausage rolls than they used to. Sandwiches were still the most popular takeaway, with people spending $420 million a year, down from $500 million in 2000. The report found that Thai, sushi, Indian and other Asian food outlets were becoming more popular, but that fish and chips shops were still the most popular independent food outlets. Growth in fast food and takeaways was estimated to average 1.5 per cent a year.

Vegemite is another Aussie obsession. A rich source of the energy-giving Vitamin B group, it's almost as much a part of Australia's heritage as kangaroos and koalas. Millions of people grew up with the black, yeasty stuff, and it was standard issue for our soldiers at war.

Spread on toast or bread or mixed with hot water to make a stimulating drink, Vegemite has a unique salty taste that most overseas people have never come to grips with. In October 1986, the *Wall Street Journal*, attempting to explain Australians' passion for Vegemite, said the national dish 'looks like axle grease and tastes like rusty nails'. Be that as it may, Australians consume 22.7 million jars of it a year, more than 4500 tonnes.

Vegemite was the brainwave of Melbourne food manufacturer Fred Walker just after World War I. He noted the popularity of Bovril, an English beef extract, approached Carlton & United Breweries, and negotiated a deal to buy their used yeast. In 1922, with a food chemist named Cyril Callister, he produced Vegemite from the yeast, adding celery, onions, salt and a few other ingredients.

The paste had no name until 1923, when Walker launched it as Vegemite after a national competition to find a name. He promoted it as a pure vegetable extract but sales were disappointing, with people preferring to dip into a similar spread called Marmite. In 1928, Walker, then owned by Kraft Cheese, changed Vegemite's name to Parwill, the theory being that 'If Marmite ... then Parwill.' But Parwill sales were also a flop, so Walker reinstated the Vegemite name.

In 1935, in an all-out attempt to make people try Vegemite, a two-year coupon redemption scheme was launched, with a jar of Vegemite given free with every purchase of another Kraft Walker food product. That did the trick. People liked it and began buying it. It had taken 14 years to become accepted.

That campaign was followed by a nationwide sales drive offering Pontiac cars as prizes. Just before World War II, the British Medical Association gave Vegemite an official endorsement – that kicked sales along as well. The spread also became standard issue for the Australian armed forces, which received supplies in tins in a range of sizes, including half-ounce (14 g) individual ration packs. But this stretched production and resulted in strict rationing at home.

When the war ended, Australia experienced a baby boom, creating another huge new market for Vegemite, which came under the Kraft Foods umbrella in 1950. The health side of the paste was continually promoted with an advertising jingle that told how 'happy little Vegemites' could eat it for 'breakfast, lunch and tea', claiming it would 'put a rose in every cheek'. The campaign continued on radio and TV until the late 1960s. In the late 1980s, Vegemite dusted off the original commercials, added some colour and began a new promotion campaign.

The original Vegemite concentrated yeast extract recipe is basically unchanged, although the salt content is now slightly lower. Vegemite has become so addictive for Australians that when they travel overseas, they pack a few jars in their bags to keep up their intake of the stuff.

Vegemite is now owned by American tobacco giant Philip Morris. Australian businessman and philanthropist Dick Smith got so hot under the collar about that that he launched a campaign to create a recipe for an Australian-made product to knock Vegemite off its perch. Now on the market, he calls that new product Ozemite. He set up Dick Smith Foods, which now sells a variety of products. Smith believes a tobacco company shouldn't own an Australian icon that is loved by children. Philip Morris was better suited to the funeral industry, he said.

Weet-Bix is a breakfast food that's been around for 100 years, the star product of a company called Sanitarium Health Food, which was established in a small Melbourne bakery in April 1898, by an American Seventh Day Adventist, Edward Halsey. He also made Australia's first batches of peanut butter and cold breakfast cereals, including Granose, a dried wheat flake biscuit that led the way for Weet-Bix, which now has 14 per cent of the cereal market.

Sanitarium, still wholly owned by the Seventh Day Adventist Church, says Weet-Bix is a staple of the national diet – and it's true, generations of Australians have been brought up on it. Every year the company makes enough of the breakfast biscuits to fill a football field to a depth of 18 metres.

Chiko rolls are another Australian phenomenon. They've been around since 1951, and the people who make them claim they're the most popular takeaway food for men between the ages of 18 and 25. Colour advertising posters have always featured a great-looking girl on a Harley-Davidson and slogans like 'You can't knock the Roll' or 'Hit the Hot Spot'. Perhaps these ads have something to do with their popularity?

Australians now eat 17.5 million Chiko rolls a year, down slightly from their heyday in the 1970s but still a huge slice of the takeaway market. Back then it was the only takeaway product besides fish and chips and hamburgers.

Bendigo boilermaker Frank McEnroe invented the Chiko roll and sold the first batch at the 1951 Wagga Wagga Agricultural Show. Chiko rolls are now made by Simplot, an American company that bought out Edgells.

Chiko rolls come in a neatly fitting paper bag so you can eat them while they're hot without dripping tomato sauce or filling down your front. And whenever you walk into a fish and chip shop you'll see them staring straight at you. They're heated in the cooking oil just like chips.

Few people seem to know exactly what the ingredients are. The shell is pastry and the tasty filling is mashed meat, vegetables and seasoning. But it appears Chiko rolls don't have a lot of export potential. The makers tried to sell them in New Guinea once, but it didn't work. They said people there 'weren't quite ready for them …'

Other icons you can eat include Arnott's biscuits and Aeroplane Jelly. The Arnott Biscuit company began in 1865 in Hunter Street, Newcastle, under the direction of William Arnott, a Scottish migrant who was a leading member of the Wesleyan Church and taught Sunday school for 24 years. Arnott's, whose biscuit packets all have a picture of a rosella on them, is the major biscuit brand on the Australian market, with 60 per cent of total sales, including the popular Tim Tams, Shapes, Saos, Jatz and Iced Vo Vos. However, it is now owned by American company Campbell Soup.

Arnott's was an extortionist's target in February 1997. A letter from an unknown source threatened to poison biscuits unless police involved in a trial in 1993 were forced to take lie detector tests. The company recalled $10 million worth of its products and destroyed them. A multi-million dollar advertising campaign got sales back on track.

Aeroplane Jelly crystals were first sold in 1927, and were advertised on the radio with the jingle: 'I like Aeroplane Jelly, Aeroplane Jelly for me. I like it for dinner, I like it for tea, a little each day is a good recipe …'

Moving away from food and onto constructions, there is one icon that stands above all others. Nothing in Australia has yet attracted a bigger crowd than the opening, on 19 March 1932, of the Sydney Harbour Bridge (affectionately called the Coathanger). More than a million people in trains, trams, buses, cars and on foot crossed the bridge in the first 24 hours. The *Sydney Morning Herald* reported that Sydney was 'a city of deserted suburbs' as the people left their homes to test the engineering marvel. The bridge was built in the height of the Depression, and was a clear signal that prosperous times were ahead.

Many of the 1000 who worked on it had previously been unemployed, and had told fibs about their skills to get the much-needed job. Climbing around the steel structure 90 metres above the water terrified them, but most eventually became as agile as mountain goats. However, 16 workers fell off the bridge during its construction and were killed. It was normal practice to collect half a day's pay from each worker for the widows.

When the bridge was finished, it was the largest single-arch bridge in the world, but the Bayonne in New York later beat it by 60 cm. Until the Sydney Harbour Tunnel was finished in 1992, the bridge was the only link between the city's centre and the north shore. More than 200,000 vehicles now race backwards and forwards across the bridge every day.

Serious accidents can cause traffic jams for several hours, but the biggest cause of delays is mechanical breakdowns, as many as 4000 vehicles a year. And around 1200 drivers a year run out of petrol on the bridge, causing more hold-ups.

In December 1975, a navy pilot flew a helicopter under the bridge, and the authorities took no action. Sydney company director John Cameron wasn't as lucky. He flew a Tiger Moth under the bridge the same year to commemorate a pioneer Australian aviator and had his licence suspended. He also copped a hefty fine.

While the bridge was being built, Sydneysiders watched in awe as the two half-arches moved towards each other from either side of the harbour. When the arches finally met in the middle in August 1930, and were joined, cynics were disappointed. They had been sure the two halves would never come together.

Huge girders were hung from the arch to support the roadway underneath. It was another two years before the bridge and its granite pylons, which serve only as additional supports for the steelwork between the main span and the approach span, was completed, at a cost around $20 million. The last of 6 million rivets had been driven home.

To reassure people that it wouldn't fall down, 92 steam locomotives were parked on the bridge at once, in a unique test of its strength. The NSW Railways was no doubt relieved that it held firm – otherwise half their fleet would have ended up at the bottom of the harbour.

At the official opening, Captain Francis De Groot, a member of a right-wing extremist group called the New Guard, rode up on his skinny horse and cut the ribbon with a sabre, stealing NSW Premier Jack Lang's thunder. De Groot appeared in court a few days later and was fined £5 for offensive behaviour.

The Coathanger received a multi-million dollar facelift for the Sydney 2000 Olympic Games. The Roads and Traffic Authority, which spends $3 million a year maintaining the bridge, increased the painting crew to 130 to make sure the new coat of grey was finished in time. There are 485,000 square metres of steel to cover with 30,000 litres of special rubberised paint that protects the metal from rust. The bridge played a big role in the Olympics. It was featured in the Opening and Closing ceremonies and was part of the course for the marathon events.

Moving from roads to cars, there is again one that stands above all: Australia's Own Car – the Holden. But the first Holden was actually designed and built by Americans, with Australia merely providing the name. The name had been around since the 1850s, when James Holden and Henry Frost established a successful saddlery and coach-building business in Adelaide. Later they turned their hand to motor bodies, and became the Holden Motor Company; eventually they merged with General Motors.

The first Holden rolled off the assembly line at a new plant at Fishermen's Bend, outside Melbourne, on 29 November 1948. It was the 48/215, and was dubbed the FX. The six-cylinder 'people's car' sold for £733 10s, and was an instant hit. The company built 163 cars in the first year and chalked up its first million vehicles in 1960.

The boss of General Motors Holden in Australia, a Pommy by the name of Laurence Hartnett, dreamed of building an Aussie car but his American superiors called the shots, and they preferred a modified version of other GM products. Hartnett resigned just before the first Holden was produced, and later built his own French-designed car; it failed after 350 were made, because contractors were unable to supply parts.

The Holden is as Australian as kangaroos and meat pies, and dominated the family car market until Ford retaliated with its Falcon in 1960. Holden fired back with a new model called the Kingswood, which became a symbol of suburban life and the name for a TV series, which starred an ocker by the name of Ted Bullpitt, whose great love was a Holden Kingswood. Holden, Ford and Toyota now battle it out for the top sales position.

Another steel icon – on a much smaller scale, and found in just about every backyard in Australia – is the Hills Hoist, a rotary clothesline that doesn't take up much room. It was invented by Adelaide motor mechanic Lance Hill, who returned from World War II to find his wife Cynthia desperate for a clothesline that fitted between two orange trees in the backyard.

He made the first from a few lengths of steel tubing, a roll of galvanised wire and cogs from a car differential, which he turned with a crank handle to raise the line so it spun easily in the breeze. Neighbours and friends who saw the contraption wanted one, and soon he couldn't keep up with orders, even though each hoist cost about £10 10s, or two weeks' wages.

Business became so good that Hill and brother-in-law Harold Ling pooled their finances to form a company. By 1948 the clotheslines were in mass production. In the 1950s they bought out a galvanising firm, a tubing manufacturer and a plating and polishing shop to set up production on the site of a former tram and railway carriage plant. The company went public in 1957, not long after Lance Hill retired.

Harold Ling became managing director and remained in that position until his death in 1965; then his son Bob took over.

To get the most from its tubing interests, Hills Industries now also makes laundry trolleys, folding chairs, swings and TV antennas. The clotheslines, also made in New Zealand, are sold in Europe, the Middle East and Asia. The largest model costs around $290.

Another Aussie invention that made life easier and became a great backyard success story was the Victa petrol-driven lawnmower. A tinkerer by the name of Mervyn Victor Richardson got sick and tired of pushing the old blade mower around, so he decided to stick a small Villiers two-stroke engine on one.

His materials included some old pipe for the frame, a peach tin, and billycart wheels. The mower was pretty bloody noisy, but went like a train.

Soon people were queuing up to buy them, and Merv was on his way to becoming a millionaire. He called the mowers Victa, after his middle name, and at first sold them from his garage, but had to build a small factory in the Sydney suburb of Concord within a year.

He used the slogan 'Turn Grass Into Lawn', advertised that the mower would cut paspalum and Paddy's lucerne of any length in one cut, left a velvet-smooth finish on good lawns and didn't require its blades to be sharpened. The mowers sold for £48 10s 6d, which was a lot in 1954. But easy payment terms were available.

The Sydney Opera House is as big a landmark as the Sydney Harbour Bridge, and is recognised the world over. Sitting on Bennelong Point and surrounded by water on three sides, it was meant to look like a sailing ship. Its sails made up part of the Sydney Olympics logo.

Labor Premier Joe Cahill took up a suggestion by Eugene Goossens, the conductor of the Sydney Symphony Orchestra and Conservatorium of Music director, that Sydney build an opera house. Opera was not the biggest pastime of Labor voters, but he accepted the challenge and held an international design competition, which attracted 216 entries from 36 countries.

The judges selected a sketch of graceful sails by a young Danish architect named Joern Utzon, who began work in 1957. The cost was estimated to be $7.5 million, which was high, but nothing like his design had been built before.

Utzon had lots of engineering headaches with his sails, and confrontations with the builders, bureaucrats and meddling politicians pushed the costs through the roof, so to speak. An Opera House lottery with a $100,000 first prize kept the money flowing as the design was changed time and again.

The brawls went on for years, and the Liberal Party – who were still in Opposition – had a field day belting the ears off the Labor Party. The Liberals won power in 1965 and new Works Minister Davis Hughes got stuck into Utzon, blaming him for most of the problems.

In February 1966, he changed Utzon's role to design consultant, and there was hell to pay. Architects and artists held protest marches and one sculptor even went on a hunger strike.

But Utzon had had enough. He went home in April 1966 and has never returned, although since then he has been given the key to Sydney. The job of finishing the building was given to Sydney architects Hall, Steele and Littlemore.

When it opened in October 1973, the cost had risen to more than $100 million. People complained about the flaws in the building, but it's a magnificent piece of architecture, and one of the modern wonders of the world.

Probably the most loved Australian icon of all, though, was a racehorse called Phar Lap, a huge, ungainly, chestnut gelding whose owners wanted to take on the world. The fact that Phar Lap was born at Timaru in New Zealand didn't make the slightest difference. He was – and still is – a national hero.

Bought by turf enthusiast David Davis for 160 guineas (£173 4s), and then leased to Sydney trainer Harry Telford for three years, Phar Lap became Australia's greatest racehorse. He won only one of his first nine races but then came good as a three-year-old after taking out the Rosehill Guineas, and went on to win 36 of his next 41 starts.

Phar Lap, nicknamed 'the Red Terror' by his fans, ran in three Melbourne Cups. In 1929, as a champion three-year-old, he started favourite and finished third, four lengths behind the winner, Nightmarch, after tiring in the straight.

But he followed that up by winning every race in sight, sometimes by 50 lengths, which made him red-hot favourite for the 1930 Melbourne Cup months beforehand.

On the Saturday morning before the race, when Phar Lap was exercising in a quiet street near the Caulfield Racecourse, a car drove up, slowed – and someone fired two shots at the champion horse. Both shots hit a paling fence. Trainer Tommy Woodcock moved Phar Lap from his stables to a secret hideout at Geelong, 65 km from Melbourne, and the horse wasn't seen again until race day, when he arrived at the course under police guard.

There had been heavy rain the night before and the track was saturated. Many people doubted whether even the mighty Phar Lap could carry 9 st 12 lb (about 62.5 kg) over the 2 miles (3200 m). His jockey, Jim Pike, soon put their minds at rest.

Pike had the Red Terror third or fourth on the rails first time round (the race goes around the track twice), but at the back of the course he let him have his head, and Phar Lap shot to the front. Turning into the straight, the horse most likely to beat him, Tregilla, issued a challenge.

Pike saw the danger, gave Phar Lap a hurry-on and tore away, leaving Tregilla and the rest of the field standing. He won, even after slowing down, by three lengths, at 11/8 on, making him the first odds-on favourite in the history of the cup.

The following year, 1931, Phar Lap was made to carry a massive 10 st 10 lb (about 68 kg), 22 lb over weight-for-age. But despite this incredible handicap, punters again sent him out the favourite, at 3/1. But Pike realised that the weight had beaten him well before the home turn and eased him back – he finished eighth.

In 1932 Phar Lap was put on a ship and taken to America for what was to be a national tour. His first race was the Agua Caliente Handicap in Tijuana, Mexico, which he won easily.

But 16 days later, at Menlo Park in California on 5 April 1932, he was dead in his stable. Australians put up several theories, many claiming he was nobbled by the Americans. The official cause was given as colic, but before devoted trainer Tommy Woodcock died in 1985, he said that he might have accidentally killed him with too much of an arsenic-based tonic.

Phar Lap's huge 6 kg heart is preserved in the Institute of Anatomy in Canberra, his stuffed hide is in a Melbourne museum and his skeleton is in a New Zealand museum. There's also a memorial at Sydney's Randwick Racecourse.

There are lots of other Aussie icons: Uluru (Ayers Rock) in central Australia, the Great Barrier Reef, Granny Smith apples and the wine cask (a plastic bag inside a cardboard box), just for a start. Australians designed the first black box for aircraft, the bionic ear and the ute (utility vehicle).

The pedal wireless was built by Alfred Traeger in 1927 for communications for the Royal Flying Doctor Service, which is an icon in itself.

Launched by the Rev. John Flynn of the Australian Inland Mission, pilot Arthur Affleck and Dr Kenyon Welsh operated the first plane: it was equipped with two stretchers and flew out of Cloncurry, in Queensland, on 17 May 1928. In their first year they flew 40,000 km and saw 255 patients.

But a colourful character named Dr Clyde Fenton was actually our first flying doctor. He bought an old Gipsy Moth, registered Uniform November India (UNI), back in 1934 for £500, which he borrowed from his mother and a Sydney MP.

Dr Fenton, operating out of Katherine in the Northern Territory, crashed the plane two months later on Victoria River Downs Station while flying in to treat a woman who had been badly gored by a bull. (UNI had a string of owners, but eventually ended up back in the Northern Territory in a museum at Katherine.)

Dr Fenton acquired other planes, but had to continually fight officialdom and red tape to pioneer aerial medical services in Australia. He once defied an aviation authority grounding to retrieve a sick patient.

Pop top cans, lamingtons, pavlova and a machine for the automatic production of crumpets are Aussie inventions, as are the billy can and the canvas waterbag.

Goanna Oil, one of Australia's oldest bush remedies, has been around since 1910, when Brisbane man Joe Marconi made up some batches of the wonder rub in his garage at home. The first product contained goanna fat, which was extracted by roasting the unfortunate lizard over a piece of iron. The modern version, a cure-all for aches and pains, uses wintergreen, another penetrating ingredient, rather than goanna fat.

Australia now has an 'official' list of living icons, nominated by 10,000 people who voted in a poll taken by the National Trust. Some of them are pretty unlikely, but the 100 'National Treasures' were selected from more than 1200 people who have supposedly made outstanding and lasting contributions.

The National Trust admitted that no two people in Australia would agree with the list, but said it was as good as they could get and covered the spectrum of society. Some of the names were predictable. No person had dominated a sport like cricketer Sir Don Bradman, who hit 271 centuries in a career lasting 20 years, retiring with a Test match average of 99.94 runs.

Former Prime Minister Gough Whitlam made the list, as well as his wife Margaret. (Many people believe Whitlam stuffed up the country before the Governor-General sacked him in 1975.) Aboriginal TV personality Ernie Dingo is there, along with soprano Dame Joan Sutherland, environmentalist Jack Mundey, country singer Slim Dusty, actor Ruth Cracknell, painter Arthur Boyd, runner Betty Cuthbert and horse trainers Bart Cummings and Gai Waterhouse.

Hazel Hawke made the list but her former husband and former Prime Minister Bob didn't. Cook Margaret Fulton, former Prime Minister Paul Keating and tennis players Evonne Cawley (née Goolagong), Rod Laver and Ken Rosewall are there. So too is feminist Germaine Greer. Slim Dusty, who died in late 2003, summed up his fellow treasures this way: 'They're a pretty good bunch of blokes and sheilas ...'

6 Where it all began

The existence of Terra Australis, of a continent in this part of the world, had been the subject of speculation since the time of the Romans. The continent was first named Australia del Espiritu Santo by Quiros, a Spanish navigator, in 1606; it was renamed New Holland by Abel Tasman, a Dutch navigator who landed in Tasmania in 1644; and then Cook, in 1770, initially called the eastern part New Wales and later New South Wales. Although the name New Holland was used in British documents up to 1849, Governor Lachlan Macquarie had officially adopted the name Australia in 1817, as it was already commonly used.

It was probably a bit of luck that Captain Arthur Phillip took a fancy to Sydney Harbour back in 1788 when he arrived from England with 11 ships in the First Fleet carrying the first settlers, 564 male and 192 female convicts, 450 crew and marines, 28 wives and 30 children, half of them belonging to the convicts. He initially parked the fleet further down the coast at Botany Bay, the spot where English authorities told him to go, but he didn't like it much because the soil looked poor, the water drained from a swamp, and the gum trees appeared to be of little use for building anything but fires. Neither were they fussed about millions of enormous black and red ants running everybloodywhere.

The Aborigines at Botany Bay watched the fleet from a safe distance, no doubt wondering what the heck was going on. The *Chronicle* correspondent wrote: 'They do not appear uncommonly hostile, although the men carry spears of great length, at one end of which is the bone of a stingray. On occasion, they seem very friendly, calling and shouting and dancing in a manner most strange. They showed some anger when a number of men from *Sirius* (one of the ships) were ordered to cut down some trees and clear the ground for saw pits.'

Phillip had a poke around a bit further north and found Port Jackson, which Captain James Cook had named in 1770 when he first discovered the Land Down Under. Phillip decided to settle there on the banks of a freshwater creek which became known as the Tank Stream. The fleet sailed out of Botany Bay and landed on the new site on 26 January, which is now celebrated as Australia Day.

Phillip had beaten French navigator La Perouse to Botany Bay by only a couple of days, so Australians could quite easily have been talking la langue étrangère nowadays instead of English. La Perouse had anchored off Botany Bay but couldn't sail in because it was too windy. His ships disappeared for a day or two but came back just as Phillip's fleet was leaving – they waved at each other as they passed.

Other than Phillip's determination, the first settlers had none of the requirements needed to establish a successful colony. The convicts, a bunch of petty crooks from the Mother Country, were mostly uneducated, had few skills, and were not the least bit interested in working for the marines.

Many of the officers and marines were equally unwilling to have a go. They lacked enthusiasm for this highly inhospitable faraway place, and contributed little to the initial development of Sydney – the town was named by Phillip as a compliment to the Home Secretary, Lord Sydney.

After a portable hospital, a canvas house for Phillip and tents for the others were put up, the women convicts, who had till now remained on board the ships, were given fresh clothing and taken ashore on 6 February 1788. A correspondent for the London Chronicle, in a despatch home, wrote: 'Within a short space of time the men convicts got among them and there were such scenes of debauchery and riot ensuing between them that it is beyond your correspondent's capabilities to describe ...'

Phillip, at the reading of his Royal Commission with great pomp and ceremony the next day, gave the convicts a dressing down about their behaviour, banned them from entering the women's camp and warned them that they would be fired upon if they tried. He also told them that stealing the most trifling item would be punished with death. They apparently got the message, and the development of Sydney began.

It was anything but orderly. The soldiers made potato rum which they used as currency, theft and prostitution were rife and anyone who stepped out of line copped a lashing. But despite the rough lifestyle, the magic of the harbour was always there, its clear blue water and golden sands shimmering in the warm sun. The London Chronicle correspondent wrote: 'It must surely be the most splendid harbour in all the world, safe from all winds and wide enough for a thousand ships to ride in.'

By 1880, Sydney was an unsophisticated seaport of 300,000 people and 3200 pubs. Steam trams and horse-drawn buses rattled up and down the streets and the residents liked a drink. So much so that a commission of inquiry in 1887 reported that compared with places of similar size, Sydney was 'unquestionably more statistically drunken than most cities in the mother country'. In fact, the report said, the only place drunker was Limerick, in Ireland.

Brandy was a popular drink, much of it made locally (and therefore pretty rough) and selling for around 23d a gallon (4.45 litres). Scotch whisky was slightly cheaper, while beer sold for 8d a gallon. Many of the pubs had 'private bars', rooms rented by girls keen to do business on a couch behind a screen or curtain. They didn't sell booze. You bought that from the main bar for a small surcharge. A newspaper reporter at the time wrote that the bars were patronised 'mainly by city johnnies and country juggins'.

But despite the seedy side of Sydney in the 1880s, the Parliament, whose members also enjoyed a degree of corruption (perhaps not everything has changed?), put up a strong fight against antisocial behaviour. Flogging, which had been abolished in 1877, was made law again in 1883, and boys as young as 10 could be given 18 lashes for minor misdeeds such as writing graffiti on a wall or picking someone else's flowers.

The authorities were determined to safeguard property, but they didn't give two hoots about crimes against people, especially the working classes. You could get ten years in the cooler for stealing a horse, but if you donged someone on the head with a four by two piece of timber, all you got was a £1 fine.

Until 1828, people in the colony had been rounded up like sheep in a muster to be counted, but when it was discovered that the governor had no right to compel free men and women to attend this counting, the free men and women refused to do it. Authorities then introduced the Census, but figures from it were kept under lock and key for many years.

The 1901 Census – held in the year of Federation – showed that there were 487,900 people in Sydney, which included a few thousand New Zealanders and 6529 visitors on 163 ships anchored in the harbour. The biggest suburb was Balmain, with 30,076 people, followed by Redfern, Newtown, North Sydney, Paddington and Glebe. And Parramatta was considered part of the bush … it certainly isn't any more!

Many think that today's Sydney, a city of 12,130 square kilometres and home to more than 3.8 million people who live in 1,426,260 dwellings, is one of the best places in the world. And former American President Bill Clinton agrees. On a visit Down Under, he reckoned wife Hillary wanted him to make her his official representative at the 2000 Olympic Games. But he sent his daughter instead. 'I cannot think of a better place in the entire world, a more shining example of how people can come together as one nation in one community, than Sydney, Australia,' he said.

Readers of the two travel magazines with the largest circulation in the world,

Conde Nast Traveler and *Travel and Leisure*, repeatedly vote Sydney the world's best city, beating the likes of Florence, Paris, Rome and Venice. Sydney also finishes a mile in front of Vancouver, San Francisco, London, New York and Vienna, according to the polls.

Travellers perceive Sydney as being friendly, open-minded and easygoing, with British visitors voting the relaxed outdoor lifestyle as the number one attraction. Like the Japanese and the Germans, they head straight for the Opera House, the Harbour Bridge and Bondi Beach. British visitors also want to pat a kangaroo, eat Australian food and tear into some Australian wine.

Americans visit Sydney because they're mad about the laidback lifestyle and the interesting people they meet. The Japanese want to see the city that hosted the 2000 Olympics, and have soft spots for the harbour and the cosmopolitan atmosphere. The restaurants and good shopping also rate high on their list.

You won't go hungry in Sydney. There are lots of places to eat, with more than 4700 cafés and restaurants scattered throughout the city. And the old traditional menus of beef, lamb and peas and potatoes have given way to culinary delights from other cultures: from the Chinese, who have been here since the gold rushes in the1850s, the Italians and Greeks, who began opening their establishments in the 1950s, and more recently from the Thais, the Vietnamese and the Indians. Not to mention the French, whose cuisine has always been a high point of European culture – there have for decades been French restaurants rated among the top in all Australia's major cities – and the Japanese, who are newcomers, but whose food exhibits a delicacy and attention to the visual that even your average Aussie now appreciates.

Luigi Coluzzi, from Bar Coluzzi in Darlinghurst, likens Sydney to Rome and Venice, but with more people choosing to sit outside to eat. And the beauty of Sydney's food is that the new generation chefs have now used their skills to add Australian ingredients like kangaroo, emu, crocodile and native peppers to their meals.

Italian restaurateurs Lucio Galletto, Steve Manfredi and Armando Percuoco, all long regarded by Sydney people as leading names in the restaurant industry, have been rewarded by the Italian Government for 'helping spread and adding value to authentic Italian cooking overseas'. They flew to Rome to receive the Insegna del Ristorante Italiano from the Italian President.

Beppe Polese, Sydney's longest-serving Italian restaurateur, was invited to Rome to receive the award of Cavaliere della Republica Italiana for services to the industry, also from the Italian President. As far as he knows, he's only the seventh Italian-born Australian to receive the award, which is the equivalent to a British knighthood.

When Beppe opened his East Sydney restaurant in 1956, he served up mussels and calamari, but Australians wouldn't have a bar of that. They regarded the dishes as fish bait, and reckoned spaghetti was the only Italian tucker they would eat. His customers now are much more open-minded and tuck into delicacies like bollito misto, a mixture of meat and sausages simmered in spicy stock, and baccala, saltwater cod.

Steve Manfredi, of bel mondo, in The Rocks in Sydney, shows how good food can be authentically Italian and still have an Australian twist. His pumpkin-filled tortelli di zucca, which his grandmother used to make in northern Italy, tastes just as good in Sydney with Queensland blue pumpkins. Steve reckons that although his food is unmistakably Italian, he speaks with an Australian accent and he cooks Italian with an Australian accent. Bellissimo, mate!

But while the food's up there with the best, liquor laws didn't kept pace with Sydney's international lifestyle: restaurants for years lobbied the State Government for a change. For example, a person who stood to propose a toast at a wedding reception in a restaurant was breaking the liquor laws. It was also illegal to drink while standing away from a table, and it was illegal to move between tables with a drink in the hand.

If you joined a group of people having lunch and had a drink with them, you were breaking the law unless you also ordered a hearty meal. The restaurant and catering association believed Sydney needed laws that suited the needs of customers. The old laws weren't really enforced, and amendments to the Liquor Act were finally put in place for the Olympics in 2000 to allow restaurants to have drinking areas for non-dining customers.

The average Sydneysider is 33 years old and married with three kids. Household incomes average $800 to $990 a week, which is higher than the Australian average ($700 to $799) and higher than what people who live in the bush earn. The average Sydney bloke works in manufacturing, construction, property or business services and has skilled trade qualifications.

The average Sydney woman works in property or business services and health and community services. She is most likely to be a professional or in mid-level clerical, sales or service work. Her educational qualifications are pretty high – women hold 48 per cent of Sydney's university degrees.

There are 38,800 people in Sydney who have Aboriginal or Torres Strait Island origins. This is around 1 per cent of the city's population. They tend to be young – a third of them are aged under 15, whereas less than a quarter of the rest of the population is under 15.

Most Sydneysiders drive themselves to work (72 per cent of men and 62 per cent of women), while nearly equal numbers of men and women, 19 per cent, use trains, buses or ferries. The rest either walk, ride their bikes or swim. On Census night in 2001, 17 per cent of Sydney homes had no wheels parked outside.

Sydneysiders are big spenders on housing, with rents and home-loan repayments way up on what they were a few years ago. Average mortgage repayments are around $1200 a month, which makes a big hole in an average pay packet. Tax Office figures show that Australia's richest people live in Sydney's inner-eastern suburbs of Darling Point, Point Piper, Edgecliff and Rushcutters Bay, where the average taxable income is $70,148. Needless to say, the garages are filled with Mercedes, BMWs and Porsches.

Bellevue Hill comes next with $61,533, followed by Northbridge $59,833, and Balmoral, Beauty Point, Mosman, The Spit and Spit Junction with $59,657. But nearly half of the people in Sydney earn less than $15,600 a year. Only 5.3 per cent earn $52,000 or more. The Australia-wide average taxable income for individuals is $25,739: for men it is $30,023 and for women, who are clearly still doing much worse, it's $20,723.

About 80 per cent of Australians speak only English at home. Those who don't are likely to speak Italian, Chinese or Greek. But in Sydney, the multilingual capital of Australia, 67 per cent speak only English, with the main alternatives Chinese, Arabic and Greek. Other popular languages include Cantonese, Vietnamese, Spanish, Croatian, Korean, German and Hindi.

Sydney is also the sexiest city in Australia. A survey by condom-maker Durex to find the nation's sexiest city resulted in Sydney receiving half the vote, while Melbourne received 34 per cent, followed by Brisbane on 12 per cent. Canberra, Darwin and Hobart are definitely un-sexy places, polling only 1 per cent between them.

The survey showed that Sydneysiders spent an average 20.7 minutes having sex each time, which was almost 3 minutes longer than the world average of 17.9 minutes. But Americans have the best staying power, averaging 25.3 minutes, with Canadians coming next with 24.4 minutes. Sydney women think Brad Pitt would be the best celebrity to go to bed with, while the men voted for Demi Moore and Sharon Stone.

For many people, Sydney is Bondi Beach, and there's little doubt it's one of the world's most famous strips of sand, packed on weekends with people looking for bronze suntans or partying in the cafés and pubs. The 1 km long beach is in a natural basin, enclosed by the north and south headlands, Ben Buckler Point and Mackenzies Point.

Bondi has always been on top of the heap in contemporary beach fashion, with topless swimming having been allowed for ages. But in days gone by, beach inspectors ordered women swimmers to wear skirts and men to wear jumpers, with trouser legs to the knee, adding a shirt on top to cover the figure.

In 1946, when the United States began testing atomic bombs at Bikini Atoll, in the Pacific Ocean, a French dude by the name of Louis Reard invented a daring two-piece swimsuit and called it the bikini – he said it was as bare as the island after the devastation of the nuclear blasts.

Australian designer Paula Stafford pioneered the bikini in Australia. But it was slow to get going at Bondi because council inspectors wouldn't allow 'bikini birds' on the beach. They were still chasing them off right up until 1961 – funnily enough, it was the same council, in 1978, that was the first in Sydney to give the OK for topless swimming on a public beach.

Bondi still brings out the exhibitionists. As well as the topless sunbakers spread along the sand like kebabs on sticks, the place is packed with lifesavers, board riders, buskers, partygoers, joggers, fishermen and tourists. Several thousand people will gather on the beach to watch a nude surfing competition where 60 naked surfers, men and women, go all out to impress the judges with their natural talents.

But despite being such a tourist hot spot – and claiming to having the oldest surf lifesaving club in the world – Bondi became noticeably shabby in more recent years, and plans to give it a much-needed boost never came to much. Redevelopment of Campbell Parade, the main drag and Sydney's most popular stretch of beachside road, was a welcome improvement, and now there is a string of cafés there, serving anything from fish and chips to coffee and gelato or international cuisine.

The local council, Waverley Council, put pressure on the Olympic organisers to contribute towards the upgrading of community facilities in return for using a section of beach for the Olympics volleyball competition. The temporary stadium, which was built on the sand and seated 10,000, was fenced, which people weren't happy about – but most reckoned the inconvenience was worth it in the long run because of the promotion the suburb received during the Olympics.

Bondi residents love their suburb and are prepared to stand up and be counted when the crunch comes. When plans for a $150 million privately owned train link between Bondi Junction and the beach were announced, more than 600 rolled up for a protest rally calling for the idea to be scrapped. Singer Kate Ceberano and her brother Phil added their voices to the protest with the song 'You Don't Know What You've Got 'Till It's Gone' and actor Michael Caton joined in a shouted chorus of 'Tell 'em they're dreamin'.'

Speakers told the protesters that Bondi Beach was a sacred site to all Australians, and it was the duty of residents to protect it. Rally co-ordinator Simon Gibson said the Bondi Beach Railway Company, a joint venture by Lend Lease and Macquarie Bank, should walk away from the plan – or be branded an 'environmental vandal'.

Bondi Beach is the site of Sydney's biggest Christmas celebration. Thousands of Pommie backpackers and others gather there every year for a non-stop party. A few years ago it turned into a drunken brawl – residents then formed a citizen's group called the Icebreakers to police the festivities and restore law and order. Tough new controls on drinking and rowdiness now help keep the peace. Grog was banned everywhere except in a tightly patrolled, fenced-in, enclosure visitors dubbed The

Cage. People queue up to ten-deep to buy wine or beer in a plastic middy glass so they can hang it around their necks in a cooler on a string.

The changes didn't impress some of the regular ragers. Scotsman Ian McDonald reckoned Bondi had lost its Christmas spirit. 'You've got to turn the place over to the people at times like this. They've neutered the bloody thing,' he said. But people still pack the beach at Christmas, and the crowd can peak at around 40,000. That's one helluva party!

Kings Cross is another Sydney icon. It's the best known few hundred metres of pavement in the city, where people live to extremes, relishing every minute of the area's once-sleazy reputation, its restaurants and bars, its trendy coffee shops, its spruikers, and the bright glow of neon lights. People flock there looking for sex, a strip club, a fix or just some plain old-fashioned fun.

Although it still has a reputation as a dangerous but exciting place, Kings Cross, home to architects and actors, witches and bankers, characters and crims, poets and sex workers, is now a far safer and better place than it was. New hotels and apartments have replaced many of the dives, and even the upmarket brothels do the right thing.

Maggies, which has the reputation of being one of the best-run houses in town, went to South Sydney Council for advice on how to become legal when the government relaxed prostitution laws. Maggie took notice of council officers and installed sprinklers in every room and put in smoke detectors and fire doors.

She won't employ girls on drugs and hasn't had any trouble for years. The worst thing that happens is a bloke passing out. Then they give him a room for the night and send him home the next day. That's service for you.

Sydney is well and truly a harbour city. As well as the 70 or so golden beaches inside the city limits, the harbour is a busy thoroughfare for ferries, launches, seaplanes, sailing boats and anything else that will float. Top Italian architect Mario Botta said it was 'a metaphorical piazza' for Sydney, the city's centre of gravity.

Sydney's Gay and Lesbian Mardi Gras, a month-long queer event, contradicts the tough, manly image Aussies like to project, but it's also one of the most popular festivals in Sydney. The first Mardi Gras was held in June 1978, and ended in a riot at Kings Cross, with the cops arresting dozens of people. The names of those arrested were published in the *Sydney Morning Herald* – now the *Herald* publishes a full guide to the offbeat event. Times change.

The monorail also gets people yakking. Entrepreneur and agent Harry M Miller says it's the most appalling piece of visual pollution he's seen anywhere in the world, only slightly behind the bombing of Hiroshima. He reckons the government should buy it and send in the demolishers. But it was built as a 1988 bicentenary project, and works well as an easy way to get to Darling Harbour.

Professor Stuart Rees of Sydney University's Centre of Peace and Conflict Studies reckons the city's greatest mistake was tearing up the tram lines. Trams were a form of transport which could have given the city character; instead, everyone now relies on the internal combustion engine and diesel buses that belch out unhealthy fumes.

Just west of Circular Quay, where the buskers perform in the sun, is the area known as The Rocks, which was Sydney's first village. From the colony's earliest days, the dark narrow streets and lanes were hideouts for crooks and street gangs.

Now preserved for its historic value, The Rocks is full of galleries and museums, gift shops, restaurants and pubs. Sydney's oldest pub, the Hero of Waterloo, is there, along with Sydney's oldest building, Cadman's Cottage, built in 1816.

A few kilometres away is Darling Harbour, which was converted from a derelict industrial waterfront site of disused wharves and stray cats into a huge entertainment, exhibition and convention centre in the heart of Sydney. It's one of the most visited places in the city, but feelings about it are still mixed. Fashion designer Marc Keighery says it's a huge blight on the landscape and describes it as vulgar. 'It's like something you would find in Surfers Paradise. It is all the things we don't want in our city.'

There are lots of ugly buildings in Sydney that come in for some harsh criticism, but the city would have had heaps more eyesores if it hadn't been for a bloke named Jack Mundey.

In the early 1970s, Jack, then secretary of the Builders' Labourers Federation, imposed what are now called green bans on old inner-city buildings earmarked for demolition by high-rise developers. Green bans were also put on new building projects the union considered environmentally undesirable.

These included cutting up the Botanic Gardens to make way for a car park for the Opera House, the redevelopment of the historic Rocks area and the preservation of low-cost housing at Woolloomooloo. The bans really stirred up the developers, and they indeed lost some of the battles, despite all their money and power.

Jack Mundey believed the green bans were probably the most exciting thing to happen in a union anywhere in the world, because they showed that workers were concerned not only about their jobs and their money but also about other people, and about bigger issues. 'We were fighting for ordinary people to have a say in what happens in their society,' he said.

It's lucky there are people who still care about the things around us. About 300 rare and endangered golden bell frogs found on the Olympics site won a reprieve from a sticky end after a five-year campaign by environmentalists. The frogs were found in a disused brick pit at Homebush Bay, and Olympic organisers spent $400,000 building a series of tunnels and ponds under Link Road to protect them – these are of course used by other animals as well.

Sydney's weather is always a talking point. No matter how wet people reckon Melbourne is, Sydney, with 1160 millimetres a year, has almost twice as much rainfall as its southern rival. And on average, Melbourne gets more sun in summer than Sydney's 7.2 hours. But in winter, Melbourne is bleak, with only 3.7 hours of sun a day compared with Sydney's 6.1. Sydney's all-year average temperature is 18°C compared with Melbourne's 15.3°C, so it's warmer all year round.

Melbourne, Australia's second city, is famous for its muddy Yarra River, which flows upside-down, and its madness for that funny game of football, Australian Rules. Also a haven for the avant-garde, visitors swear by its shopping, arts, restaurants and nightlife. And, of course, it's famous for the Australian Formula 1 Grand Prix, the Australian Open (tennis) and the Melbourne Cup (horseracing).

Home to 3.4 million people, Melbourne was established in 1835 after a bloke named John Batman bought the land from Aborigines, paying with clothing, tools and beads. The new settlement was named in 1837 and the colony of Victoria was declared in 1851.

Melbourne, the youngest city its size in the world, was boosted in the 1850s by the discovery of gold, which set the pattern for its diversified future. There was a big influx of fortune-seekers from around the world, many of them Chinese, generating lots of wealth and extravagance.

Melbourne's residents have come from all over Europe, particularly Greece, Italy, Poland and Turkey, and more recently from Cambodia and Vietnam. They have had a big influence on the city's culture and the change in eating habits – from a culinary wasteland, Melbourne now offers an enormous variety of taste sensations.

Famous also for its leafy suburbs and gardens, the Victorian transport department used to have the slogan 'The Garden State' on its number-plates. In the 1990s they changed that to 'Victoria, On the Move'. Queenslanders, who call Victorians 'Mexicans' because they arrive from south of the border, reckon that where all the Victorians move to is Queensland, to escape the cold weather.

Brisbane, Queensland's capital, got going in 1824 after an overflow of some of the toughest convicts from Sydney was dumped at Moreton Bay – authorities thought it was as good a place as any to put them. But a year later the penal settlement was moved south, to a site on the Brisbane River. The river and the city were named by Surveyor-General John Oxley in honour of the then Governor of NSW, Sir Thomas Brisbane.

Free settlers were banned from going within 50 miles (80 km) of the walled prison until the powers that be in England stopped sending convicts to Australia; the area was opened to everyone in 1842. The settlement grew into what is now Brisbane, and in 1859 Queensland separated from NSW and became a State.

With a population of 1.6 million, Brisbane is now Australia's third-largest city. For many years it was considered a big country town, but it shook off that image by promoting major events such as the 1982 Commonwealth Games and Expo 88. And Surfers Paradise is home to a round of the Indy car races.

Free settlers from England got Adelaide going in 1836, and Perth was founded as a British military colony in 1829. Darwin, which was another strategic outpost for the British, was bombed by the Japanese in World War II and almost destroyed by Cyclone Tracy on Christmas Eve 1974.

Adelaide, with a population of 1.1 million, is dubbed the 'city of churches' and is also known for its old stone buildings, green parkland, arts festivals and a pretty good drop of wine. It also had the Formula 1 Grand Prix until Melbourne stole it.

Just out of town is Hahndorf, the oldest surviving German settlement in Australia. It has lots of German-looking buildings, a Founders Day when truckloads of beer are consumed, and a genuine-style burgermeister, an honorary mayor.

Perth was founded as the Swan River Settlement, and grew slowly until convicts were brought in to boost the working force. The cons built many of the city's fine buildings, including the Town Hall and Government House.

Darwin, named after British naturalist Charles Darwin, who visited the settlement on HMS *Beagle* in 1839, has a reputation as a frontier town of buffalo-catchers, prawn fishermen, crocodile shooters and wild waterfront bars. It was the boozing capital of a thirsty nation. Yee haa!

But the Japanese took a liking to Darwin in World War II and repeatedly bombed it, forcing the evacuation of its residents and the setting up of heavy artillery. General Douglas MacArthur visited Darwin during one of the raids.

Cyclone Tracy had a bigger impact. Around 7500 homes were destroyed and damaged in the biggest natural disaster in Australia. Some of the older residents say the cyclone blew away the city's wild reputation.

Canberra, the meeting place of the nation, is where you can rub shoulders with the pollies. They'll tell you the district has never had as many top-ranking reds as the day in April 1954 when Russian diplomat Vladimir Petrov walked out of the Russian Embassy, sought political asylum and turned over sensitive documents to the Australian Government, which claimed he had been a spy for the KGB.

Now they're talking about their cool climate boutique wines – these are earning the national capital a big reputation, as are the 300 restaurants, cafés, bars, pubs and clubs which cater to its cosmopolitan lifestyle.

Parliament House is the focal point of Canberra and one of the world's most acclaimed buildings. Other interesting buildings in the Parliamentary Triangle include Old Parliament House, the National Gallery, the National Library and the High Court, along with the War Memorial and Questacon, which makes science fun.

Canberra has for years struggled to shrug off the 'shiny bum' and 'fat cat' tags that it has been given because it's a city of public servants living in their own green suburbs. But it has developed its own identity.

Having a national capital was agreed to when the colonies were federated into Australian States in 1901. The site for the capital was selected in 1908, and the name Canberra, from the Aboriginal word for meeting place, was selected in 1913.

American architect Walter Burley Griffin was given the job of designing the city after an international competition. Canberra's artificial lake, which has its own water police, was named after Burley Griffin.

That leaves Hobart. With a population around 190,000, Hobart is the capital of Tasmania, that little State of Australia across the Bass Strait that's often forgotten. And it almost wasn't part of Australia – it was claimed by Holland in 1642 and named Van Diemen's Land, then taken by the British and used as another penal colony from 1803. The Sydney to Hobart yacht race finishes there, and the State is famous for its apples.

7 Backyard playgrounds

Pixar, the clever makers of *Finding Nemo*, knew what they were doing when they used the Great Barrier Reef as the backdrop for their brilliant animated film. The colour, movement and detail, although computer-generated, showed the reef in all its glory.

The story is about an adventurous little clownfish called Nemo who gets caught in a net by divers and ends up in a fish tank in a dentist's surgery overlooking Sydney Harbour. His over-protective and timid father Marlin sets off down the reef to try to find him, spurred on by a friendly but forgetful fish called Dory.

On his epic and dangerous swim he meets schools of bizarre characters and fishy obstacles, including a trio of 'nice' great white sharks on a 12-step path to a better life ('Remember, fish are friends and not food') who speak with an Aussie accent. Their voices come from Barry Humphries, Bruce Spence and Eric Bana. It's the best advertisement the reef could ever have.

Nemo's friends in the fish tank plan a risky escape route down the sink, telling him 'all drains lead to Sydney Harbour', which no doubt upset many Sydneysiders, because it isn't true. However, Nemo makes his escape, meets up with Dad and returns to life back on the Great Barrier Reef.

The reef is one of the natural wonders of the world, and one of the world's best holiday destinations. It's also been named the most valuable coral reef system on Earth, worth about $57 billion to the international economy as a tourist destination.

A study by researchers at Yale University showed that the annual recreational benefits of the reef to Australia were around $577 million a year. Every visitor to it forks out between $500 and $1200 during their stay.

The reef's hundreds of different types of coral, fish, dugongs, green turtles (like Finding Nemo's hippie turtle called Crush) and white sandy beaches make it a magnet for tourists. The problem is, the tourists are helping stuff up the World Heritage-listed reef, which stretches 2300 km along Queensland's coast.

They're breaking the coral by walking on it and dropping boat anchors on it, and they're spilling fuel on it. Scientists say people who slap a coating of sunscreen on themselves and go swimming or snorkelling are also adding to the damage being done to the fragile coral.

But none of the damage is deliberate, and the visitors realise its worth – otherwise they wouldn't go there. And there's support from tourism operators and government agencies to develop tourism that is sustainable over the longer term.

More than two million people visit the reef each year, making tourism a major earner for the Queensland economy. Tourists are carried to the reef by more than 500 commercial vessels, and tourism is permitted through nearly all the marine park.

Fishing is restricted in some areas and animals such as whales, dolphins, green turtles and dugongs are protected. Plans are afoot to increase protected areas from five per cent of the park to more than 30 per cent.

In stark contrast to the blue waters of the Pacific is Uluru, or Ayers Rock, about 500 km southwest of Alice Springs and plumb in the middle of Australia. Rising starkly from the desert, it's probably one of the few bloody great rocks in the world that changes its colour: it looks anything from blue to red, grey to brown or orange to yellow, particularly at sunrise and sunset.

Photographers sit around for days with their cameras recording its different colours. The rock dominates the flat countryside – it is 335 metres high, and its circumference is 8.8 km. It and the nearby Olgas, another amazing place, are in the Kata Tjuta National Park, which is now owned and run by the local Anangu Aborigines, who have lived around there for thousands of years. The Federal Government returned the land to them in 1985, and the Anangu in turn leased the land back to the government to be reserved as a national park for 99 years.

The Aborigines say there's an energy source below the ground they call Tjukurpa – the dreamtime. The name is also used to refer to the record of all activities of an ancestor, from the beginning of their travels to the end. Anangu say the area around Uluru is inhabited by dozens of ancestral beings whose activities are recorded at many different places. At each site, the events that took place there can be recounted. There's also some sort of physical feature at each site which represents the activities of the ancestral being and the living presence of Tjukurpa, which could be a rock, tree or a sand hill. For all of these, the creative essence remains forever within the physical form – information about them is kept secret, and never disclosed to people who aren't Aboriginal.

The Aborigines don't like people climbing the rock, but hundreds still do. Some of them come to a sticky end from heart attacks, heat exhaustion, falling over the side or, maybe, some sort of spiritual intervention! It's OK to walk around the base.

There's plenty of accommodation at Uluru, some of it very expensive. The new Longitude 131 resort charges $1500 a night but says guests want for nothing, except a sprinkler system. In October 2003 fire tore through the camp-like resort, causing millions of dollars' worth of damage to the self-contained luxury villas. Three days later a second fire broke out, forcing mass evacuations.

The Olgas are about 30 km from Uluru. They are 36 rounded domes; the tallest, Mt Olga, is 546 metres high. Visitors have the choice of two walks. The Valley of the Winds is a 7 km track that circles several of the Olgas, but if the temperature is likely to be more than 36°C, the track is closed. The other walk is the Olga Gorge, which is a 2 km walk.

The Blue Mountains for years gave the colony a headache, because none of the explorers could find a way across. Finally, Blaxland, Wentworth and Lawson did the job in 1813. Heading across the mountains now you'll roughly follow the same track the three explorers blazed across this seemingly insurmountable barrier to open up desperately needed fertile grazing lands in the west.

There's lots of reminders of the pioneering days. Aboriginal rock carvings, convict-built stone bridges, historic buildings, old coach houses and inns. Energetic people can take in the wild side of the scenery, the invigorating air and unforgettable views on one of the more than 40 marked walks.

On the way you'll pass the Blue Mountains' best known hotel, the imposing Hydro Majestic at Medlow Bath. It was used in World War II by the US Army as a hospital for soldiers wounded in the Pacific.

Legend has it that in the 1920s and 1930s a bell was rung each morning to let guests know that it was time to return to their own beds. Not so, says Mary Shaw, of Megalong Valley, whose grandfather Mark Foy built the pub. A dressing bell sounded at 8 am for guests to get ready for breakfast and a siren sounded two hours earlier for staff to start work, but she insists there was no bell for philanderers. Her grandfather always threatened to sue anyone who repeated the rumour.

Katoomba's Carrington Hotel is another building worth seeing. It originally supplied the water and electricity for the whole town and now, after total restoration, it is an icon of tourism heritage.

The former home of flamboyant artist Norman Lindsay can be found at

Faulconbridge. He is well known for his voluptuous nudes, painted in the early 1900s, when most people frowned on that sort of thing. The gallery and museum houses some of his most important works, and you can have a picnic in the landscaped gardens. Lindsay also illustrated books and magazines.

There are also other touristy things on the mountains: Katoomba's most famous natural attraction, the Three Sisters; a Scenic Railway down the steepest railway incline in the world to the valley floor below; the Sceniscender aerial cable car for a trip through World Heritage-listed rainforest; and for people who like heights, the Scenic Skyway.

Leura, known as the Jewel in the Mountains' Crown, has gardens everywhere, dozens of little specialty shops, restaurants, galleries and tea and coffee houses. Some of the Blue Mountains' most spectacular waterfalls are in the Wentworth Falls/Lawson/Hazelbrook area.

But be warned. The people who live on the mountains are very protective of their World Heritage-listed area and are prepared to fight when they feel it is threatened. Low-level joyflights by ex-military fighter jets annoyed local residents so much that they campaigned to have them totally banned. The jets were operating the joyflights on permits that were meant to be used for demonstration flights and intense lobbying by local pollies resulted in the permits being revoked. Residents said they had no problem with people having joyflights in jet fighters, but zooming low over houses and down through some of the valleys really got them annoyed.

Locals are also dead against the Golden Arches becoming part of their community. An action group called Mountains Against McDonalds threatened to send out calls worldwide if need be to help convince the fast-food giant to leave Katoomba a Mac-free zone.

The group said the mountains stretched for 75 km but the cultures were different in different parts of the mountains. Glenbrook, Blaxland and Springwood were basically commuter suburbs of Sydney, they said, but Katoomba had a tourism industry and a different appeal for visitors. A McDonalds drive-through was completely inappropriate, the group said; they were ready to go into action if Big Mac lodged a development application. So far, it hasn't happened.

People looking for neon lights, nightlife and surf and sand flock to Queensland's Gold Coast. It's also the sixth-largest city in Australia, with around 425,500 people.

Not so long ago, the Gold Coast was a vast expanse of nearly nothing. A bloke named Bruce Small, who sold pushbikes, got it going. He was the mayor for years and introduced innovations like meter maids to push the tourism side.

Now there are more than 500 restaurants and cafés, hotels, casino, theme parks like Warner Brothers Movie World, Sea World, Dreamworld and Wet 'n' Wild, as well as several wildlife parks. The city hosts a string of sporting events – the Indy car race, the Gold Coast marathon, the Asia Pacific Masters Games, horseraces, triathlons and the Australian surf lifesaving championships.

But high up there on the publicity stakes is schoolies week. Thousands of kids converge on the Gold Coast every November to hang out with their mates. Drinking takes top priority, along with sex and generally mucking up. There are usually lots of arrests for various offensive, unruly and drunken behaviours, but according to the academics, that's part of a necessary transition to adulthood.

University psychologist Phil Harker says young people who don't mark the beginning of adulthood with rituals of some kind – whether they are like schoolies week or not – in which parental controls are relaxed, might have more difficulty believing they have grown up. Who knew that denying teenagers the chance to act like idiots could result in them relying on their parents for guidance until they were 26 or 30 years old!

The Snowy Mountains, in southern NSW and northeastern Victoria, are Australia's winter playground. The High Country is a magnet for skiers and other people who like the snow, and in summer the bushwalkers and mountain bike riders take over the alpine resorts.

Bushfires, started by lightning strikes in January 2003, burnt out 400,000 hectares of Kosciuszko National Park, adjacent forests and pastures, but failed to stop the booming tourism trade. The NSW National Parks & Wildlife Service promoted the burnt-out area, saying that people had the opportunity to see something they would not see again in their lifetime: nature's rebirthing of an entire landscape.

Mt Kosciuszko, Australia's highest mountain at 2228 metres, was first climbed and named by a mysterious bloke who arrived in Sydney in April 1839, on the French ship *Justine*. He had the colony wondering about his bona fides from day one, because he had visited a string of countries around the world before he turned up in NSW and seemed to have an endless supply of money.

Paul Edmund de Strzelecki, who called himself a count and was later knighted, made friends easily with people in high places. He walked an estimated 11,200 km on his expeditions in Australia. Strzelecki, accompanied by James Macarthur, James Riley and an Aborigine named Charlie Tarra, set out in early 1840 to explore the Alps and the area now known as Gippsland, which he named.

On 15 February 1840, Strzelecki climbed the highest point in Australia. When he reached the summit, he thought the scenery resembled a mound over the tomb of his hero, freedom-fighter Tadeusz Kosciuszko, at Krakow in Poland. Later, in a letter to his lady friend Adyna Turno, he wrote: 'Although in a foreign country, on foreign ground, but amongst a free people who appreciate freedom and its votaries, I could not refrain from giving it the name Mt Kosciuszko.'

Strzelecki spelt Kosciuszko without a z. The z was put back in the name in the 1990s, after intense lobbying by an interested group of people convinced the Geographical Names Board that it should be there.

In the meantime the National Parks & Wildlife Service, getting over the disastrous bushfires, commissioned a report called 'Between a rock and a hard place', which looked at a number of options for environmentally friendly dunnies on the walk to the summit of Kosciuszko. The service installed temporary toilets for the 70,000 people who trekked through the national park in summer, but reckoned these were unsightly, sitting among the boulders of a sensitive alpine environment. Such unique circumstances called for some imaginative and constructive solutions, the service's Snowy Mountains regional manager Dave Darlington said. They would be Australia's highest loos. By 2004 the service still had no solution to the problem and was still looking for suitable designs.

When William Dampier in his leaky Admiralty cast-off ship HMS *Roebuck* was sailing along Australia's west coast for the second time, back in 1699, he discovered and named Shark Bay, probably because he thought there were lots of sharks there. It turned out they were dolphins.

Shark Bay is behind Hartog Island, one of an island group found by Dirk Hartog in 1616. He looked around for a couple of days, nailed a pewter plate with a record of his visit etched on it to a post and then sailed off in his ship *Eendracht*. That's how close Australians came to speaking Dutch!

There are two towns at Shark Bay now. One, with the strange name of Monkey Mia, still attracts the dolphins, which swim in to the beach to say g'day to the visitors. You can hop in the water and go for a dip with them – a pretty amazing experience.

Shark Bay, about 800 km north of Perth, was listed as a World Heritage area in 1991 because of its spectacular landforms, bays and inlets and wildlife. There's been no major development there because of a lack of fresh water, something Dampier noticed as well.

Tasmania's Cradle Mountain is part of another World Heritage area. Between Launceston and Devonport, it's one of the most popular places in Tasmania,

Named in 1827 by explorer Joe Fossey because he thought it looked like a cradle, the mountain is part of a rugged national park that has 25 major peaks. It was first climbed in 1831 by Henry Hellyer. Then the prospectors, trappers and settlers moved in, but it's still a wilderness region.

Kakadu in the Northern Territory is another backyard Australians like to go to.

It is the largest national park in Australia, and is teeming with animal, reptile, bird and insect life. And you don't have to look too far to find saltwater crocodiles.

The historians reckon Aborigines have been living in the Kakadu area for 40,000 years. They back up their argument with the nearly 5000 rock art galleries of Aboriginal paintings that have been found in the Arnhem Land escarpment.

The Anbangbang Gallery near Nourlangie Rock has depictions of Namarrgon the Lightning Man and Nabulwinjbulwinj, a dangerous spirit who eats women after banging them on the head with a yam. Namarrgon wears his lightning as a band that connects his arms, legs and head. Stone axes on his elbows and knees make the thunder. When he wants to make lightning, he strikes the stone axes on the ground or against the clouds. The actual lightning is his children, collectively called Aljurr, which means 'little lightning'.

8   The shearers

A city slicker walks into the pub at Tilpa, sits at the corner of the bar and orders a Bacardi and coke. A group of curious shearers wonder who he is.

'Somebody go and ask him,' one says, so big Norm walks over.

'G'day mate,' Norm says in his rough voice. 'Whatcha doin' round these parts?'

'Just here for a few days,' the visitor says. 'I'm a taxidermist and I've been looking for some animals to stuff. Yesterday I stuffed an emu and this morning I stuffed a big red kangaroo. Tomorrow I want to stuff a merino sheep if I can find one.'

Norm goes back to his mates, who are anxiously waiting to hear what the visitor had to say. 'He reckons he's a taxi driver,' Norm tells them. 'But I think he's really a shearer like us.'

Since the early days of the 19th century Australia 'rode on the sheep's back', economically speaking, and shearers have played a colourful and important role in that. They've helped make Australia great – and they've been a pretty militant lot over the years. Between 1860 and 1890 they went on strike more than 3000 times, trying to win better conditions from station owners who paid them meagre wages and then fined them if they cut sheep or broke the fleece.

The shearers began by getting together in informal groups. These groups amalgamated in 1886 to become the Queensland Shearers Union, and 18 years later the powerful Australian Workers Union.

The shearers really put it to the graziers in the Great Strike of 1891. This involved thousands of men in camps all around western Queensland. That time, the graziers were able to convince the government to use the military to break the picket lines.

The shearers had burnt sheds and station stores, and their strike leaders ended up locked up.

There was more trouble in the early 1900s when machine shears were first introduced. Couldn't have any new-fangled automation, but they were gradually accepted, although some die-hards continued to use hand shears in mechanised sheds until the 1920s. There were blues again in the 1980s when New Zealand shearers hit our shores. They brought in the wide comb, which infuriated the Aussies, because the Kiwis could get through 20 per cent more sheep in a day by using it. The wide comb too is now accepted.

Shearers had some unique rituals. First, they elected their cooks by secret ballot, and second, if they wanted a day off, they would have a 'wet' or 'dry' vote – handling wet sheep wasn't good for the health, so if the sheep were wet, the shearers should not shear that day. The only way to find out if the sheep were wet was to test them. Each shearer would finish two sheep and then the 'rep', their spokesman with the management, gave them all two pieces of paper, one with 'dry' written on it and the other with 'wet'. The shearers put the appropriate piece of paper in a tin with a slot in the top. The majority ruled, and the decision was final; there was no appeal. If the decision was 'wet', it meant a day off; if 'dry', it was back to work.

Australia's most famous shearer was Crooked Mick from the Speewah, a mythical character from beyond the outback whose mighty deeds are recounted from Bourke to the Barcoo. He had feet so big he had to go outside the shearing shed to turn around, and he smoked so heavily that a rouseabout worked fulltime cutting tobacco to fill his pipe.

He worked at such a rate that his shears were red hot, and often he had half a dozen pairs cooling off in the water pot. When he was really firing, it took three pressers to handle the wool from his shears and they had to work overtime to keep the bins clear. But he refused to work in sheds that faced north.

He usually ate two sheep each meal if they were small merinos and one and a half if they were crossbred wethers. Between sheds (shearing jobs) he went fencing, and he used an axe in each hand to cut the posts. Digging the holes was a breeze, with a crowbar in one hand and a shovel in the other. It's little wonder shearers talked with awe about his exploits – for the benefit of the new boys in the shed.

Jackie Howe has gone down in history as our real 'gun' shearer – a gun shearer is the fastest shearer in a shearing shed. On 10 October 1892, using hand-operated blade shears, he sheared 321 sheep in 7 hours 40 minutes at Alice Downs, in the Blackall district of central Queensland. This feat (with blades) has never been bettered, but the record with the machines is 563 lambs in 8 hours, set by David Lawrence, of Western Australia.

In competition, Hilton Barrett, from the NSW town of Wellington, won the national championship shearing 15 merino wethers in 20 minutes 54 seconds. Points are lost for cutting the sheep and leaving tufts of wool.

West Australian brothers Michael-James and Cartwright Terry set a record in 2003 for two individual shearing stands, shearing 924 merino ewes in 8 hours. They gave up drinking nine months before the record attempt, and got fit by swimming and cycling, but they celebrated with a few beers.

There are few shearers left who can use blades. Ray Hamblin, of Ganmain, in southern NSW, is one. He sheared his first sheep on the family property at Trangie, in western NSW, when he was five. It was his sister's poddy (calf) and he got a swift kick in the arse for his efforts.

By the time he was 14 he was highly skilled with the blades and worked in two sheds. His tally totals more than a million sheep, a performance that would make Crooked Mick proud. Ray was the gun shearer in many of the sheds in NSW and Queensland – the best he chalked up in one day, using the machines, was 301 at Cloncurry (Queensland) in 1934. That was a pretty amazing tally: a record of 325 was set in 1947 by Daniel Cooper, of Perth, and it stood for many years.

Ray remembers shearing in sheds made of cane grass, especially around Bourke, in far western NSW, and sleeping out in swags under tarpaulins 'borrowed' from the railway. He sheared 30,000 sheep with the blades, averaging 100 a day, in the 1930s, and was paid £1 a day. On one run he sheared 28,000 sheep without a day's break.

In the early days, shearers were itinerants, going from shed to shed, living in rough corrugated iron quarters and spending their weekends at the nearest pub – this was where their contractor paid them their weekly wage, and where they usually spent it.

A typical working day for a shearer was divided into four two-hour sessions with exactly an hour for lunch and two half-hour smokos, mid-morning and mid-afternoon. After work there was little to do apart from eat and drink. In the 1960s, many shearers owned cars, and some went home on their days off.

But traditional shearing took on new mobility for a few months with a mob called ShearExpress, who ran a mobile chain shearing system from the back of trucks. It was claimed that each truck (they were staffed by up to eight people) could shear up to 1000 sheep a day and transfer the fleece to a trailer to be weighed, classed and pressed.

The company began with four units, each worth $500,000, and said its method would reduce shearing costs and do away with the need for farms to have shearing sheds and other equipment. The aim was to have, by 2015, 300 trucks tearing around Australia, shearing 65 per cent of the wool clip.

Traditional shearers were wary of the scheme, of course. They reckoned robot shearing machines had never been successful in the sheds. And indeed two attempts

– one in the 1980s and another in the early 1990s – to replace the blue singlet humans with a machine had both failed.

They were right. Australian Wool Innovation Ltd, which had spent $6 million developing the prototype ShearExpress, pulled the pin and parked the machines in 2003.

Shearing is not without its hazards. A woman sued her husband's boss for damages because she claimed a back injury he received while he was a shearer ruined her sex life. In a separate action, the shearer concerned took out a workers compensation claim against his employer for the injury, which he alleged resulted from years in the job. The National Farmers' Federation said the wife's claim alleged that because her husband had been shearing 200 sheep (or more) a day for 20 years, he could no longer provide the services a wife would normally expect from a husband. She alleged that he could no longer bend his back for her in the way he used to. And he couldn't do things like mowing the lawn. She wanted damages for the pain and suffering and mental torture that this had caused her.

After almost total male dominance of the industry for more than 120 years, women are beginning to appear in the sheds. And they're doing a pretty good job. They can chalk up 120 or 130 sheep a day, and that's not a bad tally, especially if they're big sheep. Kylie Hamilton, a young New Zealander working the sheds in western NSW, relies on her gear, technique and style rather than brute strength to throw the sheep around. She uses her hands and feet and works harder at getting the sheep in the right position than a bloke, who can lift and overpower a big ewe without much trouble.

Bob Houghton, the owner of Wongy Station, near Gulargambone in NSW, was shocked when Kylie turned up with the shearing team – it was the first time in 140 years that a woman had worked in the shed. But he said she never complained, and she got through 130 big sheep a day. She had made history.

Shearers are now more fashion conscious than they were. The traditional blue cotton singlets and dirty denim jeans are slowly being replaced by more comfortable black or navy shearing denim, which is actually a cotton, polyester and nylon blend with the traditional high-cut waist, double front and extra double panelling on the back of the legs. Add a belt and a coloured singlet with extra long tails at the back and you've got a smarter image as well as better protection against drafts while you're bending over. The coloured singlets are designed to break the monotony. The smarter image helps the industry promote its approved 'clip care' sheds, where smoking and dogs are banned. Holed and frayed trousers could shed bits of cotton into the wool clip, and that affects quality and the price.

Shearing contractor Peter Hamilton was one of the first employers to fit out his shearers in the colourful new look. He adds to the changed image by carrying his handpiece in a briefcase.

Maori shearers probably helped push along the Aussies' change of dress. The Maoris team black trousers with pink, lemon or green tops. Clothes like that didn't detract from their toughness.

The back-breaking deeds of shearers are now commemorated in a $4.6 million hall of fame called Shear Outback at Hay, a town in the Riverina area of NSW – and the heart of a prime wool-growing district. The timber and corrugated iron centre was originally a shearing shed built in 1928 on the banks of the Murray River on Murray Downs Station, near Swan Hill in Victoria. It was relocated to Hay, and now sits on an old stock route (at the junction of the Sturt and Cobb highways). The centre has all sorts of memorabilia, including a list of shearing records and shearing equipment, new and old. It also has interactive displays, audiovisuals, shearing demonstrations and training programs. It hopes to attract more than 60,000 visitors a year. It ran into financial troubles in 2003, but Hay Shire Council put up money to help pay its debts. The council's general manager, Bob Behl, said he was sure the museum would have a bright future if it received help from the NSW and the federal governments.

9   'The Man from Snowy River'

There was movement at the station, for the word had passed around
That the colt from Old Regret had got away,
And had joined the wild bush horses – he was worth a thousand pound,
So all the cracks had gathered to the fray.

All the tried and noted riders from the stations near and far
Had mustered at the homestead overnight,
For the bushmen love hard riding where the wild bush horses are,
And the stock-horse snuffs the battle with delight.

'The Man from Snowy River', written more than a century ago by bush bard Banjo Paterson, has a touch of everything typically Australian. The poem embodies our character. It tells us something about ourselves and our heritage – traditionally this has been a country of battlers and supporters of the underdog.

Perhaps it was the 'tough and wiry' rider on the 'small and weedy beast' who captured our imagination. His courage, horsemanship and never-say-die attitude as he raced down the mountainside 'while the others stopped and watched in very fear' could well have played a small but vital role in our development as a nation. Achievement against the odds.

Historian and special events promoter Dr Jonathan King believes it's important to keep the spirit of 'The Man from Snowy River' alive. He wants to protect that part of our culture from changes in social attitudes. Dr King directed slap-up celebrations in the High Country town of Corryong for the 100th anniversary of the publication of

Banjo Paterson's book, *The Man from Snowy River and Other Verses*, which remains Australia's most popular book of poetry, chalking up sales of more than 100,000.

King is concerned that the so-called politically correct do-gooders are chipping away at Australian society. He believes attitudes are changing rapidly, with the community drifting into ambivalence over things like equal gender representation and recognition of gays and other minority groups.

But he believes there will always be genuine bushmen and bushwomen in the Snowy River tradition, and he thinks that's important, because 'The Man from Snowy River' has an appeal for many Australians, especially those in the bush who are worried that city lifestyles are undermining their culture. And he thinks they're frightened that saying – or perhaps even thinking! – things that aren't politically correct will soon be completely outlawed socially.

When he approached sponsors, film-making companies and TV networks to support the centenary celebrations in Corryong, he was knocked back: they reckoned 'The Man from Snowy River' was too sexist. One network said it would consider doing something if there was a name change to 'The Person from Snowy River', and asked him to put in an application that gave an equal balance to genders so that women were featured in the story ... along with other ethnic groups and gay groups. Of course King would not do this; it would be a betrayal of the original poem and all it has meant to Australians past and present. King believes there's still a big disparity between rural and urban Australians, and that the urban Australian often idealises the life of people in the bush. Banjo Paterson himself was a city lawyer and he idealised the bush in poems like 'Clancy of the Overflow' and 'The Man from Snowy River'.

King says Paterson and his works can play a major role in helping break down the Americanisation of our culture. He says there are too many American TV programs, too much American language, American music, fashion and clothing.

'If we want to hang on to the original Australian culture, which I believe city people derive great sustenance from, we have to promote and preserve "Waltzing Matilda", "The Man from Snowy River" and other Paterson works. And Paterson was pretty anti-English. He wanted Australia to stand on its own feet: he wanted to get rid of that cultural cringe, he wanted Australians to be Australian, and more than 100 years later I reckon we don't have the problem of British culture being too dominant. I think we should use the same Paterson material to stop Australia becoming too American.'

Banjo Paterson's poems tell Australians a lot about themselves. And they give us pride in achievement. 'The Man from Snowy River', alone and unassisted, brought the wild horses back with the colt from Old Regret after his amazing ride down the mountainside. He wouldn't say die, and that really strikes a chord with Australians.

Corryong was selected for 'The Man from Snowy River' centenary celebrations because Elyne Mitchell, who wrote the Silver Brumby books and who was dubbed the

Queen of the Snowy Mountains, told King the story of how Paterson went there in 1889 and stayed with Walter Mitchell at Bringenbrong Station. Mitchell then took Paterson to Tom Groggin Station, to meet head musterer Jack Riley.

Riley told Paterson how, as a young man, he had chased wild mobs of brumbies when good stockhorses got caught up with them. That's the basis of the story of the colt from Old Regret in 'The Man from Snowy River'. Riley also told Paterson how he and others had had to ride hard down terrible descents to get the horses back. Paterson then wrote 'The Man from Snowy River', and it was published in *The Bulletin* on 26 April 1890. It was hugely popular, and in 1895 was published in a book with other poems.

A string of riders have claimed to be The Man from Snowy River. They include Jack Riley, Jack Clark from Adaminaby, Owen Cummings from the Northern Territory, Jim Troy from Queensland, Bill Hedger from Melbourne and Bill Spencer from Tumut. Riley is the closest to Paterson's character, who 'bore the badge of gameness in his bright and fiery eye ...' Riley died in 1914, and is buried at Corryong – 'The Man from Snowy River' is engraved on his headstone. A local newspaper report 19 years after Paterson's book was published reported the death of 'The Man from Snowy River'.

But Paterson often made up composite characters, like Clancy of the Overflow. Because no one is really sure who The Man was, there's an annual competition to find a modern-day Man from Snowy River, which carries a big prize. A field of around 50 riders, including women, from around Australia go to Corryong to take part in 10 different horseriding events.

There are plans in the Snowy region for a Snowy Mountains Muster, an annual two-week event to pay tribute to the Australian stockhorse and its place in the nation's culture, as reflected in Paterson's poems. Ignatius Jones, who directed 'The Man From Snowy River' theme at the opening of the Sydney Olympics at Stadium Australia, and Bruce Rowland, who composed the theme music for *The Man from Snowy River* movie in 1982, are both involved.

The stockhorse segment at the Olympics Opening Ceremony was one of its most memorable moments. Horseman Steve Jefferys, who strangely enough lives just outside Sydney, nowhere near the Snowy Mountains, played The Man. He charged into the stadium on his horse Ammo, reared on cue to thousands of camera flashes, cracked his whip and tore off. That was the signal for 120 stockmen and women carrying white Olympic flags to ride into the stadium to Rowland's music. The segment was a big hit, not just in Australia but overseas, where billions of people watched it on TV.

The Muster, which is also aimed at promoting continuing moves by the NSW and Victorian governments to get the Snowy River running again, is loosely based on the Canadian Calgary Stampede, which started as a weekend event with a budget of $12,000 and now attracts a million people.

Sydney man Richard Whalan believes his great-grandfather George Hedger was the original Man from Snowy River. He has copies of a letter written to his father by author Frank Clune, and a Sydney newspaper report in 1912 about George Hedger's death, which referred to him as 'The Man from Snowy River.' The report said: 'George Hedger was a bush Australian to the bones and marrow. Over mountain range, down precipice and into deep recess of ravine, over rugged acclivity and ground encumbered by rock or felled tree, he rode his horse, hunted the wild mob, and by coo-ee, with crack of stockwhip and bark of dog, rounded in the unbranded beasts in a manner that astounded all. Banjo Paterson proved his genius in the discovery of a subject so congenial to illustrate the intrepidity so graphically described in his rollicking lines ...'

George Hedger was buried in Manly cemetery – he had moved there from the Monaro region in southern NSW after, as he often said, 'the banks broke me'.

Now for the poet. Andrew Barton Paterson was born at Narambla, just out of Orange, on 17 February 1864, at the home of his great-uncle JA Templer. His father was Andrew Bogle Paterson, a grazier of Buckinbah Station at Obley, near Yeoval in central western NSW.

Paterson's mother, Rose Isabella Paterson, formerly Barton, of Boree, was a grand-daughter of Major Edward Darvall, and through her he could claim kinship with Sir Edmund Barton, Australia's first Prime Minister. Compared with Henry Lawson, the son of a gold miner, Paterson was off to a flying start.

He was baptised at Mr Templer's home on 11 March 1864, by Rev. Robert Mayne, the rector of Holy Trinity Church at Orange, who had married his parents at Boree on 8 April the previous year. His birth was registered at Orange Court House.

Paterson spent his early years on the family property at Obley, but later moved to Illalong, Yass. He attended Sydney Grammar School, later studied law and was admitted as a solicitor of the Supreme Court.

As a young man he began contributing to *The Bulletin*, and the pen-name The Banjo appeared first in that journal in 1886. A banjo, in bush parlance, was a frying pan, but some say he used the name because one of his father's racehorses was called Banjo.

In the 1890s he contributed lots of writing to *The Bulletin*, moving ever further from the law. He loved the bush and its people and jumped to their defence when other writers stressed the harshness and cruelty. In 1895 he published his first book, *The Man From Snowy River, and Other Verses*, and it was an immediate success.

In 1900 he gave up law altogether and covered the Boer War as a correspondent for the *Sydney Morning Herald* and the *Melbourne Argus*. He was always keen to be a country Australian, and bought a property near Yass called Coodra Vale, but he sailed for England soon after moving there – World War I had started, and he was hoping for an appointment as a war correspondent. He was unsuccessful in this aim, and after a brief stay in France, returned to Sydney and joined the Australian Remounts (though he was over military age). He served in the Middle East for the remainder of the war and rose to the rank of major. When he returned home in 1919, he resumed life as a journalist and later edited the *Sydney Sportsman*.

He kept up his journalism, and between 1904 and 1906 edited the *Sydney Evening News*. In 1907–08 he edited the *Town and Country Journal*, and he later edited the *Sydney Sportsman* and the *Sydney Mail*. He continued to contribute to various literary journals until his death in 1941, although his main interests by then were pastoral pursuits.

Now back to Elyne Mitchell. The daughter of Australia's greatest warrior horseman, Sir Harry Chauvel, who led the fabled Desert Corps of 34,000 horsemen in battles across the Sinai, Palestine and Gaza to Jerusalem, Jordan, Damascus and beyond, she was an accomplished horsewoman herself. In 1936 she married Tom Mitchell, the son of the man who had taken Banjo Paterson to meet Jack Riley.

Elyne Mitchell rode and tramped the length and breadth of the Snowy Mountains, and while her husband was in a prisoner-of-war camp in Singapore, she ran the family cattle and sheep station. For recreation she wrote a book called *Australia's Alps*, which was about her interests in the mountains and its wild horses. It also described her trip down the entire western face of the mountains on skis.

She followed that with *Speak to the Earth*, a book on the environment, and a string of others, including 12 Silver Brumby children's novels. The first Silver Brumby book in 1993 was made into a feature film starring Russell Crowe and called *The Silver Brumby*.

Elyne Mitchell died, at the age of 88, in March 2002 in Corryong Hospital. Towong Hill Station, a few kilometres from Corryong, is now run by her son.

10　Big things

Former Federal Tourism Minister John Brown once made the comment that anyone who didn't like the Big Merino (in Goulburn, southern NSW) was not a true Australian. Forgetting that he also described the koala as a piddling, flea-ridden, scratching, rotten little thing, his views on the Big Merino are probably pretty well on the mark.

Big Things, like the Big Merino, the Big Yabbie, the Big Banana, the Big Pineapple, the Big Bull, the Big Wine Barrel, the Big Trout, the Big Oyster, the Big Peanut, the Big Avocado and the Big Beer Can, have sprung up all over the countryside, and although many people still believe they're gross and tasteless, they've become hugely popular landmarks.

The concrete and fibreglass colossuses exert magnetic powers of attraction over tens of thousands of tourists, who find it impossible to drive past without at least buying a hot dog or some petrol, or clicking off a couple of photos.

The Big Merino, made from fibreglass reinforced concrete over a steel rod frame, is 15 metres high, 18 metres long and weighs 200 tonnes. It houses a complex which sells woollen clothing, sheepskin products, toys and souvenirs, and is attached to a petrol outlet and restaurant.

The Big Merino, the Big Prawn at Ballina, the Big Oyster at Taree and a partly built Big Giraffe at Dubbo, were part of the gargantuan world of Louie and Attilla Mokany's LA Development company. But the company went bust and its assets were sold – to new investors who believed there was still money to be made out of them.

Businessman Norm Newton, who also has a luxurious Cadillac Fleetwood once owned by film star Mary Pickford, couldn't resist buying the Big Prawn; he turned it into a major attraction after spending $1 million on renovations. He admitted that the reinforced concrete crustacean, which sits on top of a block of specialty shops at the southern entrance to Ballina, on the NSW north coast, was an eyesore, but he knew he could make it work.

He bought an adjoining service station and restaurant as part of the package, added a bus depot and thought about adding a motel, to help feed the Big Prawn's ten specialty shops. People have been critical of the Big Prawn in the past, but it's an attraction that people do stop to look at. And because Ballina has around 36 trawlers – it is the biggest prawning port on the coast – the theme fits in.

The original designer of the Big Prawn is sculptor James Martin, a technical officer with the University of South Australia's Art School. He made it clear that working on Big Things is not the kind of work he normally does, and admits that other artists would probably shy away from doing it. But he also understands that the purpose of Big Things is to attract travellers off the highway and sees that they seem to do a pretty good job of that.

When he sat down to work on the Big Prawn, he bought the biggest tiger prawn he could get in Ballina, and with a magnifying glass drew it from many angles. He also tried to give it an expression, but found that difficult to do! James also worked on Taree's Big Oyster, and believes that people get pleasure from Big Things. Although they are often described as gross and tasteless, he says, everyone seems to smile when talking about them.

Wauchope, in the mid-north coast area of NSW, has the world's biggest man-made bull: it stands five storeys (14 metres) high. It's a unique complex, and contains an animal nursery, a children's playground, an educational farm, a restaurant and a gift shop – and, according to the owner, offers panoramic views from the bull's eye lookout.

Tamworth, in northern NSW, promotes its image as Australia's country music capital with a 12 metre-high Big Guitar on the New England Highway. It's a replica of the Country Music Awards Golden Guitar trophy and was unveiled – no doubt with some difficulty! – by Aussie country music icon Slim Dusty. To continue the theme, the Tamworth Visitors Information Centre was built in the shape of a Big Guitar, and the Alandale Motel has a guitar-shaped swimming pool.

Stanthorpe, in Queensland, has plans for a Big Thermometer to celebrate being the coldest town in Queensland. Its chamber of commerce wants the thermometer to include an electronic temperature display and a cut-out bulb at the bottom that people can stick their heads through for photographs.

Dr Ian Henderson, of the Department of Visual Arts and Design at the University of New England, in Armidale, believes that as time goes by, Big Things become an accepted part of the landscape – they often to take on a life of their own, even though they might appear brash to start off with. Dr Henderson, who has a particular interest in graffiti and the way we use art in our surroundings, says that things like the Big Prawn and the Big Banana become major features because they do in fact represent a particular area or have some particular connection to it. They tend to be markers or pinpointers for towns that want a special sort of character or definition. It is quite understandable that the banana growers at Coffs Harbour, for instance, would come up with a plan to build a Big Banana – bananas are the single most significant commercial activity in this part of the NSW north coast.

A good example of something that almost accidentally became a marker is Thunderbolt's Rock at Uralla (not far from Armidale). Although it already had some history attached to it, it kept being covered with graffiti – and the graffiti kept changing. When it was first spray painted, people said it was terrible, but now the rock and its graffiti are so well known and so often photographed that everyone knows they are just out of Uralla when they see it.

Many artists want to create big things, and most want as many people as possible to see their work. John and Ros Moriarty have been there, done that. One night Ros decided she wanted to paint a jumbo jet – and eventually she talked Qantas into letting her do it. The first 747 she painted rolled out of the hangar covered in indigenous art-inspired motifs. It was called Wunala Dreaming. It has been followed by a second, called Nalanji Dreaming. Both are seen around the world.

11 Native animals

The Sydney Olympic Games organising committee selected Syd the platypus, along with Millie the echidna and Olly the kookaburra, as Olympic mascots because it reckoned the kangaroo and koala were overdone. All three were almost unknown overseas before the Olympics, and the committee's belief that they would turn into wildlife favourites by the time the Games came around turned out to be pretty correct.

People had jumped up and down in an awful flap when Australian Olympic organisers rolled out kids in kangaroo suits riding pushbikes to promote the Sydney Games at the Atlanta Games Closing Ceremony. Corny, they said, but the man in charge of Australia's seven-minute performance, Ric Birch, noted that the Americans had clapped and applauded. It would only be corny in Australia.

Birch, who had previously worked on the opening and closing ceremonies for both the Los Angeles and the Barcelona Olympics, used the kangaroo theme in Atlanta so that people would know 'we were talking about Australia …' The idea was to push Sydney's 2000 Games, and the kids wobbling around on their bikes, one with the kangaroo tail stuck in the spokes, did just that.

But we ended up with Syd, Milly and Olly as official mascots. The decision to have three was supposed to represent the third millennium as well as air, earth and water; it was not, organisers said, intended to raise more money in toy mascot sales.

Syd, Millie and Olly were the creations of Sydney designers Matthew Hatton and Helena Harris, who produced the original series of the children's program *Bananas In Pyjamas*. Sculptures of their form were developed by Jozef Szekeres, an animator on Walt Disney's *Aladdin*.

The official Olympic blurb described Syd as a team player and a natural leader. Like all platypuses, he was strong and supple, and his sturdy body and muscular limbs gave him the speed, agility and power to excel at most sports, although swimming was his favourite.

Millie the echidna was the brains of the trio. A born optimist and information guru, her eye was firmly focused on the future, except when she was peering into ant holes in search of a tasty snack.

Olly the kookaburra was gregarious, honest, enthusiastic and open-hearted, and embodied the Olympic spirit of generosity and universal friendship. A chuckling raconteur with a devilish glint in his eye, Olly loved a yarn and catching up on the latest gossip, and was a comedian who could make a joke out of anything.

Few people were happier than David Goldney when organisers selected Syd the platypus as one of the Olympic mascots. Associate Professor Goldney has studied the small aquatic animal for years and believes it's one of the most fascinating mammals in the world.

But he's also concerned that while the platypus is not yet classified as endangered, it could end up on the endangered list unless something is done to improve the quality of inland rivers. Professor Goldney, head of Charles Sturt University's environmental studies unit at Bathurst, in central NSW, carried out a two-year study which found that 80 per cent of the platypuses he had earlier caught and tagged had disappeared.

There would have been a natural mortality rate, plus attacks by foxes and other predators, and some may have been caught in illegal gill nets. But he thinks the major cause is the lack of quality habitat. This is the result of the silting up of rivers, the loss of trees along the banks and the subsequent bank collapse.

In some river systems the platypuses have gone altogether, because they can't dig their burrows in the collapsed banks. Professor Goldney would like to see the Federal Government's Landcare program, which involves groups of people looking after pieces of land by planting trees and shrubs, put more emphasis on rehabilitating the rivers – this would make a big difference to platypus numbers.

The egg-laying platypus, a fauna emblem of NSW, has a bony, duck-like, beak and a flattened tail. The largest is around 60 cm long and weighs up to 3 kg. The females are smaller, and weigh around 1.3 kg. The males have two spurs on the back legs and can badly bruise anyone they take a dislike to. Platypuses are found only in the eastern rivers, as far north as Cooktown in Queensland and as far west as Condobolin (on the Lachlan) and Wellington (on the Bell and Macquarie) in NSW.

Several overseas bidders put out feelers to buy a platypus when it seemed their fame would go through the roof because of the Olympics, but Australian zoos weren't interested. One overseas zoo apparently offered millions of dollars for one, but couldn't get a taker.

The two native animals proudly displayed on Australia's coat of arms, the kangaroo and emu, might be national icons, but they can cause a fair bit of havoc for people on the land, especially during a drought. Travelling in huge mobs in search of food and water, they compete with starving stock for what little grass is left, and when they get really hungry they venture into towns to attack gardens, lawns, sports ovals and golf courses. One mob of about 400 emus swam the Murray River near Wentworth in southwest NSW on the Victorian border, on a desperate trek south to try to find something to eat.

Kangaroos and emus can also be a major traffic hazard.

The roos are blinded by car and truck headlights and run head-on into them, killing themselves instantly and causing thousands of dollars' worth of damage to vehicles. Drivers who swerve to miss them often end up having more serious accidents as they run off the road.

Kangaroos are a bit like the short-sighted cartoon character Mr Magoo. They haven't got good eyesight; they rely on their hearing, but the sound of approaching vehicles confuses them, and they become particularly disoriented when nearby vehicles are travelling at high speed.

Emus, the second-largest bird in the world – the ostrich is the biggest – run at fences and smash them down, causing no end of headaches for farmers. Emus are protected in NSW by the National Parks and Wildlife Act, but they can be farmed (under licence) for their meat, oil, skin and feathers. They will eat almost anything, including flowers, seeds and insects like grasshoppers. They have reached plague proportions in the outback, which upsets farmers no end.

Michael Lawrence, a ranger with the Broken Hill Rural Lands Protection Board, gets hot under the collar about it; he reckons the National Parks & Wildlife Service has a lot to answer for. He says it isn't the emus' fault there are so many of them: we created the conditions that allow them to breed so prolifically and we therefore have an obligation to keep them under control, he says. You can't shoot either emus or roos without having a licence to do so.

Both emus and kangaroos come into outback towns to feed on the ovals – and they even walk up the middle of streets. They're on golf courses and sporting ovals and they destroy gardens.

In the 2002–03 drought in the north west, thousands of kangaroos tried to get through the high fence, built to keep dingos out, to head south to look for feed. Because they couldn't find any, they threw their joeys out of their pouches and left them to fend for themselves.

Kangaroos can jump fences but emus can't: they go back about 100 metres and charge at a fence until they smash it down. Mrs Pat Glennie, of Muddall, near

Nyngan in western NSW, says kangaroos eat every rose leaf in her garden, and that as the daffodil bulbs come up, they attack them at ground level.

'Fences won't stop them,' she says. 'A big roo on our front lawn cleared a 2 metre fence as if it wasn't there. And thousands of them came in from further west looking for something to eat.'

But kangaroos are high on the popularity list of visitors to Australia. Matilda, a giant kangaroo made from steel and fibreglass for the 1982 Commonwealth Games in Brisbane, is a leading attraction at the entrance to the Wet 'n' Wild theme park on Queensland's Gold Coast. Forget the water slides and wave pools in the park – about 80 per cent of all visitors stop to have their photo taken with Matilda, which stands 13 metres high. The giant roo weighs 6 tonnes and towers over a grassed picnic area just inside the gates.

And a real-life kangaroo called Lulu became a hero when she barked like a dog to attract help for a farmer (from Morwell, in southeastern Victoria) who had been knocked unconscious by a falling tree branch. After Lulu had been 'barking' for about 15 minutes, farmer Len Richards' family went to investigate – and found him about 300 metres from the house. The kangaroo was standing guard over the farmer with her chest puffed out. Len was taken to hospital, where he made a full recovery.

Lulu was a family pet. She had been adopted as a joey (a baby) after her mother was hit by a car and killed, and had been reared on the farm. Mr Richards' daughter Celeste said 10-year-old Lulu was friendly and smart, and followed her father around the farm. RSPCA president Dr Hugh Wirth said Lulu should be nominated for a bravery award.

The koala, a marsupial from the same family as the kangaroo, is another Australian icon. But former federal Tourism Minister John Brown caused an outcry when he described the koala as a 'piddling, flea-ridden, scratching, rotten little thing'. He later mellowed and joined a Save the Koala campaign.

His views weren't shared by former US President Bill Clinton. Mr Clinton and his wife Hillary gave the OK to the Rainforest Habitat sanctuary (on the outskirts of Port Douglas, in Queensland) to name a baby koala Chelsea, after their daughter. They saw the koala on a visit to the sanctuary, where they also met and fed some kangaroos.

Mrs Clinton commented to a TV cameraman: 'It's sort of as fuzzy as your microphone ...' Bill Clinton put in his two bob's worth as well: 'Great, huh? It's the first time I've seen a koala. I like it. And it's the first time I've fed kangaroos. They were pretty friendly.'

We give full marks to people like Ruth Barrett, a member of a Lismore volunteer group called Friends of the Koala, who has spent years looking after koalas who are unlucky enough to be injured or orphaned. They've also been rescued from power poles, and one was found stuck in bamboo. Members of the group began working from their own homes, but after years of fundraising they have managed to build a modern koala care centre on a piece of bushland made available to them by Southern Cross University.

An average 130 koalas a year are taken to the centre. The injured ones are nursed back to health and then released into the wild. Ruth becomes fond of her charges, and often gives them names: one she called Lady Luck because it was rescued three or four times before it settled in a nature reserve, and another was called PC, after the koala's scientific name – *Phascolarctos cinereus*.

The Australian Koala Foundation, which raises money for conservation of Australia's most well-known wildlife attraction, estimates that there are fewer than 100,000 koalas left. There are three main reasons for this: much of their habitat has been destroyed, many are hit by cars and many die from disease. One of the things that makes conservation of koalas difficult is that even though there are lots of different species of eucalypts available to them, they are fussy creatures and will only eat leaves from forest red gum, swamp mahogany and tallow wood.

We also have a little-known Aussie native animal that is about the size of a rabbit, has big ears, a long snout, lots of sharp teeth and a black and white tail, and lives in a burrow in the ground. It's a bilby, but you could be forgiven for not knowing.

This near-extinct marsupial once had the run of about 70 per cent of the country, but now is found in only three small pockets in outback Australia and is fast disappearing. Wildlife experts in the Queensland outback have tried to monitor their movements with small radio transmitters attached to a collar, but this hasn't really helped much. The main reason for their disappearance seems to be grazing pressure – from domestic stock, both cattle and sheep, rabbits, which compete for both food and living space, and foxes, dingoes and wild cats. They can't compete with foxes and wild cats, so their only hope now is fauna sanctuaries.

The National Parks & Wildlife Service team at Charleville in Queensland carried out a research project on bilbies at Davenport Downs cattle station, about 160 km east of Bedourie; the research included looking into what the bilby eats and when it breeds. Bilbies there were living in open Mitchell grass country; those in the other two pockets where they've survived (one in the Northern Territory and one in Western Australia) are living in sandy spinifex country and mulga.

The Western Plains Zoo, at Dubbo in central western NSW, is dedicated to saving the bilby from extinction and has a successful captive breeding program under way.

And at Easter, people can now buy chocolate bilbies as well as – or instead of – chocolate bunnies. It's a campaign to keep the noxious rabbits in their place!

About 40 schools in the northern rivers region of NSW grew special rainforest vines to help save a rare and endangered butterfly. Called the Richmond Birdwing, the colourful butterfly depends on the *Aristolochia praevenosa* vine, which has now almost disappeared because of rainforest destruction through the years. The butterflies were once common in the NSW north coast and southern Queensland Big Scrub rainforest areas, but as the rainforest disappeared to make way for farming, so did the butterflies. The male butterfly has brilliant panels of lime green and gold on its wings, surrounded by a velvet black border, and has a red thorax. The female, which is slightly larger – it is up to 18 cm across the wings – is smoky grey with a yellow panel and has black spots on its wings.

National Parks & Wildlife Service ranger Bob Moffatt, based at Alstonville, was confident that the almost extinct butterflies would breed again if people grew the vine in their backyards. His own experiments at home showed that the butterflies would then be attracted to the garden to feed and lay eggs.

The Balunyah Nursery at Coraki, run by the local Aboriginal community, grew the vines. The National Parks & Wildlife Service gave them away throughout the region – in the area roughly between Lismore, Byron Bay and Ballina – and they were also sold through northern rivers nurseries. People planted vines in their yards, over a fence or stump.

Butterfly numbers are still low, but the more vines are planted, the sooner they will return. The project was a good opportunity for urban dwellers to easily contribute towards a conservation program – all they had to do was grow a vine in their backyard. Let's hope the butterflies can be saved by the backyard and school vine-growing programs.

A few people have caught sight of a gruesome bush beast called a bunyip, also known as a yowie. You could probably best describe them as the Aussie cousin to North America's Big Foot.

A bunyip was seen back in the late 1950s in the Byng district, between Bathurst and Orange in central NSW. It was about 1.1 metres high and mostly grey, and had two big red eyes, long hair and a bushy tail.

Bunyips are creatures of Aboriginal legend, and are said to haunt rushy swamps and billabongs. The yowie seems to favour Queensland: a bloke named Dean Harrison claimed to have seen one near Beenleigh in 1997. He reckoned it roared like a bear and a lion in one. It had a vocal capacity no human could match. A more recent sighting was at Springbrook (also in Queensland) in 1999; in this case the yowie was blamed for the death of some horses.

Dr Helmet Loofs-Wissowa, a specialist in Asian exotic animals who works at the Australian National University in Canberra, said there was evidence of similar creatures in Asia. He wanted the sceptics to prove they didn't exist. Although a string of yowie hunters have tried to catch one for years, none has had any success.

The Byng bunyip first appeared about 1956 near an old cemetery in the Byng district near the central western city of Orange, after being caught in the glare of the headlights of a car driven by one of the local cockies. Residents searched the cemetery the next day and found huge footprints and flattened grass where something appeared to have been sleeping – but the scary creature was nowhere to be found.

In December 1959 three Sydney men saw the bunyip on the Byng Road. It hopped around on its hind legs a couple of times and then ran off into thick scrub and disappeared. The local radio station broadcast an appeal for volunteers with spotlights to help look for it, but search parties of up to 40 people failed to find any trace.

A more mundane Aussie creature is the wombat. Something like a furry pig to look at, wombats live in burrows unless they're pampered and kept as house pets.

Farmer Virginia Wykes, of Yeoval, in central NSW, had a wombat called Samantha which liked to go walkabout in style. Sam had been hand-reared since she was a few days old, after her mother was run over by a car.

One night, when she was two years old, she wandered away from the farm and crossed a heavily timbered mountain range more than 300 metres high. She eventually came across a homestead, about 18 km away, found an open door and wandered into the kitchen. Tallisan Fleming, then 12, was doing his homework in the kitchen and couldn't believe his eyes.

Sam was well and truly tuckered out after her marathon four-day trek, but she was also pretty hungry. She got into a cupboard and devoured a packet of muesli breakfast cereal, then attacked a bag of nuts. Tallisan phoned his artist father, Dr Eris Fleming, who was in Sydney – he had to talk hard and fast to convince his father that there was a wombat running around inside the house.

There was nothing Tallisan could do, so he called the wildlife rescue service. They turned up the next day, by which time Sam had retired under the veranda for a well-earned kip. All efforts to coax her out failed.

The only thing her would-be rescuers could do was rip up the floorboards, so they did, and eventually Sam was collared, loaded into the back of a ute and taken away. Meanwhile, back at Yeoval, Virginia Wykes was fretting over the disappearance of her wombat.

'Samantha normally went for a wander around the farm at night, and when she scratched on the door around 2 am, I'd get out of bed and let her in,' she said. 'But after she had been missing for seven days, I thought something must have happened to her. I'd crawled under the house and the shearing shed floor to see if she was there.

'When the woman from the wildlife rescue service phoned to ask me what to feed a wombat, I knew she had Sam, and I wasted no time getting her back.' Mrs

Wykes was worried that Sam might have done some damage to Dr Fleming's house and paintings but she wasn't game enough to phone him to ask. Five years were to pass before Mrs Wykes told Dr Fleming (who had repaired the house damage) that she owned the wombat. He was amused by the incident.

The welfare of animals is under the control of the Animal Welfare Unit, which is run by NSW Primary Industries. Animals used in research, films and TV commercials, zoos and circuses, and the treatment of sheep, cattle, cats, dogs, birds and horses, pet shops and grooming parlours also come under the watchful eye of the unit, which is based at the department's head office at Orange. Its powers have recently been widened to take in restaurants that cook lobsters, crayfish and prawns while they're still alive.

The unit is advised by three formal committees, the Animal Welfare Advisory Council, the Animal Research Review Panel and the Exhibited Animals Advisory Committee. Members of these committees are appointed by the agriculture minister. They include representatives of other government departments, animal welfare groups, the Zoological Parks Board, rural lands protection boards, farmers and the animal industry. Unit manager Renata Brooks says the unit's main role is to ensure that animals are protected from unreasonable, unjustifiable or unnecessary pain and distress.

And the unit's Exhibited Animals Protection Committee can flex its muscles when the need arises. The Federal Airports Corporation wanted to build a 5000 square metre enclosure near the international terminal at Sydney Airport to house 18 kangaroos – as an attraction for overseas visitors. The committee ruled against the plan because of aircraft and vehicle noise and kerosene on the ground.

Other matters that have come before the committee include attacks on keepers at a private zoo by a bear and a jaguar, a burst fish tank at Sydney Aquarium, and escapes of animals from circuses (including several lions at Broken Hill). Each incident is investigated to see whether the correct safety procedures were in place and the security of enclosures was up to standard.

Circus acts from overseas are also checked for their suitability, which includes care and treatment of the animals.

In one of the more unusual cases, someone wanted to run a bullfight on the NSW south coast. This time, legislation had to be amended in order to stop it. However, it turned out that the amendments affected rodeos as well, so a special code of practice was set up to cover them.

Another unusual case was a female stripper who used a large python in her act. It was checked, and everything was OK, so she received the registration she needed for the python.

The unit has a code of practice under the Prevention of Cruelty to Animals Act to cover the use of animals in film and theatre. There were some concerns when

The Man from Snowy River was being filmed in 1982, and a code was set up then, but it has since been reviewed.

The treatment of crustaceans in restaurants and other places where food is prepared for consumption has also been reviewed. Traditional methods of preparation, cooking or eating these animals while they're still alive have been prohibited.

Laws about confining birds by ring and chain, using dogs in hunting, firebranding animals like cattle, tethering pigs, and carrying dogs on the back of moving vehicles have also been tightened.

12 Native flora

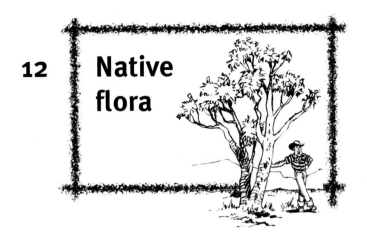

Herbal medicine is big business. More than 50 per cent of Australians use the plant substances at least once a year in an effort to stay healthier, stronger and more energetic. Echinacea, horse radish, astragalus, wild yam, valerian, dandelion root, celery seed, St John's wort and passion flower are just some of the plants offered as alternative solutions to problems like viruses, influenza, weakened immune systems, headache, insomnia, fatigue, infections, hay fever, ulcers, arthritis and diabetes.

The natural therapy industry has even developed a plant-based sex performance enhancer for men and women called Veromax, which it says has no harmful side effects. The increasingly popular notion that if it's natural it's better, and the fact that herbs account for less than 1 per cent of all toxic reactions to medicines, has resulted in a boom.

The industry in Australia is worth $140 million a year; worldwide, it is worth $22 billion. And it is growing at the healthy rate of 15 per cent. Southern Cross University at Lismore has decided that this boom is worth working with, and has established the world's first herbal medicine quality assurance centre, which works alongside its research and development facility. Herbal medicine manufacturers have been invited to shift their operations there. A variety of herbs will be grown on-site and by contract growers in the district. The university's Pro Vice-Chancellor of Research, Professor Peter Baverstock, says the plan is that the centre will become the Silicon Valley of herbal medicine.

If you're in herbal medicine anywhere in the world and you do not have something happening in this centre, in some ways, you are nowhere. Professor

Baverstock and his team have worked closely with the industry, forming the Cellulose Valley Advisory Group, which includes representatives of all the major herbal medicine manufacturers in Australia.

Professor Baverstock says the medical establishment is still sceptical of herbal medicine but the pharmacy establishment is moving rapidly towards its use – pharmacy shelves contain 60 per cent herbal medicines. The main consumers are 30 to 40-year-old professional women.

Although the widespread use of herbal medicine is relatively new, country cures and bush remedies have been around for a long time. Whether they work or not is anybody's guess, but many people grew up with them.

Carrying a potato around in your pocket was a popular old-time cure for rheumatism. Wearing a red flannel belt was a remedy for backaches and chills, a vinegar compress cured headaches, garlic in the shoes stopped coughs and a cut-up onion bound to the soles of the feet reduced a fever.

For infected fingers, old-timers often resorted to breaking a hole in a raw egg, pushing the finger into the yolk and then bandaging the egg and finger together. For persistent sore throats, a dirty sock wrapped around the neck was believed to work wonders.

Brandy and salt restored the hair, although sheep dip was held by some to be much better. Goanna oil was a popular remedy for many complaints. People believed its penetrating power was so strong it could seep through a glass bottle.

Another popular cure-all on the market that apparently does wonders for all sorts of aches and pains is emu oil. It's used for muscular aches and pains, sunburn, windburn, rheumatism and arthritis. Aborigines have used it for hundreds of years, and now we've discovered it. The oil is a good seller for Virginia Wykes. She and her husband Lyle farm emus.

They stock it at their Yeoval angora farm, near Dubbo in western NSW, and it's usually the first thing visitors ask for. People try it, discover it works, and write or ring and order more.

Aborigines ate lots of native flora, of course. They sucked the nectar from bottlebrush, banksia, grevillea and the grass tree flowers. Putting the flowers in water made a sweet-tasting drink.

Nowadays, people are turning bush tucker into profitable businesses. The boom was probably kicked off by Les Hiddins, who became well known through a TV series called *Bush Tucker Man*. When he was an Army officer, Les introduced bush tucker survival guides to the Defence Department. He reckoned they would still be relevant 50 years later, and no doubt he's right.

Some of the native delicacies, if that's the right word, include billygoat plum, a deciduous tree common in savannah bush in Australia's Top End. The foodies changed its name to Kakadu plum, presumably to get away from any association with goats. The plums, chock-a-block with vitamin C, are used extensively in jams and chutneys. The gum from the tree's bark can also be eaten and is used to treat sores, boils, backache and ringworm.

When Captain Cook was sailing around the place, he called in at Botany Bay to look for some greens for his crew. He collected a good supply of *Tetragonia tetragonoides*, best known as Warrigal greens (or New Zealand spinach – it's also found there). The arrow-shaped leaves have a spinach flavour and are used in quiches and stuffings. However, like some other edible native plants, they have a high oxalate concentration: this means that only leaves and young stems should be eaten, and then only after they have been immersed in boiling water for at least three minutes, or until they turn white.

The yam was a major part of the Aboriginal menu. It's a climbing plant that produces new stems in the northern Australia wet season and survives the dry season underground. Yams can grow up to a metre long. The flesh is white and tastes something like a sweet potato. They can be eaten raw or roasted in the traditional way – in a ground oven. They're usually dug up after the wet season, because this is when they're the fattest and sweetest, but caution is needed if you want to dine out on them: some of the species are toxic.

Another native used for medicinal purposes is the milky plum, a small tree common in open woodlands and forests in northern Australia. The fruit stays green even when it's ripe, but the ones that are ripe are soft to touch; that's when they're ready to eat (but the taste is a bit off). To treat coughs and chest infections, drink a leaf infusion or chew the leaves. Boil the inner bark in water and you have an eye wash or a solution for ear problems. The Aborigines used the hard timber from the tree to make boomerangs, woomeras and axe handles. Nothing was wasted.

You can make a coarse bread out of the seeds of cycads, palm-like plants that are common around Darwin. The 'bread' tastes fine, but smells awful. It's quite a complicated process: first the seeds are cooked in a fire. Then they are chipped into small pieces, put in a bag and left in a running creek for a few days to get rid of the toxins in them. Then the soggy mess that's left is shaped into cakes, wrapped in bark from a melaleuca (a paperbark tree) and roasted overnight. The cooked cakes, or loaves, last for up to six months.

The quandong is an amazing fruit, and again, all parts of it can be used. It makes tasty pies, jams and chutneys and can be used as a glaze. Quandong wine is not a bad drop, and the fruit goes well in brandy. Dried quandongs are similar to beef jerky. The large seed in the centre, called a bully, is attached to a piece of string and used by kids to make a conker – and is also used to make jewellery. Aborigines used the kernel as a contraceptive and also rubbed the kernels on cuts. And quandong leaves make a good cup of tea.

Quandongs, *Santalum acuminatum*, have a tangy taste, something like a mixture of peach and rhubarb. They grow naturally in the wild and are harvested there, but moves are being made to cultivate them, especially around Broken Hill, in the far west of NSW.

It takes four to six years for the fruit to appear, and then the trees last for up to 90 years. But there's only about a ten per cent survival rate growing them from scratch.

Gum trees are everybloodywhere. More than 600 species of eucalypts dominate the Australian landscape. They range in size from small trees to forest giants, and have a range of kinds of flowers and pods.

Gumnuts, the hardened flower cups of the eucalyptus, are used to make craft items, and inspired author May Gibbs to write kids' books with a gumnut theme. Like *Snugglepot and Cuddlepie*.

Haberfields, a food company based in Albury, on the NSW-Victoria border, is also using eucalypt to produce a truly Aussie cheese like no other; they are also wrapping it in gum leaves. Called Mungabareena, an Aboriginal word meaning a pleasant place of tall talk, the cheese is unique – it has a soft texture, something like a French brie, and a hint of eucalypt flavour. Haberfields reckon it is their 'pièce de resistance', dinky-di Australian and absolutely delicious.

Tea tree oil, credited with amazing healing qualities for everything from rashes, abrasions, insect bites and athlete's foot to sunburn, arthritis and sore throats, is back on the shelves in a whole range of products, and doing better than ever. Industry estimates are that worldwide demand for this unique Australian product are outstripping supply.

Tea tree oil is distilled from the leaves of the *Melaleuca alternifolia*, which is native to northern NSW. Europeans first encountered the tree when botanist Sir Joseph Banks collected leaf samples and brewed up a cup of tea; this is apparently how the tree got its common name, tea tree.

But long before that the Aborigines were crushing the leaves and using them to help heal cuts and wounds. Members of the Bunjalong tribe who lived near Lismore were great believers in its healing magic. When the first settlers and cedar cutters moved into northern NSW they borrowed many of the Aborigines' natural cures, so it wasn't long before the leaves of this miracle tree were being used to treat a string of ailments.

In 1925, after extensive research, Dr Arthur Penfold, from the Museum of Applied Arts and Sciences in Sydney, came up with some amazing results. He had a brief to investigate the commercial possibilities of native flora generally, and of the more than 200 species available to study, the species he focused on was the *Melaleuca alternifolia*. He extracted the oil by steam distillation, and after a series of trials found it had an antiseptic power more than 10 times greater than carbolic acid, which was the standard antiseptic of the time. He also found it killed bugs, bacteria and fungus much more quickly, was safe on skin tissue, and was highly solvent. And it had local anaesthetic properties – it produced a soothing feeling, minimising pain from cuts and abrasions. Dr Penfold published his papers in the late 1920s, and there was an immediate rush by other scientists to develop tea tree products which could be sold commercially.

The trees were unique to the area from north of Port Macquarie to the Queensland border, particularly in the floodplain country of the Tweed, Nambucca, Richmond and Clarence rivers, and bush stills soon sprang up throughout the area. Cutters brought in the leaves, which were put in big pots about a quarter-filled with water, with a wood fire underneath. The hot water sent steam through the leaves and the vapour was condensed and cooled. The oil, which is lighter than water, floated to the top of a collecting drum and was then scooped off with a jar.

The industry boomed. As well as being used as an everyday remedy for most ills, dentists used the oil as a mouthwash, and even for sterilising cavities before filling them.

During World War II, tea tree oil was used extensively by the Australian Army in first aid kits issued to soldiers in the Pacific region. Not only did it help heal minor injuries; it also repelled insects. The soldiers dabbed it on their faces, arms and clothes, and if they were bitten, the oil neutralised the venom.

The Federal Government considered the oil so essential to the war effort that it exempted the cutters and other industry workers from war service. But around the same time new synthetic medicines, such as penicillin, were discovered; that, combined with unreliable tea tree oil supplies, resulted in a major downturn in the industry.

By the 1960s, only about a dozen stills remained and the industry was going nowhere. Small supplies of oil were being sent by brokers to America to be sold. It was basically a yesterday's industry.

But a family who settled in Australia from Kenya in 1961 would eventually change all that. They established a highly successful tea tree oil operation at Ballina on the far north coast, in the heart of the area where Dr Penfold had found the best-quality tea trees back in 1925.

It took about three years of red tape and hard talking by a former Australian Broadcasting Commission employee Eric White, the stepfather of Chris, Peter and Mike Dean, to tie up the Crown lease on the 100 acre block he wanted, but eventually he got approval – on a Thursday in 1976. So he called the land Thursday Plantation.

The name was something of a joke to start with, but it stuck, and today it's synonymous with the tea tree oil industry worldwide. Ill health forced White to bow out, but Chris and his wife Lynda carried on, doing it pretty tough. They lived in a shed made of scrap iron, a shed that doubled as home and distillery. They were in the deep heart of Bungawalbyn State Forest, and had no running water, no power and no telephone. They had to drive 30 km to Evans Head to pick up their phone messages and mail orders, go back and fill the orders, then take the oil to the train at Casino.

Word of mouth was their earliest and most effective marketing tool. They began by taking a table and a supply of small bottles of tea tree oil to the local street markets, particularly at Shannon, between Lismore and Nimbin. They handed out literature with their sales, and sales increased each week as word spread, confirming their belief that there was a market for their product. Thursday Plantation is now a thriving business that has expanded into other natural health products and has a worldwide market.

One of our most publicised trees is the prehistoric Wollemi pine – up until 1994 it had lived undetected in its own Jurassic Park in the Blue Mountains, west of Sydney. The previously unknown trees, some of which were 40 metres high and had a three-metre girth, were found by National Parks & Wildlife Service officer David Noble in thick bushland in a deep gorge in the Wollemi National Park.

He was on a weekend bushwalk, and had abseiled 600 metres into the gorge, when he came across the 23 mature and 16 young trees. They were like nothing he had seen before, with knobbly trunks that looked as if they had been sprayed with the children's breakfast cereal Coco Pops.

Professor Carrick Chambers, Director of Sydney's Royal Botanic Gardens, said at the time that the discovery was the equivalent of finding a small dinosaur still alive on Earth. The location of the trees has been kept secret, to protect them, but scientists have a propagation program under way and people will eventually get the opportunity to buy one for their garden.

Australia's national flower is the wattle, a member of the acacia family. There are more than 600 species, but the best-known ones are Gold Dust, Cootamundra, Black, Sydney Golden and Queensland Silver. The masses of fluffy yellow flowers bloom in late winter or early spring. It was the wattle's contrasting green and yellow that became Australia's sporting colours of green and gold.

The Waratah is the floral emblem of NSW and the name of a string of sporting teams representing the State. The botanical name is *Telopea*, which comes from the Greek Telopos, which means seen from afar. Nobody knows the meaning of Waratah, which was the Aboriginal name. It has spectacular cones of vivid red flowers.

Western Australia's emblem is the Kangaroo Paw. It has velvety claw-shaped blooms in red, green and black and grows naturally from the Murchison River in the north to Lake Muir in the east and around Busselton in the south.

Sturt's Desert Rose is the Northern Territory's emblem. It's a member of the cotton family, not the rose family, so perhaps Australian Cotton is a more apt name. The small bushy plant has mauve petals with deep red markings at the base, similar to the hibiscus, which in fact belongs to the same family of the Cotton genus, *Gossypium*.

South Australia's emblem is Sturt's Desert Pea, a plant first collected by William Dampier when he visited the northwestern coast of this country in the 17th century. The long and curiously shaped flowers are usually scarlet or blood red with a large blue–black blotch at the base. The plant flowers in clusters of six to eight on short, thick stalks.

The Common Heath is Victoria's emblem. Its flowers, which are showy and bell-like, range from white to pink and red and are found on the upper part of the branches; they all point in the same direction.

Tasmania has the Flowering Blue Gum, which grows to 60 metres and has rough grey bark. The 'blue' in the name refers to the colour of the leaves, which are borne in opposite pairs on square stems. The trees are extensively used for pit props which hold up the roof in mines, burning in fires and for paper pulp.

The Australian Capital Territory, well known for its annual Floriade Festival, the capital's 30-day floral extravaganza of flowers and fun to celebrate spring, has the Royal Bluebell as its emblem. It is a small perennial herb with violet–blue flowers that grow around 3 cm in diameter.

Queensland's floral emblem is the Cooktown Orchid. Each plant flowers for up to six weeks. The flowers are usually purple, but some have white or white spotted flowers.

13 Our Prime Ministers

I'm glad that I'm Australian,
I'm glad that I am free,
But I wish I was a little dog
And the Prime Minister was a tree.

Conrad Black, a Canadian media magnate and former owner of Fairfax newspapers, didn't think much of Australian politicians. When he sold his shares in the company and left our shores he took a parting shot at them, saying they were 'impenetrably insular and juvenile' compared with their British, Canadian and American counterparts.

Black said Bob Hawke in his last days as Prime Minister, when he (Hawke) was under no political pressure to do so, had blocked him (Black) from taking over more of Fairfax – and that annoyed him no end. Black said that Hawke's successor, Paul Keating, was at first a refreshing change after Hawke, and promised to let him raise his shareholding in Fairfax to 35 per cent, but then 'suffered a merciless attack of amnesia' after winning the 1993 election.

Despite this, Black said that he found Keating, whom he described as the 'king of larrikins with a tongue that could clip a hedge', hard to dislike. He was pretty right about the tongue.

In Parliament, Keating regularly took the mickey out of Liberal leaders with comments like: 'John Hewson's performance is like being flogged with a warm lettuce leaf ...' Or, referring to Andrew Peacock: 'We're not interested in the views of painted, perfumed gigolos.'

Keating also raised eyebrows with other infamous comments: Australia was the 'arse-end of the world' and the economic downturn we had in the early 1990s was 'the recession we had to have'. Neither did he win any friends when he told Adelaide students protesting over university fees that they should 'get a job'. His description of Malaysian Prime Minister Dr Mahathir Mohamad as 'recalcitrant' triggered a diplomatic fracas between Canberra and Kuala Lumpur. It took months before the ruffled feathers were soothed.

Bob Hawke, otherwise known as the Silver Bodgie, was a knockabout Prime Minister who was famous for his affinity with people. When he was a young bloke, he had also been known for his drinking, and even earned a place in the *Guinness Book of Records* for skolling 2.5 pints of beer in 12 seconds.

After ten years as president of the Australian Council of Trade Unions, Hawke entered Parliament. He became a teetotaller when he realised that his alcohol consumption could ruin any chance he had of becoming Prime Minister. He failed in his first bid to lead the Labor party but ousted Bill Hayden on 3 February 1983, the same day that Malcolm Fraser called an election for 5 March. Hawke won in a landslide.

Hawke won three more elections before a restless Paul Keating, who had a deal with Hawke (on which the latter reneged) that he take over the job after a certain time, launched a challenge and won a Cabinet spill a couple of days before Christmas in 1991. Hawke retired to the backbenches and resigned from Parliament in February 1992.

But Hawke, who remains the longest-serving Labor Prime Minister, chalked up a number of memorable moments. Among them were changing the national anthem to 'Advance Australia Fair' and admitting on TV that he had been unfaithful to his wife, Hazel. (He divorced her after 40 years of marriage, and wed journalist Blanche d'Alpuget, who wrote his biography.)

One of his fearless election promises in 1987 – one that has not yet come true – was that after 1990, no Australian child need live in poverty. He was also fond of shedding a tear in public. And when Australia won the America's Cup, he said on national TV that any boss who docked staff for being late to work was a bum.

One of Hawke's proudest achievements was saving Antarctica from being destroyed. Members of his Cabinet had told him that it was a lost cause because an agreement had been reached to open up the whole area to exploration and mining. Any breach of the agreement would result in international ridicule, they said. Hawke disagreed, and made an alliance with the French to protect it as a nature reserve, so that it would be used only for science.

He's been busy since he retired from politics with business consultancies and speaking on the international circuit. He also reckons he remains a happy agnostic, a keen punter and a fiercely competitive golfer.

Robert Gordon Menzies, otherwise known as Merciless Ming or Pig-iron Bob, was a master of wit. He was also Australia's longest-serving Prime Minister. He led the country through the 1950s and 1960s.

He also took the helm between 1939 and 1941, after the then Prime Minister, Joe Lyons, died, but after one long trip overseas – cheering on the troops in the Middle East and spending weekends with Winston Churchill, his colleagues turned on him and he was forced to resign. Acting Prime Minister Artie Fadden took the helm, but was beaten in the election in 1941 by Labor's John Curtin.

Menzies formed the Liberal Party and stormed back to office in December 1949. He was Prime Minister from then until he retired, on Australia Day 1966. He handed over office to Harold Holt.

Menzies had no major achievements to his name other than presiding over a period of economic growth and security, introducing national service for 20-year-olds and then committing them and regular Australian troops to the war in Vietnam. He also spent much of his 17-year reign attacking communism and 'Reds under the bed'.

Menzies picked up the nickname Pig-iron Bob in 1938, after forcing waterside workers at Port Kembla to load scrap iron for Japan. They had refused, on the grounds that it was being used to make shrapnel. Later, he often used the name to his advantage. On an election campaign he told a rowdy meeting: 'The 40-hour week is no benefit to our economy. Let us take the steel industry …' Hecklers in the audience shouted 'Pig-iron Bob!' and Menzies replied, 'OK, let us take the pig industry. Will a 40-hour week produce more and better pigs?'

When the Queen installed Menzies as the first Australian Knight of the Thistle, Scotland's highest order, she pronounced his name in the Scottish way as Ming-ees. From that it was a logical step to the nickname Ming; later, Merciless was added – it was the name of an outer space ruler in a newspaper cartoon strip. It remained a press gallery nickname until journalist Massey Stanley let the cat out of the bag in the *Sydney Sunday Telegraph*. From then on, Ming stuck.

But people best remember Menzies for his wit. He was quick to put down hecklers and reply to taunts in the House of Representatives.

A woman at an election meeting yelled out: 'I wouldn't vote for you if you were the Archangel Gabriel.' Menzies replied: 'Madam, if I were the Archangel Gabriel, you would not be in my constituency.' And when he was being questioned in the House about whether 'Advance Australia Fair' – the alternative was 'God Save the Queen' – would be played at the Melbourne Olympic Games in 1956, Labor MP Arthur Greenup called out: 'Waltzing Matilda.' Menzies replied: 'I've heard it around the world. I say nothing about the lamentable moral defects of the hero of the poem, but as an air it stirs the mind.'

Another time, an opposition MP asked whether or not the Prime Minister was aware that a jockey had been suspended for life for having pulled another jockey's leg during a race. He went on: 'Seeing that Mr Menzies has been pulling other people's legs for years, why has he not been given life disqualification?' Menzies replied: 'I am under the impression that I have been practically given a life sentence by the people [who keep electing me].'

He once told 400 delegates at an International Federation of Business and Professional Women's meeting in Canberra: 'Opinions differ whether men understand women, but I am one of the few men honest enough to admit I don't understand them. This is the first time I have walked into a room where the entire audience has been respectfully silent …'

In 1972, Edward Gough Whitlam used the slogan 'It's Time' to lead the Labor party to its first election win in 23 years. Three years later he became the only Prime Minister to be sacked by the Governor-General.

But during his whirlwind term he ended national service, brought the troops home from Vietnam, established a national health scheme … and sent inflation and unemployment sky-high. Some of his ministers were involved in dubious deals to borrow huge amounts of money from unusual sources in the Middle East.

When Labor's popularity was on the ropes, the Liberal–Country Coalition in the Senate blocked supply, cutting off money to government departments and authorities. The Governor-General, Sir John Kerr, did a controversial thing by calling in Whitlam, giving him the boot and then swearing in Opposition Leader Malcolm Fraser, who had been waiting in another room.

Ironically it happened on Remembrance Day, 11 November 1975, a national day of mourning. Whitlam, in a speech to supporters from the steps of Parliament House, said: 'Well may we say "God save the Queen", because nothing will save the Governor-General. The proclamation which you have just heard read by the Governor-General's official secretary was countersigned by Malcolm Fraser, who will no doubt go down in history from Remembrance Day 1975 as "Kerr's cur".'

There was a federal election and Whitlam was defeated in a landslide. He stayed on as Labor leader but lost another election in 1977 and then retired from Parliament. His reforms had come too thick and fast for many in the electorate.

Malcolm Fraser, who won elections in 1975, 1977 and 1980, may be best remembered for losing his trousers. One morning in October 1986 the conservative former Prime Minister wandered into the lobby of a hotel in Memphis, Tennessee in a dazed condition, wearing a towel around his waist and no trousers. He was attending a conference in the city, and had apparently been drugged and robbed by a woman he met in a bar.

Fraser, dubbed The Prefect because of his serious manner, resigned from Parliament after losing to Bob Hawke in 1983.

Australia's first Prime Minister, Edmund Barton, who took office on 1 January 1901, got the job by default. Nicknamed Tosspot Toby because of his fondness for food and wine, he was the second choice in what was probably the first stuff-up of Federation.

Australia's first Governor-General, Lord Hopetoun, first invited NSW Premier Sir William Lyne, who was an anti-federationist, to form a federal government until elections could be held. This was two weeks after Lord H had arrived in Australia from England, and clearly he hadn't quite got a handle on the place or people yet. Lyne couldn't find enough people to help him run the country so Hopetoun had to bite his tongue and ask Barton to be Australia's first Prime Minister instead.

Barton was a popular choice with the people, and he at least had been prominent in the drafting of the Constitution. He resigned as Prime Minister in September 1903 to become a judge on the new High Court, where he sat for 17 years.

Alfred Deakin, or Affable Alf, took over from Barton — but kept his hand in as a journalist. He had worked on the *Melbourne Age* until 1883, even while he was a Victorian Member of Parliament. While he was Prime Minister, he wrote an anonymous weekly column for London's *Morning Post* until 1913 and articles for London's *National Review* until 1905.

There were a string of Prime Ministers after Deakin who weren't too interesting. Joseph Cook, who had 15 months in the job, from June 1913 to September 1914, started as a Labor MP for the State seat of Hartley in NSW, but resigned from the party after refusing to take the pledge to accept caucus direction.

He entered Federal Parliament as the Member for Parramatta in 1901, and after Deakin's resignation he became leader and then Prime Minister. The former Lithgow coalminer believed in the virtues of self-improvement and was opposed to drinking, smoking, gambling and other frivolous activities.

William Morris (Billy) Hughes, known as the Little Digger, was another MP who began his parliamentary career in the Labor party in 1894 and did the rounds of a string of other parties in his 58 years in politics. The Labor party booted him out because of his support for national service. After he had been a Labor Prime Minister for only 13 months, he first formed the National Labor Party (he was Prime Minister and their leader for three months), and then joined the Liberals to form the Nationalist Party in 1917 (he was Prime Minister with them until 1923). They expelled him in 1925 for criticising the government, and in 1929 he led a group of dissidents to bring them down. Next he joined Joseph Lyons' new United Australia Party, and then Menzies' Liberal Party. He remained an MP until he died, in 1952.

Joseph Benedict (Ben) Chifley, an engine driver from Bathurst, in central western NSW, was a popular Prime Minister from July 1945 until December 1949. His achievements included the Snowy Mountains hydro-electric scheme, setting up Trans Australia Airways, nationalising Qantas and sponsoring General Motors Holden's plan for an Australian car. But when he tried to nationalise the banks, his government got the boot. Drawn-out petrol rationing after the war didn't help.

Chifley spent most of his youth living on his grandfather's farm just out of Bathurst – he slept in a chaff bag bed in a four-roomed wattle and daub shack with whitewashed walls and an earth floor. He and his wife Elizabeth kept their modest cottage at 10 Busby Street, Bathurst, all their lives, and never lost their Bathurst connections. The cottage is now a memorial.

In 1942 he took on an additional role as Minister for Postwar Reconstruction and set the foundations for a new social order. In his policy speech in 1949 he said it was the duty of the community to see that less fortunate people were protected and not left without hope – this was the beacon, the light on the hill, to which efforts should always be directed.

Mystery still surrounds the demise of Harold Holt, who went swimming in heavy surf at Portsea, south of Melbourne, in Victoria, on 17 December 1967 and was never seen again. The rumours about his death make it sound like a thriller movie. Besides murder and suicide, there were allegations that he was a spy for China and didn't drown at all: two frogmen picked him up in an artificial air bubble, took him to a waiting submarine and off he went to China, where he was given asylum. Then there were people who reckoned he committed suicide. But Holt was a man who enjoyed himself, so this seems unlikely.

There's nothing to remind anyone of him other than a memorial swimming pool in Melbourne. He will simply go down in history as the Prime Minister who had a mysterious death.

14 Our wine

The first grape vines were brought to Australia by Captain Arthur Phillip in the First Fleet in 1788, no doubt because the colonists at the time liked a tipple. The vines were planted at Farm Cove, the present site of the Sydney Botanic Gardens, but they didn't grow too well, so they were dug up, taken further inland to Parramatta and replanted there.

It's lucky the people weren't relying on the wine from the grapes to quench their thirst, because Captain Phillip's three acre (1.2 ha) vineyard didn't produce any worthwhile results. Others in the following years also tried to establish grape growing and winemaking ventures in the colony, but also without success.

The colony's biggest farmer, John Macarthur, was establishing a profitable wool industry – but he was always arguing with the colony's administration, too. William Bligh, the infamous captain of the *Bounty*, had replaced Philip Gidley King as governor and he wasted no time getting a campaign going to break up the rum trade and the lucrative commercial monopoly John Macarthur and officers of the Rum Corps were involved in. Governor Bligh, who had no interest whatever in the future of wool, wanted to take back land grants made to free settlers, including Macarthur. This was causing a deal of unrest in the colony.

The Rum Corps commander, Major George Johnston, was eventually persuaded by his senior officers and John Macarthur that Bligh should be booted out of office. Major Johnston marched on Government House on 26 January 1808, put Bligh under house arrest and assumed office as lieutenant governor. He appointed Macarthur to the new position of Secretary to the Colony.

But several months later, Major Johnston was summoned back to England to face a court martial and was found guilty of mutiny against Bligh. He was dismissed from service but allowed to return to the colony to work his farm. John Macarthur, who had gone with him to offer support, had to remain in England in exile because of an order in New South Wales that he be brought to trial for his part in the rebellion. During all this time his wife Elizabeth was doing a good job of running his farm at Camden Park, 48 kilometres out of Sydney.

In 1817, Macarthur was allowed to return to Sydney, after giving an undertaking that he would have nothing to do with the affairs of the colony. While he'd been in exile, he and his two young sons, James and William, became interested in grape growing. They travelled through France and Switzerland to look at vineyards and the production of olive oil. When they returned to NSW, they brought hundreds of vine cuttings with them, and planted them at Camden Park.

The first vineyard was on a hill about a mile (1.6 km) from the estate's garden. This was abandoned in 1830, and the best varieties of vines were transferred to a new site after the soil was prepared for planting. The vineyard was about 22 acres (8.8 hectares) in size, and was on a natural terrace.

Because the transportation of convicts was being phased out in the 1830s, the government offered financial incentives to landholders to bring out immigrants from Europe to work in specialised areas. The Macarthurs were quick off the mark with this, and got six German vine-dressers from the Rhine Valley in 1839. The same year William Macarthur also imported cuttings from the Rhine vineyards; these too were planted at Camden Park.

More than 22,250 litres of wine were produced in 1841, and selected varieties won gold medals in England. Vine exports included 24,000 cuttings sent to Adelaide in 1844. The Macarthurs also regularly advertised cuttings for sale in the *Sydney Morning Herald* and other newspapers.

In 1845 Camden Park produced about 44,500 litres of wine; by this time, their wine had an international reputation. With 1458 bottles in the cellars by 1845, Camden Park's vineyard and winery had one of the best names in the colony. The annual vintage was harvested almost exclusively by women living on the estate.

Another 12 German families arrived in 1852 to work in the vineyards – some of their descendants still live in the town of Camden. Around 1882 a *Phylloxera* epidemic wiped out the Camden Park vineyards. They were replaced by new plantings in 1889 of 4.5 acres (1.8 hectares), but winemaking then was only a sideline to growing table grapes.

Explorer Gregory Blaxland also got into the industry, though in a much smaller way. In 1822 he shipped 122 litres of wine to London, where it won a Silver Medal of the Society for the Encouragement of Arts, Manufactures and Commerce. Five years later he sent a larger shipment – 1800 litres – and won the Gold Ceres Medal.

Since those early days, vines have been gradually planted right across Australia, and by the end of World War II, 117 million litres of wine a year was being churned out. But it was the postwar migrants from European countries such as Italy that really got the Australian wine industry going. The annual production in 2003 was around 1100 million litres – the sixth highest in the world after France (5900 million litres), Italy (5200), Spain (3200), the US (2400) and Argentina (1250).

About 48 per cent of Australian wine is exported. We export to more than 104 countries, but the main markets are the US, the UK and Japan. People in those countries buy the wine at less than half the price they would be able to in Australia because competition in the overseas markets is so tough.

On the consumption side, Aussies don't do too well. Per head of population, we drink a modest 20.9 litres a year, which puts us in 18th place in the world. That compares with 110.5 litres per head of soft drink, 2.4 kilograms per head of coffee and 0.9 kilograms per head of tea. France tops the list of wine consumption, with each person there downing 59.5 litres a year, followed by Italy (52.3 litres) and Portugal (50.2 litres).

White wine is the favourite Aussie drink. In 2003, sales of whites, with Chardonnay the most popular, totalled more than 344,000 litres. Sales of reds totalled 142,800 litres, with Cabernet Sauvignon the most popular. South Australia is the State that makes the most wine, producing 506 million litres in 2003. NSW was next, with 337 million litres, followed by Victoria (153 million litres), Western Australia (38 million litres), Tasmania (1.8 million litres) and Queensland (700,000 litres).

Stephanie Rose Helm is probably Australia's youngest successful winemaker. At the age of 12 she won a silver medal at the Southern NSW Wine Show for her 1996 Merlot, which she made when she was only ten.

Stephanie, brought up on her parents' vineyard at Murrumbateman, near Canberra, tested for sugar and taste before selecting her own grapes. She crushed them herself, and after school each day kept a close eye on the fermentation. Although well under the legal drinking age, she had 'a little taste' now and then to check how things were going.

Her first effort was a Chardonnay, made when she was nine, and it missed winning a medal at the Cowra Wine Show, in central western NSW, by a mere half a point. But she scored the same points as her father Ken's commercial Chardonnay.

Ken Helm, a former mayor of Yass, near Canberra, says Stephanie is an independent young lady. She is enthusiastic about everything she does, he says. She plays the piano and knows practically everything there is to know about horses, although she doesn't own one. She reads a lot and picks things up quickly.

She might ask, 'What should I do now?' He tells her what happens to the wine if you do this or do that, but also tells her that she should make up her own mind – and she has done that pretty successfully.

Stephanie would like to be a winemaker, but also wants to do other things. 'I like making wine because you're not sure how it will turn out,' she says. 'The taste of a Chardonnay I made wasn't quite right. The following year I made a Cabernet. I tasted the grapes, selected the ones I wanted – we picked them on my 10th birthday – and I made around 300 bottles.'

She wasn't allowed in the tasting room at the Cowra Wine Show because of her age, even though she reckoned she only wanted to have a look. The judge, Gerry Sissingh, was full of praise for Stephanie's medal-winning Merlot. His comments were: 'The colour was a nice red with a slight purple still in it, there was a strong rich fruit blackberry-like flavour, a good balance of wood ageing character and good crisp acid. A nice wine.' He was amazed someone so young was able to make such a good wine. 'I hope she decides to become a professional winemaker,' he said.

The maximum score for a wine is 20 points. If a wine scores 18.5 points it's awarded a gold medal, if it gets 17 points it's a silver, and if it gets 15.5 it wins a bronze medal.

Stephanie's father Ken grew up with wine. Mr Helm's great-grandfather, Peter Fraunfelder, came to Australia in 1850s on a contract to grow grapes at Albury, on the NSW–Victoria border. In the 1870s there were 1000 acres (400 hectares) of vines in the area, which made it the largest wine-producing district in Australia – it turned out 4.4 million litres of wine a year. Ken's grandfather followed the tradition, but as wines began to disappear at the turn of the century, they turned to other businesses, becoming wheelwrights and blacksmiths.

The Yass–Murrumbateman–Canberra region is proud of its cool-climate boutique wines, which are earning a big reputation and a string of medals. Lots of sunshine, warm days, dry autumns and cool nights ensure that the grapes ripen slowly, bringing out a great fruit flavour and enriching the colour of the local reds – Cabernet Sauvignon, Merlot and Shiraz. The main whites produced in the area are Chardonnay, Sauvignon Blanc and Riesling.

The weather is similar to that in the Bordeaux region in France, so it's little wonder that bigger companies like BRL Hardy and the Ron Bell Management Group are cashing in on the region's potential. There are around 25 wineries in the area, most of them in Yass Shire; Murrumbateman is the hub, but the district is still small and friendly.

You walk in and there's the winemaker. He's shovelling the grapes, he's making the wine, he's standing at the counter selling it and he's telling people how he made it. Winemaking isn't new to the district. Soon after the discovery of the Yass Plains by explorer Hamilton Hume in 1821, the new settlers planted grape vines, and between 1869 and 1874, 12 vineyards produced 190,000 litres of wine. But strong competition from the warmer wine-growing regions, the momentum of the temperance movement, which kept consumption down, and Federation, which removed trade barriers between the States, resulted in the disappearance of the Yass wine-growing industry. The last recorded winery, called Ainsbury, just out of Yass, closed down in 1908.

It was academics, mainly from the Commonwealth Scientific and Industrial Research Organisation and the Australian National University at Canberra – described as 'the PhD vignerons' – who revived interest in the area in the 1970s. Dr John Kirk set up his small vineyard at Murrumbateman and produced the first commercial vintage (under the Clonakilla label) in the district in 1975. The other vineyards have shot up since then.

Apart from Macarthur's Sydney efforts, the Hunter Valley is the oldest – and now the most visited – wine region in Australia. The Lower Hunter's Pokolbin–Rothbury area attracts more than 500,000 visitors a year, even though the whole Hunter produces only three to four per cent of NSW's wine. It's less than a two-hour drive from Sydney, so people can hop from one winery to the next, from the big-name wineries like Draytons, Lindemans, McGuigan, McWilliam's, Tyrrells and Rothbury to the one-winemaker boutiques.

The Upper Hunter region, centred on the town of Denman, is an hour's drive from Pokolbin, and locals here brag that they have NSW's best Chardonnay (maybe even Australia's, they reckon): Rosemount Estate Roxburgh Chardonnay, which has won a string of medals. It is predominantly a white wine area.

Wine grapes were first introduced to the Hunter around 1820, after convicts had built the Great North Road from Windsor, west of Sydney, to Jerry's Plains, between the present towns of Muswellbrook and Singleton. Free settlers flowed into the area and the grapes were planted. By 1823, 20 acres (eight hectares) were flourishing, with more going in every year. Some of the pioneers were George Wyndham, James King and William Kelman.

Amateur viticulturist James Busby added to the development when he returned to the colony after extensive study tours of Europe's wine-growing regions – and with 500 vine cuttings from selected vineyards. Some were planted in Sydney's Botanic Gardens, but they failed because of mismanagement and official neglect. A duplicate collection of 300 varieties was planted on the Hunter River by James' sister Catherine and brother-in-law William Kelman. These were the grapes that really got the industry going, and by 1840 the Hunter's registered vineyard area totalled more than 500 acres (200 hectares).

The Riverina is the biggest wine-producing region in NSW, with 60 per cent of the market. It churns out 260,000 tonnes of grapes a year, dwarfing the Hunter Valley harvest of around 30,000 tonnes. Growers there rejoiced in 2004 because their big harvest was all made into wine; in 2003, grapes were left on the vines because there was a glut of wine worldwide, and no ready market.

Their good fortune is mainly due to the remarkable expansion of Griffith company Casella Estate, which took 70,000 tonnes of local grapes in 2004. Family-owned Casella, established on a small farm in 1969 by Filippo and Maria Casella, who migrated from Italy in the early 1950s, and now managed by second generation John, Joe and Marcello, also buys grapes from other regions, such as Orange, Forbes and the Barossa, to keep its production line churning out 24,000 bottles an hour, 24 hours a day, six days a week.

Nearly all the wine, 97 per cent, goes overseas under the yellow tail label, with exports topping 10 million cases in 2004. Three years ago the company exported only 500,000 cases.

Sales and marketing manager John Soutter said nearly every vineyard owner in southeast Australia had received some benefit from the success of the yellow tail range of Chardonnay, Merlot, Shiraz and Cabernet Sauvignon wines: besides buying grapes, Casella had been able to absorb a lot of the wine other companies have had left over from the 2000, 2001, 2002 and 2003 vintages.

Casella tripled the size of its winery in 2004, going from a 50,000 tonne crush capacity to 150,000 tonnes, but manufacturers couldn't make enough stainless steel tanks in time – otherwise the company would have crushed even more grapes than it did. Casella's biggest market is the US, where yellow tail is the biggest-selling Australian wine brand. Other countries that love yellow tail include Canada, Germany and the UK.

Orange, in central western NSW, found a new spot on the map with its cool-climate grapes grown in volcanic soil on the slopes of Mt Canobolas. At more than 900 metres, the vineyards are some of the highest in Australia, and this combination of an altitude-induced, cool-to-mild climate and superb soils has guaranteed the city a major role in the viticultural future of NSW. It was the Bloodwood Estate that took the first step to establishing a major wine-growing industry, planting a vineyard in 1983, followed by Hunter's Rosemount in 1989, after recognising the potential of the district as a grape-growing area. Orange now has more than 50 vineyards.

Mudgee is another smaller central western NSW region producing good Cabernet Sauvignon and Shiraz. Vines were first planted in 1858 by the Roth family, and it was from their Craigmoor vineyard that the rest of the country's early chardonnay plantings were sourced. Mudgee has a string of boutique winemakers.

Cowra Estate likes to take the credit for developing the booming grape industry, which began almost by accident in 1973. A Department of Agriculture feasibility study in 1970 found the area well suited to viticulture, but apparently nobody took much notice except an American mail order company called Reading Dynamics.

The company selected 600 acres (240 hectares) of land several kilometres out of Cowra on the Boorowa Road for their vineyard, but went broke before they could even start. Then along came another prospective buyer, who was mainly interested in establishing a tax shelter; he took out an option on the land, with the intention of subdividing it and selling it bit by bit.

Sydney real estate agent Tony Gray tried hard to talk him out of the idea. Mr Gray had read the Department of Agriculture study on grape growing and thought the land was better suited to that. When he couldn't get the owner to change his mind, Mr Gray bought the option himself, for $25,000, with plans to develop it as a close farming scheme – basically, managing vineyards for collective owners.

His idea was to use a small part of the property as one acre (0.4 hectare) residential blocks and sell off five acre (two hectare) blocks of vineyards. But that plan didn't get off the ground either, and Mr Gray finished up with the lot himself. What he did next was a risky move, because he had no experience at all in grape growing, but he went ahead and planted 50 acres (20 hectares) of chardonnay and cabernet sauvignon vines anyway; he planted another 40 acres (16 hectares) in the next two years. The first vintage was made by Montrose Wines at Mudgee in 1976. The same year Mr Gray planted another 100 acres (40 hectares) and sold off some of the land he didn't need, to be used for housing.

In 1979 he recruited Greg Johnston, a viticulturist who worked for Rothbury Estate, as vineyard manager. Mr Johnston bought 25 acres (10 hectares) of vineyard himself. In 1981, to finance more development, Mr Gray sold a piece of the established vineyard to Rothbury, which by now was taking a keen interest in what was happening at Cowra. Other big companies followed, and Cowra is now a major grape-growing centre, specialising in chardonnay and verdelho.

The far-flung Margaret River region in Western Australia, about three and a half hours by car south of Perth, boasts that it produces some of the best Chardonnay in the world. Cullen Wines holds an international Chardonnay tasting each year, pitting the local wines against the top of the variety from around the world, such as California's Beringer, Kistler and Gallo. And there are always locals – such as Leeuwin Estate, Pierro, Voyager, Cullen and Cape Mentelle – that are placed in the top bracket. Leeuwin Art Series Chardonnay won in 1999, making it officially the best in the world.

Victoria's Yarra Valley is another of Australia's great wine-producing regions – the people there will tell you it is also one of the world's greatest. Home to around 55 wineries, it was the birthplace of the industry in Victoria in 1838, when a vineyard was planted on what is now Yering Station.

Pinot Noir and sparkling wines are Yarra Valley's specialties, though the region is also a quality producer of Chardonnay, Shiraz and Cabernet Sauvignon.

South Australia is Australia's biggest wine-producing State. Its Barossa Valley region is the best known, with more than 50 wineries and cellar doors, ranging from small family enterprises crushing up to 50 tonnes to national companies crushing more than 10,000 tonnes.

Unlike the eastern convict colonies of NSW, Victoria and Tasmania, South Australia was a free settlement from the beginning. It was planned in 1836 by English philanthropists, who saw an opportunity for people to develop the land by growing grapes, fruit and corn. But there was a typical Aussie stuff-up in the name of the wine-producing region. It was initially called Barrosa by the colony's surveyor-general, Colonel William Light, after the site of a victory by the English over the French in the Spanish Peninsular War. But the people who drew the maps misspelt the name and it turned out Barossa, which it remains to this day. Only in Australia.

German and Lutheran settlers moved into the region in the 1840s, and they established their own vineyards and made wine. The richer Poms living there put up the money for a commercial wine industry in the 1860s, but the major growth took place in the 1880s. The Barossa now has more than 500 expert vignerons who mix their knowledge of the old ways with modern wine-making practices.

There are now thousands of hectares of meticulously maintained vineyards in the Barossa region, with some of the old shiraz vines going back to the first days of settlement in the 1840s. More than 500 growers, some of them sixth generation, supply about 60,000 tonnes of grapes to the local wineries every vintage.

Because there are people in Europe and the US who have both a fondness for Australian premium wines and an eye for contemporary Aboriginal art, a Sydney company has combined the two. In a first for the industry, their wine comes in bottles that have been individually hand-painted by a team of northern NSW and central Queensland Aboriginal artists.

The artists were given a free rein in relation to what they paint on the bottles, and no two are the same. The wine, sourced from South Australia's Barossa Valley, comes at a premium price: $230 a bottle. A six-pack sells for around $1200.

Sydney company International Australian Wine Export reckons the wines are collectors' items and make good corporate gifts for overseas and local art lovers. The company says the aim was to export something that was uniquely Australian and to present wine to the international market in a novel way. It was also something that would benefit the Aboriginal community. It hoped people would buy the wine, put it on the mantelpiece for four or five years, until it was at its best, then drink it, and keep the bottle as a work of art.

About 28 Aboriginal artists are involved, most of them full-blooded. They paint about 800 bottles a week using a variety of tools, including sticks and brushes. To stop the paint coming off the bottle, it is covered with a special coating. Each artist also writes a small card to go with each bottle, which explains what the painting is about – it might tell the story of what the artist comes across when hunting, the animals the artist sees and the landscape. Called the Aboriginal Art Work range, the wines include a Cabernet Merlot, Cabernet Sauvignon and a Shiraz, all from the Barossa Valley.

Big is definitely better when it comes to wine barrels, so the experts say. Cassegrain Wines at Port Macquarie, on the NSW north coast, imported two huge 4500 litre wooden barrels from France for its best vintages. The barrels cost about $40,000 each, excluding shipping, but the winery reckons the final product will make the expense well worthwhile.

Cassegrain, which instigated the rebirth of viticulture in the north coast Hastings River district in 1980, is the first winery to use the giant barrels, which are made at Taransaud, near Bordeaux, in France. Brand manager Donna Carrier said the bigger the barrel, the better the elegance and characteristic flavours of the wine. 'We put lots of emphasis on ensuring that we use the highest quality grapes, and we want to maintain and enhance that in the winemaking process,' she said. 'With the large French oak barrels, the tannins will be much finer and we will get a softer wine and better flavour. We will use them to mature our best Reserve Shiraz and Cabernet Merlot, which will stay there for at least two years.'

Now, here's something wine connoisseurs might not want to read! The old Aussie term 'cracking a tinnie' has taken on a whole new meaning. As well as beer, drinkers can now get a Chardonnay, Cabernet Shiraz and a sweet white in a ring-pull can. The company game enough to buck the traditionalists says there is no tainting from the aluminium and the wine tastes great.

Woomba Wines at Toowoomba in Queensland initially developed the wine in cans for the overseas market, but in 2003 released limited quantities in Australia and intends to extend its outlets. The canned wine is sold in Downtown Duty Free stores at national airports and when a general acceptance is built up, it will be spread through the domestic market.

Sales manager James Newberry said Woomba Wines focused on the tourist trade because the name 'Aussie Wine' was aimed at that market and the export market. He said there would obviously be people with a traditional view on how wine should be packaged who may not be too enthusiastic about buying it in cans, but most people who did liked it. The company aimed at a younger market, but Newberry reckons people across the board, regardless of their age, are buying it.

Before the wine went on sale, the company carried out extensive testing over a 12 to 18 month period and there was no tainting of the wine from the 250 ml slimline can. And the cans were well received overseas. At the launch in London, people had been cautious but when they tasted the product they went away happy. The company has a Chardonnay and a Cabernet-Shiraz for the UK, south-east Asian and Japanese markets, and a sweet white for the United States.

Other Australian wine companies are cautious about producing wine in cans. Steph O'Dea of Windowrie Estate at Canowindra in central western NSW said there was consumer resistance to a change from cork to screw caps so he thought wine in cans 'could be pushing it uphill'. But he thinks eventually the move towards variety in packaging will gather pace, which could include cans.

Greg Johnston of Cowra Wines said that when he worked with Rothbury Estate in the Hunter in the early seventies, the company's chief financial officer suggested wine should be sold in cans. Wine connoisseur Len Evans was the chairman at the time and Greg remembers tears came to his eyes at the mere suggestion. He thinks it would be a definite no-no for most people.

15 Watering holes

An old bushie who had never left his lifelong home at Mt Hope, a tiny speck in the middle of nowhere in western NSW, won a bus trip to Sydney in a raffle. As he was leaving, his mates asked him where he was staying in case they needed to contact him while he was away. 'At the bloody pub, of course,' he replied.

Where else?

Sydney, where settlement Down Under all began, has hundreds of pubs. Many have a history as long as your arm. The oldest is the Lord Nelson – it received its licence in 1842. Another historically important watering hole is the Napoleon in Sussex Street. The Federation-style pub was once a wharfie haunt but now its patrons are office workers.

Oldtimers say there was a trapdoor near the bar at the Hero of Waterloo, at Millers Point, and that back in the mid-1850s, when ships needed more crew, the barmen would get a bloke drunk and drop him through the floor. Underneath were tunnels that led to the wharves. By the time the unsuspecting men had sobered up, they were out to sea and had to work their passage back home.

One of the most popular pubs in Sydney, the Hero was made from hand-hewn blocks of stone by convicts. But it's unlikely any of them ever got to have a beer inside. Patrons now sit on church pews and take in an atmosphere not found in most other pubs. The Hero is also a popular target for tourist buses, which unleash hundreds of passengers armed with clicking cameras.

The Friend in Hand in Cowper Street, Glebe, is packed with hundreds of pictures and bits and pieces of junk. There's road signs, street signs, number plates, police signs and newspaper clippings all over the walls, along with a bear's head, surf ski and a huge cage for Joe, the resident cockatoo.

Publicans Peter Snr and Peter Jnr Byrne wanted the bar to have a 'unique feel.' They certainly did that. Their regulars included Glebe's bohemians, yuppies, labourers and students. Hermit crabs are raced at the pub every week and there are also jelly-eating contests.

An Australian Hotels Association award winner, the Friend has its own set of rules for drinkers. They include the checking in of all guns at the bar, no promises to pay later, no screaming, no begging or crawling and no stupid questions. Males with no shoes or shirts will not be served, but females with no shoes or shirts get their drinks free. There's Irish music on Sundays. Constructive criticism is not allowed and customers are not always right.

The historic Dundee Arms Hotel, built in 1849 but renovated to become part of the new Hotel Nikko complex in Sussex Street, has its own ghost, called Victoria. An architect is the only person who has seen her, but others reckon they've felt her presence. Victoria slams doors, breaks glasses and switches on electrical appliances. The architect who spotted her says she was wearing a long flowing bridal dress.

The story goes that a brothel-keeper murdered the young Victoria in the late 1880s, when there were lots of bawdy goings-on at the Dundee Arms. But apparently she holds no grudges; hotel staff say Victoria is a friendly ghost and hasn't harmed anyone.

The pub's beverage manager first came across Victoria in the hotel's cellar. He was trying to lock the door late one night, but someone on the other side kept pushing it back open. It happened three times, so he took off. He could feel a force, he said, and it wasn't the wind. Another time, a senior staff member heard footsteps up and down the stairs, giggling and even a scream, which gave him goose bumps. When he checked, there was nobody there.

The Australian Youth Hotel at Glebe has a raised floor behind the bar. A former publican was a jockey, and because he was so short, he had trouble talking to patrons. He fixed the problem by building a false floor 30 cm above the real floor.

Sydney is the only city that can boast that it has pubs made by convicts, but Hobart, the capital of Tasmania, is not far behind. The second-oldest city in Australia, Hobart was established in 1804 on the mouth of the Derwent River after Governor Philip Gidley King sent a small party of marines and convicts there to get things going.

His main aim was to keep the French out, but Hobart became an important port. It was a wild and unruly place, and by the 1830s, it had a pub for every 200 people. Named after the Secretary of State for War and the Colonies at the time, Robert Hobart, the town was frequented by sailors, whalers, sealers, traders, crooks and convicts and, as you do, they all liked a drink.

The oldest watering hole in Hobart, and one of the oldest continuously licensed pubs in Australia, is the Hope and Anchor – named after many others in the Old Dart.

The Hope and Anchor was built in 1807 and is still an important part of Hobart's pub culture.

The Georgian-style Knopwood's Retreat and Whaler's Return, later named Irish Murphy's, is another of Hobart's famous pubs. It was at one time run by a woman called Ma Dwyer, and earned the nickname Ma's Blues House because of the regular fights there. It was also a popular haunt for crooks, because it had three lanes at the back which provided speedy escape routes when the place was raided by cops.

Back on the mainland, Melbourne has some top watering holes, especially the Railway Hotel in the city's west. A quiet back-street pub, you get the feeling you're going back in time when you step inside. Leadlights above the bar add to the old-world ambience and the well-worn but comfortable feeling. The no-nonsense management expects drinkers to keep a lid on their enthusiasm.

Adelaide has some stately pubs, but they're not of the same era as the Sydney pubs. The Corus Grosvenor is a reminder of the past, and although it was refurbished in 2002, it retains its classic marble façade.

The Union Hotel in Waymouth Street was a venue for cock fighting in the old days. It was also the favourite watering hole of journos from the Adelaide *Advertiser*.

The Stag and the Crown and Sceptre in the east end of Adelaide, near the wholesale fruit and veg markets, which are now apartments for yuppies, had special licences allowing them to open at something like 2 am to serve the market gardeners after they'd delivered their produce.

The Earl of Aberdeen, in the city, has its own brewery, which is all behind glass and can be viewed by patrons. The Cathedral hotel in North Adelaide, which is opposite the city's famous Anglican cathedral, is another famous watering hole that is worth a look.

Canberra, meeting place of the nation and an everything-goes city, has more than 300 restaurants, cafés and bars, pubs and clubs to cater to its cosmopolitan population. You can rub shoulders with the pollies at a number of watering holes, but the Holy Grail in Green Square, in trendy Kingston, is the most popular.

Almost next door is Filthy McFaddens' Irish pub, a cosy and dimly lit joint with buckets of atmosphere and almost any drop of brew you could want. PJ O'Reilly's, the Wig 'n Pen and King O'Malley's are other popular Irish-inspired waterholes – but remember, they're all pretty new.

Australians like a drink. We down the equivalent of 253 stubbies (375ml bottles) each a year. If under-age people are taken out of the calculations, the average Aussie drinks 127 litres a year, equal to 339 tinnies (cans of beer). But we're amateurs compared with some Europeans, who are the best drinkers in the world. Austrians guzzle 165 litres of beer each a year, while the Irish down 144 litres. Americans are low on the list, with 75 litres.

Australians are now drinking more low-alcohol beer. One in every four beers consumed is now low-alcohol – 23.9 litres per year for each drinker. Wine consumption is also on the increase, with Australians now drinking 18.8 litres each a year.

Pubs stay open for long hours now. Some never shut. But it wasn't always like that. In World War I, after vigorous campaigning by temperance groups, 6 pm closing was introduced. When the war ended, the early closing hours remained, producing an infamous Australian institution known as the Six O'clock Swill.

It usually reached its peak between 5 pm (when offices shut) and 6 pm, and featured hordes of shouting, gesticulating drinkers who fought, pushed and elbowed their way to the bar in an attempt to consume as much beer as they could before the dreaded closing hour of 6 pm arrived. This was quite the opposite of what the temperance groups had had in mind and it amazed overseas visitors. People voted in a referendum to discontinue 6 pm closing.

Running a small pub these days is far from being all froth and bubble. In fact, in most cases it's hard, backbreaking work 15 hours a day with little reward at the end of a seven-day week. The once continual clink of glasses, loud laughter and a cheerful red-faced publican who seemed to enjoy himself as much as the patrons are things of the past. Faced with reduced profits as a result of several factors – random breath testing, higher overheads and a general decline in alcohol consumption in pubs (as opposed to homes) because of discounted packaged beer – many small pubs are fighting for their survival.

If they are to succeed today, publicans must have a multitude of skills: financial adviser, money lender, postman, diplomat and marriage counsellor, to name just a few. And as the old-style pubs disappear, the old-style barmaids who knew how to pull a perfect beer and called everyone 'luv' and 'darl' are going with them.

The Australian Hotels Association says pub staff are now more likely to be young part-time actors and models and students and travellers, usually aged between 18 and 28, who are filling in time behind the bar until they find other work. The long-time barmaids in their 50s and 60s have been edged out by new marketing strategies designed to increase trade. It seems that a young bird has a better chance of attracting more drinkers.

There's a slow change in publicans, too. In the trendy Sydney suburbs, rather than ex-footballers, ex-coppers and ex-bookmakers, publicans are more likely to be restaurateurs, chefs or businessmen and women in the 30-40 age group. Their emphasis is on style, sophistication, a pleasant atmosphere and good service.

But the traditional family-owned pubs are still solidly there. Greg Loveridge, whose family has owned Booligal's Duke of Edinburgh Hotel for more than 40 years, has no pretensions about his small business. And he and his wife Bernadette wouldn't live anywhere else. 'It's hot, we get a few dust storms, heaps of flies and the mozzies are bigger than rabbits,' Greg says. 'We have to pump our own water from the river and if it comes out dirty, that's just bad luck, because there's nothing you can do about it. But life isn't too bad.'

Booligal, population 49, is the Riverina town bush bard Banjo Paterson in one of his poems likened to being worse than hell. The poem, in part, goes: 'Oh, send us to our just reward in Hay or hell, but, gracious Lord, deliver us from Booligal!'

Booligal was once a stopover for Cobb and Co. coaches and the wagons that travelled the black soil plains to Ivanhoe and the Darling River port at Wilcannia. Some time ago, Greg's father moved the Duke of Edinburgh about 100 m, so that it would be closer to the Cobb Highway and perhaps attract more passing trade, but the council shifted the road and now they're no better off.

However, the Duke of Edinburgh has at least been able to survive all these years – the One Tree Hotel, in a desolate spot in the desert between Hay and Booligal, Paterson's earthly hell, served its last round of drinks more than 50 years ago.

Retired schoolmaster Sam Willis, of Hay, remembers the publican, an interesting character called Frank McQuade: 'We were on our way to Booligal to play cricket and we called in to see Frank. After I was introduced as a new blow-in teacher and we ordered our drinks, Frank reached down behind the bar and came up with a couple of dusty bottles of lukewarm Victoria Bitter which he poured into lukewarm glasses. "Excuse me, Mr McQuade," I said, "but are those bottles off the ice?" "Yes, of course they're off the ice," he replied, "20 bloody miles off."'

Pubs are tourist attractions in their own right. They're also important rest stops, particularly when you're travelling hundreds of kilometres in the inhospitable outback. And they all have a story to tell. Take the Blue Heeler at Kynuna, on the Matilda Highway in central western Queensland, between the Channel Country and the Gulf, for instance.

Country music singer and former jackeroo James Blundell wrote a song, appropriately called *Blue Heeler*, for the watering hole's 100th birthday. The song goes, in part: 'Drovers with mobs, road trains and dogs, were part of the trade that she's known. A hundred years on the Diamantina, the test of time for the old Blue Heeler …'

A mate of one of the owners, Blundell has had his share of pots at the Blue Heeler, and was special guest at a centenary birthday party that attracted 600 partygoers, who came in cars, planes and boats. Some people stranded by the flooded Jessamine Creek were given a lift by the Army. They polished off 10 bullocks, a dozen sheep, 200 dozen bread rolls and more than a tonne of vegetables, not to mention what they washed it down with.

Kynuna, home to around 20 people, is easy to miss if you're in a hurry. But local cockies Bill Cooper and Russell Parsons, who bought the pub so they could drink free beer whenever they liked, solved the problem. They installed a gaudy, flashing blue sign – a picture of a cattle dog – on the roof. It lights up so brightly that they say pilots flying across Australia use it as a navigational beacon.

Back in the 1970s, the then publican, a former ringer, drover, stock inspector and colourful character called Barry Patrick, boosted business by bailing up passing buses with a shotgun. Eventually he built up such a rapport with the bus companies that the Blue Heeler became an official refreshment stop. But he still produced the shotgun when a bus drove into sight.

And even though Kynuna is about 1000 km from the nearest beach, Patrick formed a surf lifesaving club and was able to convince visitors that the ocean was just over the rise. Those adventurous enough to don their swimmers and go with him found only the dry, dusty, Diamantina riverbed.

Besides the pub, Kynuna has only a petrol station and a couple of houses, but it remains an important place in Australian history. In 1895, Banjo Paterson wrote the words for 'Waltzing Matilda', Australia's best liked song, at nearby Dagworth Station (now called Belfast).

Just down the road to the north of Kynuna, at McKinlay, is the Walkabout Creek Hotel, where film crews shot the town scenes for Paul Hogan's movie *Crocodile Dundee*. The small single-storey building in the town's dusty main street was originally called The Federal, and licensed in 1901, but after its rise to fame, the owners decided to keep the movie name.

Now hundreds of people turn up every day in tourist buses to look at the pub and the stills from the movie, provided by Hogan, that are stuck all over the walls.

The North Gregory Hotel in Winton, also in western Queensland, was built in 1878 by two blokes named Corfield and Fitzmaurice. Like many old bush pubs, it was destroyed by fire, the first time in 1900. It was burnt down again in 1915, and a third time in 1946. The town's council realised the need for a good pub, so they put a levy on the rates, and by a special Act of Parliament, the North Gregory was raised from the ashes a third time. It was reopened in 1955, with a full silver service, bellboys and room service, and was one of the largest employers in the town.

Banjo Paterson was one of the hotel's famous visitors, and former American President Lyndon B Johnson was another – but well before he became President. On 11 June 1942, a US Air Force Flying Fortress called 'The Swoose', piloted by Major Frank Kurtz, made a forced landing at sunset on Carisbrooke Station, 85 km west of Winton. The compass had packed it in on the flight, which was supposed to be from Darwin to Cloncurry, and being low on fuel, the only option was to put the plane down among the cattle and the gibbers. US Navy commander LBJ was on board. The air crew all headed off to Winton in the station owner's car and booked in to the North Gregory Hotel for the night.

Still in central western Queensland, Betoota, population 1, lost its pub and the only business when the only resident decided to retire in 1997 when he was 87. Simon Remienko reckoned he needed a break, so he shut shop, painted over the beer signs and put his feet up. The sixth owner in 115 years, Simon bought the pub in 1959 after migrating to Australia from Germany. He picked up the language and soon got to know the people from the outlying stations and the passing tourists who called in for a cold drink to wash down the red bulldust.

Betoota is on a dusty rutted track between Birdsville, 165 km to the west, and Windorah, 230 km to the east. Motorists now face a longer trip between watering holes, a thirsty drive indeed through the mulga and gidgee scrub and salt pans. But Windorah's Western Star Hotel, just across Cooper Creek in the heart of Queensland's channel country, has loads of character and good service. It will help ease the pain of Betoota's closure.

The Birdsville pub, another must-call-in watering hole for thirsty outback travellers, really comes to life at the annual Birdsville races. Most of the people who go there have no interest in horses. They just like to drink.

The pub sells 35 tonnes of beer over the race weekend. That's 80,000 tinnies. Patrons get excited and behave in ways they never would at home, like doing nude handstands on the pub's chimney, or jumping off the roof. Cleaning up the layer of empty cans that spills into the street takes days. But it's all legend, mate.

An almost empty reminder of western Queensland's golden past is the once magnificent Hotel Corones at Charleville. This is probably Australia's biggest outback pub. The Duke of York has slept there and waved from the balcony to a cheering crowd below.

Built by Greek immigrant Harry Corones between 1924 and 1929, the hotel has lots of silky oak and cedar panelling, embossed plaster ceilings, stained glass windows, a grand staircase and a foyer of Italian marble tiles. Besides a ballroom, there are about 40 rooms upstairs, of which four had ensuites even in the 1920s, which was pretty modern thinking.

The Corones has its own hall next door, which was used for movies and race day balls – it is part of the pub. More recently the Corones has suffered financial problems, but there's little doubt it will survive, just like it did when it was flooded in 1990.

Pubs play an important part in life in the bush. Most people reckon that if a town hasn't got a pub, it's not really on the map. It was the other way round at Table Top, 15 km north of Albury, on the NSW-Victoria border: in this case the 'Mob' from the famous Ettamogah Pub needed a good excuse to work up a thirst, so they built a town.

The timber watering hole, a replica from Ken Maynard's long-running Ettamogah Mob cartoon in *Australasian Post* magazine (now shut down), has a number of added attractions – a 'Comedy Cop Shop', a lock-up (prison cell), pottery and blacksmith shops, a winery, a restaurant and a café.

The complex attracts thousands of people a year. One of the managers, Sef Spencer, who boasts that he can drink a beer in four seconds while standing on his head, reckons he has the best of two worlds and could never work in another pub after the Ettamogah. It just wouldn't be the same, he says. He meets so many different types of people every day, it is like a college of knowledge.

Albury businessman Lindsay Cooper, who originally had just a winery on the site, let his imagination run wild when he built the pub as a tourist attraction – straight out of Ken Maynard's cartoons, complete with sloping walls, balconies and staircases. Some of the locals feature in the Ettamogah Mob cartoons, but on the other hand, they also mimic some of the cartoon characters.

The pub has about 50 regular patrons from the district. Some of them helped build the place. And as in the cartoon strip, the Ettamogah Mob play an annual football match against Yackandandah, which is 30 km south. The rules are pretty simple: every man on the team has to have a tinnie in his hand at all times (this rule also applies when they play cricket), and the visitors have to run uphill. This makes it hard for them – which, after all, is the reason for the rule – because the oval falls 1.8 metres from one end to the other.

Another old pub that's one of a kind is the Lion of Waterloo, built back in 1842 by a young Belgian named Nicholas Hyeronimus to cater for Cobb and Co. passengers, teamsters and miners. Looking pretty much the same as it did all those years ago, the Lion is the oldest hotel west of the Blue Mountains. It has been classified by the National Trust, and attracts lots of interest.

It's on the junction of the Bell and Macquarie rivers at Montefiores in western NSW. The small community here led to the settlement of the now much larger town of Wellington. Montefiores was a Cobb and Co. staging post, and for years it was the only town beyond Bathurst, but when a bridge was built over the Macquarie River, Wellington sprang up on the opposite bank and Montefiores was bypassed.

The Lion of Waterloo's licence, number 98, was issued on 19 April 1842. The Lion's first owner was elected to State Parliament in 1859 as the Member for Wellington, but he died the following year and not a lot is known about the hotel since then.

The licence eventually lapsed, and in more recent times the hotel was used as a plumbing shop. But then it was bought by Maryvale farmer Trevor Wykes, who spent four years meticulously restoring the building. The front wall is original, along with some of the flooring and the pit-sawn timber rafters. The shingles are still on the roof, but they have been covered with iron to make the building more weatherproof. It was reopened in November 1993 after the licence was renewed.

There's more history in Teamsters Park, just across the road from the Lion. In 1854 it was the site of the last recorded duel fought in Australia, between Dr Samuel Curtis and a Mr Sheridan. History records that due to both men being drunk, 'there were no fatalities ...'

The pub closest to the centre of Australia is the Ti-Tree Roadhouse, on the Stuart Highway near Central Mt Stuart, 190 km north of Alice Springs in the Northern Territory. It's almost bang in the middle of the country, serves up icy cold beer, and has motel rooms and a caravan park for travellers.

Probably the most photographed pub in Australia is the Silverton Hotel at Silverton, near Broken Hill, in outback NSW. It's been used in lots of movies, including *A Town Like Alice*, *Razorback*, *Mad Max II* and *Scorpio*, and in dozens of TV commercials, including Coke ads of a sky surfer.

Former publican Ines McLeod, who was awarded an Order of Australia Medal in 2003, took it all in her stride. 'We didn't charge anything for them to use the pub, so long as they left it the way it was before they started,' she says. 'They painted it a different colour each time but always restored it to original. And the pub has had eight different names for the movies, including McNally's Ridge for *Blue Lightning*, the Gummulla Hotel for *Razorback* and The Diggers Rest for *Outback Bound*.'

Regulars over the years included a parrot called Mister Mac. He spent most of his time flapping around the beer garden upending the empty tinnies in the rubbish bins. Ines, who bought the pub from her father in 1973, says he was often hung over. She tried to keep an eye on him, she says, but people gave him all sorts of things to drink and he never said no because beer was his favourite drink.

Mister Mac became something of a star after making a TV commercial for brewing company Castlemaine Perkins. But he wasn't the only offbeat regular at the pub, which sits like an oasis in the desert, 25 km west of Broken Hill. Misty, an ageing hack, was there for 12 years, most of the time on the front veranda, after choosing not to chum up with the brumbies (wild horses) that roamed the area.

Darwin, Australia's frontier capital, has a liking for Irish pubs. Kitty O'Shea's Irish Bar and Café is a lively establishment that attracts all sorts of people who want a good night out in a friendly atmosphere. Shenanigans is another Irish pub where you can drink pints of genuine Guinness and other Irish beers. In outer Darwin, Dolly O'Reillys is the place to go if it's Irish hospitality you want.

The Victoria Hotel, known to locals as the Vic, is a survivor of both the Japanese air attack in World War II and Cyclone Tracy, which devastated Darwin on Christmas Eve in 1974. The Vic was called the North Australian Hotel when it was built in 1894. Since then it's had three or four major reconstructions, but has retained its original architecture and most of the original stone. It's a popular waterhole for both locals and backpackers, though the Globe Trotters Bar and Lodge caters specifically for backpackers.

The Hotel Darwin is the Northern Territory's oldest pub, and advertised accommodation 'suitable for ladies' when it opened in 1883. Locals call it a mini-Raffles, because its architect looked at Singapore's Raffles, Penang's Eastern and Oriental and Bangkok's Grand hotels before he did the design work. The original hotel survived the Japanese bombing but then burnt down. It was also shut for nearly two years after Cyclone Tracy caused major damage.

There are the makings of a mystery buried under the 135-year-old Albion Hotel at Forbes, in central NSW. While carrying out renovations, a former publican, Jeff Nicholson, unblocked the entrance to a series of tunnels that apparently run under nearby shops: the adjoining newsagency, the Grace Bros store and the National Bank. There were also brick rooms down there.

Forbes was founded by the goldrush in 1861, when 30,000 miners arrived and set up a shanty town. The Albion Hotel was built the same year, and quickly won the reputation of having the highest bar takings in Australia. It was partly destroyed by fire in the 1880s and rebuilt in brick in 1889. A lookout with a bugle used a tower on the roof to watch for approaching coaches so that fresh horses could be brought out from the stables in the hotel yard.

Some locals believe the tunnels were used to secretly move gold to the hotel, where it was loaded onto coaches headed for the city – the hotel was a staging post for Cobb and Co. – but there's no firm evidence either way. Bushranger Ben Hall and his gang were active in the district at the time, and in one daring raid on the Forbes mail coach the gang escaped with 2700 ounces of the precious metal and £3700 in cash.

Townspeople also say the underground rooms in the hotel were used for drinking, gambling and opium smoking by the Chinese, who flocked to the goldfields to seek their fortune. But that theory could be doubtful too, because there was plenty of trouble between European and Chinese miners.

After several unsuccessful attempts by European miners at the Lambing Flat fields, now Young, to drive the Chinese out of the goldfields, 3000 European miners launched a major attack on a large Chinese camp in June 1861. In response, the NSW Government restricted Chinese immigration. When the centre of mining moved to Forbes, Chinese miners were officially excluded. But gradually they were allowed back, and many turned to market gardening. Eventually hostility towards them declined.

Jeff Nicholson unblocked the tunnels and turned them and the underground brick rooms into a mini-museum. But he was never able to crack the mystery of who dug the tunnels and whether or not the Chinese actually used the rooms. He established that a Stockman's Bank was directly opposite the hotel and the tunnels headed that way in the goldmining days, but doesn't know where the other banks were. What seems clear is that townspeople at the time were terrified of the bushrangers.

The old Tom Paine's pub at Menindee, a small town of 500 people on the Darling River, 110 km southeast of Broken Hill, has a chequered history. Robert O'Hara Burke and William John Wills stayed there before they headed off into the desert on their expedition to the top of Australia in 1860 – they were never seen again.

Explorer Thomas Mitchell in 1835 followed the Bogan and Darling rivers down to where Menindee and the surrounding lakes are today, which he named Laidley's Chain of Ponds after the deputy commissary-general of NSW (the Barkindji called them 'Wontanella' meaning 'many waters'). He camped there on a sandhill.

The same area was visited by Charles Sturt in 1844 and Menindee was then at the edge of the known world, and Tom Paine's pub was the last watering hole for overlanders and settlers. When Burke and Wills were there the town had only a couple of shacks, a store owned by a riverboat operator, Captain Cadell, and well-established river port facilities.

Burke and Wills wanted to be the first to cross Australia from Melbourne to the Gulf, but rival explorer McDougall Stuart set out from Adelaide on a similar expedition a week or so before them. Burke, a determined man who bragged that 'he'd give 'em a show' and 'if it's a race Stuart wants, he'll get one', set out with Wills from Royal Park with 19 men, 28 horses, 27 camels, six wagons and 21 tons of equipment and supplies – amid criticism that he'd lost his way on 20 miles (32 km) of good road between Beechworth and Wangaratta, so what hope did he have of crossing Australia?

The top-heavy expedition arrived in Menindee two months later, after 500 miles (800 km) of hard going, and Burke picked up with local Bill Wright, who was supposed to know the country like the back of his hand. They set up a base at Tom Paine's pub to organise supplies, but there were lots of arguments, mainly over alcohol and the sheer size of the group.

Burke agreed to split the expedition into two smaller parties and set up a new base camp seven miles (about 10 km) north of Menindee, at Pamamaroo. The first part of the expedition left there with nine men, 15 horses and 16 camels. Wright was in charge of the second team, and was to leave later for Cooper Creek with fresh supplies for Burke and Wills' return, but he spent most of the following 11 weeks at Paine's pub after a wrangle over his pay. This delay was one of the main causes of the failure of the expedition. A Royal Commission into the failed expedition put much of the blame on Wright for taking so long to follow up the expedition with supplies, but for years there has been considerable dispute about the true sources of failure and where blame should be directed. (Burke left Menindee on 19 October 1860; Wright did not follow with supplies until 26 January 1861, and he made very slow progress. Burke had left Cooper Creek on 16 December.)

Burke and Wills and Charles Gray did reach the Gulf of Carpentaria, and got there before Stuart, but Gray died on the way back to Cooper Creek. Burke perished at Cooper Creek in April 1861, soon after Wills. The party waiting at Cooper Creek to resupply them had left only hours before Burke and Wills arrived, and their rations ran out. John King, the only survivor, was found and cared for by Aborigines – a search party for Burke and Wills found him in 1861 and he and was taken back to Melbourne.

Paine sold the pub in 1890 to the Maiden family, and it became known as Maiden's Hotel Menindee. It stayed in the family for 89 years, until it was sold again in 1979. The pub was badly damaged by fire in 1999, but was restored to much the same state as it had been in when Burke and Wills became its most famous guests, and reopened in 2000.

Harry, a local whose speech mightn't shock a shearer but would certainly leave him blinking, graphically complains that the 'bloody people who made the Burke and Wills film didn't even bloody well come here. You'd have thought they'd bloody well shoot some of the film where it bloody happened,' he says. 'This bloody pub has a bloody history longer than your bloody arm. And by the way, I hope you don't mind me bloody swearing. Everyone bloody well talks like that round here …'

16 The gamblers

A punter slightly under the weather sees a sign on the pub wall which reads 'Lunch 12 to 1'. He thinks that's pretty good odds so he says to the barman: 'Can I have $20 on Lunch.'

'Come off it,' the barman replies. 'You've had too much to drink.'

The punter staggers down the street to the next pub and it's got a sign that says 'Lunch 11 to 2'. That's worse odds, but he badly wants a bet so he rushes up to the barman and asks to have $20 on Lunch. 'You're drunk,' the barman says, and kicks him out.

Down the road there's a third pub, so the punter staggers in there. The sign on the wall reads 'Lunch 1 to 2'. Odds on, he thinks. Not worth having a bet.

A minute or so later the barman yells an order to the cook. 'Steak and salad, one.'

The punter gives a huge sigh. 'Bloody glad I didn't back Lunch.'

Australians, they say, will bet on two flies crawling up the wall. And it's pretty true. For many years we patronised illegal two-up schools and SP (starting price) bookmakers in back rooms in pubs. Now, having a bet is regarded as respectable, and we gamble away more than $11 billion every year, most of it in poker machines.

Australian Bureau of Statistics figures show that the biggest losers are in NSW, where every adult loses an average $963 a year. That compares with the national average of $790 a head. The figures climbed 42 per cent in the 3 years up to June 1999. Victorians are pretty keen gamblers, too. They lose $6 million a day, or $69 a second, on poker machines.

Young people are also getting in on the act. A judge ordered a 16-year-old boy to have counselling after he lost $3000 of his savings before stealing $10,000 in gambling chips at Brisbane's casino. His mother blamed TV commercials making casinos look good. And a 17-year-old girl stole an engagement ring and documents from a friend's grandfather, cashed them in for $30,000 and then, with two friends, lost the lot in one night at Jupiters Casino.

There are 180,000 poker machines in Australia, and Australia accounts for 21 per cent of the world's gaming machines. We have more than any other country except the United States.

Poker machines, especially in hotels, grew in numbers in NSW by 60 per cent in the six years between 1997 and 2003. The Penrith Panthers Rugby League Club tops the NSW pokies list, with a staggering 1167 machines. Rooty Hill RSL is next, with 776, followed by Bankstown District Sports Club (739), Bulldog Leagues Club (649) and Western Suburbs (Newcastle) Leagues Club (589). The average annual profit from each machine is $35,500. In hotels, where there are generally just 4–6 machines, they reap an even bigger profit, averaging $46,700 a year.

New machines are so technically advanced that they are almost the ultimate money-making business. They're noisier, brighter and faster, and computer programmed to ensure that they always turn in a profit. They can suck in a $100 note in 1.5 seconds and accept up to $90 a spin.

The amount of money people are gambling on the machines forced the NSW Government to introduce half-hearted measures to try to dampen our enthusiasm for losing the shirts off our backs. For one, you can't play pokies around the clock any more: clubs and pubs are required to shut down the rolling reels for at least six hours each day.

Neon signs promoting the machines are now outlawed, and the total number of machines in the State has been cut to 104,000. New clubs aren't allowed to have more than 450 machines. Promotions in club foyers – such as the chance to win cars and overseas trips – to lure players into the club's gaming area have been limited to $1000 in value.

However, all governments do well out of poker machines. The NSW Government's $750 million take in taxes is expected to climb to around $907 million, through an increased rate of tax. The Victorian Government collects around $1 billion a year, which accounts for 9.2 per cent of its revenue.

More than 80 per cent of Australians gamble each year – on anything from chook raffles in pubs, sweeps, lottery tickets, Lotto, scratch tickets, horse and dog racing, casinos and poker machines. A counsellor with the NSW Problem Gambling group said Australia was a nation of poker machine players – the days of horse racing being the main game for punters were gone, he said.

But try to tell that to a nation that comes to a standstill on Melbourne Cup Day. More than 350 million people in 120 countries, many of whom wouldn't know a horse's hindquarters from its head, tune in their TV sets on the first Tuesday in November to watch the running of the race, which has become a national institution. And Melbourne is probably the only city in the world that has a public holiday for a horse race.

A handicap for three-year-olds, the first Cup, run in 1861 over two miles (about 3200 metres), was won by a horse called Archer, who happened to get up again in 1862 – by a record ten lengths. Unfortunately, the horse's nomination for 1863 was refused, because it arrived late. In 1972 the distance was officially changed to the marginally shorter 3200 metres.

More than $100 million is splurged on the Cup on totes all around the country. In Victoria, punters bet around $30 million, but nobody knows how much goes on sweeps, which are held in practically every business house, office and pub in Australia.

Bookmakers are right in there for their share too. The first on-course bookie was a bloke named Robert Servier, who came here from England in the late 1800s. He was soon followed by others who delighted in fighting battles of wits and wallets with punters in the betting ring.

There have been some colourful bookies through the years, like 'Gentleman' Jim Hackett, who claimed some of Australia's richest people as his clients in the 1920s, and Andy Kerr, known as the 'Coogee Bunyip', who lost his fortune when Amounis and Phar Lap won the Caulfield Cup–Melbourne Cup double in 1930.

The magnetism of the Melbourne Cup, especially for people who bet on only that one day of the year, is no different in the bush. Take Quandialla, a small town in the southwest of NSW, for instance. The people do it tough here. In the Big Drought in 1995 they ran out of tap water and had to wash out of buckets.

But although Australian Tax Office figures show that Quandialla people have among the lowest taxable incomes in the State – around $18,100 per person per year – they still kick up their heels on Cup Day. There's a calcutta (in which people pay to draw horses in the race) the night before, and on Cup Day, while the more affluent are sipping champagne and lunching on chicken and cucumber sandwiches on the lush green lawns at Melbourne's Flemington racecourse, the people of Quandialla are happy with a few beers and savouries at the local pub, The Bland, as they watch the race on TV.

The Cup is one of the biggest events of the year at Quandialla. It's a day when the close-knit community can forget its worries, its battles for survival against the elements – and the stock prices and the GST – for a few hours. The town's only garage and bank shut down a few years ago and the few remaining businesses are struggling.

Quandialla, like dozens of other small bush towns, still lives in hope that politicians and bureaucrats will one day spare it more than a casual thought. In the meantime, the locals put on a brave face and look forward to the Melbourne Cup festivities.

Chris Condon isn't an avid follower of the sport of kings, but he paid $55,200 for the 1938 Melbourne Cup. The 18 carat gold cup, which was won by New Zealand horse Catalogue, the oldest horse to ever take out the race and the first winner trained by a woman, now sits in a glass case on the bar of his Lennox Point Hotel on the far north coast of NSW.

He bid by phone when the cup was put up for auction by Sothebys on behalf of the family who owned it. It had been locked away in a bank vault for 44 years. Condon offered $30,000 beforehand but the owners decided to let it go to auction – and the auction was over in a few minutes. The bidding began at $10,000 and went up in $1000 lots. Only Condon and one other bidder were left after the $34,000 mark. He thought he'd had it at $28,000. The auctioneer was about to hit it for the third time … but the others decided to carry on.

Catalogue, an 8-year-old gelding, was owned by Mrs A Jamieson. It was trained by Mrs A McDonald, but it ran in her husband's name because the VRC (Victorian Racing Club) wouldn't recognise women trainers. A nephew talked Mrs Jamieson into entering the 80/1 long shot, which was ridden by F Shean, and the cup was handed down to him. He left it to his wife, and she gave it to her son, who decided to sell – against the wishes of other family members.

'We have a good collection of memorabilia and we wanted to add to that,' Condon said. 'When we found out the cup was being auctioned we thought we would have a go because it would add a new dimension to the hotel. There was a suggestion it would go for around $25,000, but the 1913 cup went for $68,000 so we knew it would be around that mark.

'The interesting thing was that another buyer who was too late for the sale offered us $70,000 afterwards and $100,000 three days later. My wife said I was lucky she didn't answer the phone, because she would have sold it.' The cup weighs 900 grams, which would bring around $13,000 for the gold if it was melted down.

Two-up, a game played extensively in both world wars by Australian soldiers, and once called Australia's national game, is illegal everywhere except in casinos and in Broken Hill (in the far west of NSW) – and in pubs and licensed clubs on Anzac Day. It was originally called pitch and toss, and then swy, and has been played since soon after settlement.

Two coins are tossed in the air by a person (called the spinner), from a small piece of board (called a kip), and players bet on whether the coins will land heads or tails up. Visitors to Broken Hill can play two-up in the Musicians' Club, which has been given special permission by the NSW Government because the mining city was a traditional home of the game.

17 Saturday night at the flicks

It's been more than 100 years since the Lumière brothers first showed their flickering images in public in the billiards room of a French café. The story goes that 32 people turned up and paid 1 franc each to watch the 50 second films, which included workers leaving a factory and a horse pulling a wagon. But the Lumiere technique quickly blossomed into a new and exciting industry: the cinema.

Australia was quick off the mark with this new-fangled technology, and in 1900, 4000 people turned out to watch the religious epic, *Soldiers of the Cross*. Billed as soul-thrilling stories of the martyrs and 'illustrated by the most beautiful living pictures by kinematographe', it was believed to be the world's first dramatic presentation which included film. Made by the Salvation Army's Limelight Division, *Soldiers of the Cross* was an enormous box office success.

Australia can also claim the world's first full-length feature film, *The Story of the Kelly Gang*. It was made on weekends by two entrepreneurs, John and Charles Tait, and had voices and sound effects supplied by people standing behind the screen. Soon Australians became hooked on the flickering new marvel of cinematography, and theatres sprang up everywhere.

Travelling picture shows did a roaring trade in the bush, setting up in the open air, in marquees and in local halls. By the 1930s, nearly every town and village had its own movie theatre, and people came from miles around to watch the talkies and the weekly newsreels, which covered everything from bushfires to sopranos singing duets with kookaburras.

They swooned over romantic epics like *Gone with the Wind*, with Clark Gable and Vivien Leigh, were spellbound by the spectacular screen version of *Ben Hur* with

132

Charlton Heston, and cried their eyes out at *Goodbye Mr Chips*, a brilliant 1939 movie starring Robert Donat and Greer Garson.

One of our early stars was a bloke called John Goffage, a true blue man of the Australian bush best known to moviegoers as Chips Rafferty. Rafferty, who was given his first role as an actor by director Charles Chauvel, in the World War I blockbuster *Forty Thousand Horsemen*, was born in 1909 in the outback mining town of Broken Hill, in NSW.

He appeared in dozens of films over more than 30 years, including *The Overlanders, Bush Christmas* and the *Smiley* series. His only Hollywood role was in the remake of *Mutiny on the Bounty*, with Marlon Brando.

Rafferty always held the view Australia should develop its own film industry; he believed we could match the world in terms of production crews, actors and writers. And he was right. As well as a host of home-grown films that have done well at the box office in the past few years, overseas companies are now coming to Australia more frequently to make their movies using our talent, our unique outdoor locations and our professional crews.

Rafferty, who died in 1974, would be proud that his home town, Broken Hill, has established itself as a movie-making centre. Dozens of big-budget movies and TV series have been made there in the past 25 years. In fact, Rafferty starred in Broken Hill's first feature film, in 1970. It was called *Wake In Fright* (also known as *Outback*). Also starring the UK's Donald Pleasence and Australia's Gary Bond, Sylvia Kay and Jack Thompson, the film was about a sensitive schoolteacher whose personality went to pieces after she became involved with the so-called rough men of the Australian outback. Bobbie Pickup, who runs a Broken Hill casting agency, was an extra in the film, as were other members of her family, including her youngest daughter, who was seven at the time; that daughter now works with her sister as a TV camerawomen.

Wake In Fright made audiences squirm in their seats. It had its share of sex and booze and mindless slaughter of kangaroos, which didn't help Australia's image especially, but it was one of the first Australian films to make the Cannes Festival.

Based on an Australian novel, scripted by Englishman Evan Jones, who never visited Australia, and directed by Canadian Ted Kotcheff, who later directed *Rambo* and is now executive producer of the American TV series *Law & Order*, *Wake In Fright* was an excellent portrait of Australian outback life and our male psyche.

The opening scene of a Christmas party was shot at the Broken Hill RSL Club. In those days the extras were given real beer rather than coloured water, and by the end of the day, everyone was well and truly primed. It was also 'badge show' day in Broken Hill, when every employee has to wear a badge to show they are members of a trade union. This meant that all the extras had to wear their union badges, and the badges can clearly be seen in the film.

The next movie made there was an Italian production called *Girl in Australia*, which starred Claudia Cardinale and Alberto Sordi. Most of the film was shot on a train shunting back and forth between Broken Hill and Menindee.

Bobbie Pickup opened her casting agency after years of unofficially finding extras for TV documentaries and movie-makers, and says that things snowballed from there. The budding actors on her books, all from the Broken Hill region, are what she describes as 'real people, real characters', and they seem to be what film-makers want.

She's had some unusual requests for extras. In 1985 she had to find a team of men no taller than 160 cm (5 ft 3 in) for a sequence on the Mundi Mundi plains for a film called *Comrades*. It was about the Tolpuddle Martyrs, six farm labourers who attempted to form a union in 1834 and were sentenced to transportation to NSW for administering unlawful oaths.

That was a complete contrast to finding a team of men for the film *Priscilla, Queen of the Desert*. This time, they had to be taller than 183 cm – to match the actors when they were in their drag queen outfits, which of course included stiletto heels. Townspeople got the shock of their lives when they began to film the opening scene for that one! They didn't know what to make of the actors at first, but they got used to it.

Broken Hill has a rosy future as a film-making location. The city can offer pretty much everything except snow and rainforest. There is a huge expanse of desert on the Mundi Mundi plains, there are claypans, rocky outcrops, dry creek beds, sand dunes, ruins, red dirt roads, minescapes, lunar landscapes, saltbush scrub, country pubs, a ghost town, sheep and cattle stations and homesteads.

There is plenty of native fauna, pollution-free air, lots of sunlight, minimal rainfall, and spectacular sunsets. As well as this, local authorities do everything they can to help film production companies. But it's not always easy.

Finding 250 extras for one film was a challenge because these extras had to be lookalikes to extras already used in Sydney. And about 15 Japanese people were needed. That was particularly difficult, because there aren't any Japanese people living in Broken Hill. Trips to the local Chinese restaurants to look for people were made, and two Chinese medical students at the hospital were recruited to help out.

Lighting doubles had to be found for James Belushi and Halle Berry when they were working on *Race The Sun*, another movie which was filmed mainly at Broken Hill. This one was inspired by a true story.

One of the joint producers and the film's writer, Barry Morrow, who won an Academy Award for the original screenplay of *Rain Man*, lived in Hawaii in the 1960s, and on one of his trips back there he was told by a friend about some local school kids who, against all odds, had built and raced their own solar car in the World Solar Challenge from Darwin to Adelaide in 1990. The kids were all from local working-class Hawaiian families, and it was easy to think of them as underdogs – but that's not how they saw themselves.

In the film, their science teacher (Halle Berry) sends them off to a trade fair to find some inspiration for their senior science exam. There they see a magnificent solar car and are suddenly filled with a common desire to build one, which at first appeared to be way beyond their grasp. But they did it, won a local solar car race and then automatically gained entry to the World Solar Challenge in Australia.

Most of the race scenes were shot on the Mundi Mundi plains, about 35 km from Broken Hill.

It was the first time in the Australian outback for producer Richard Heus. He said the terrain was unique. There was no other place in the world like it, and TriStar never imagined doing it anywhere else, he said. Besides that, Broken Hill had great geographic diversity and gave a clear sense of vastness. And the light was excellent for film-making.

Heus says he had worked with Australian crews in 1985 on *Mosquito Coast*, which was directed by Peter Weir and starred Harrison Ford and Helen Mirren, and had been trying to get back to Australia ever since. Australian crews were as good as any in the world and did their job with a lot less nonsense, he added, and noted that they were also used to physically tough conditions.

Some of the other Aussie movies that made the world sit up and look included the historical drama *Breaker Morant*, *Mad Max*, *Babe*, *Gallipoli* and *Newsfront*. *Breaker Morant*, starring Edward Woodward, was based on the real-life trial and execution of Australian soldier Harry 'Breaker' Morant, who was fighting in the Boer War in 1901 and was found guilty by a British military court of murdering Boer prisoners. It was nominated for an Academy award in 1980 for its screenplay.

Mad Max was a low-budget film in which Max, played by Mel Gibson – fresh from drama school – loses his wife and child and vows to seek vengeance on the offending bikies. It was imitated around the world and was the model for a string of Hollywood copies. *Mad Max 2* was filmed two years afterwards, and was the first Australian film to get American distribution.

Babe was all about a little pig that was taken to a farm to be fattened up for eating, and who was adopted by a family of border collies and of course then dreamed of becoming a sheep herder. *Gallipoli*, written by David Williamson and directed by Peter Weir, was a historical drama about the friendship between two young men, played by Mel Gibson and Mark Lee, who go into battle.

Newsfront, directed by Phillip Noyce, was acclaimed for the way it used real film footage mixed with fiction. It was about two brothers, Len (Bill Hunter), a true blue Aussie who was a cameraman for Cinetone News (soon to close down), and Frank (Gerard Kennedy), who worked for the American-owned Newsco and wanted a career in Hollywood. It was ground-breaking stuff.

Ned Kelly, made for the third time in 2003, was a box office success. It starred Heath Ledger as Ned, Orlando Bloom as Joe Byrne, and Naomi Watts and Geoffrey

Rush, and was hailed by critics. Some people who saw it claimed it wasn't true to life, but what movie is?

Not all Australian films have been successful, though. There have been some shockers, among them *Wendy Cracked a Walnut*, *Reckless Kelly*, *Garbo*, *The Delinquents*, in which Kylie Minogue tried to break into films, and Paul Hogan's *Lightning Jack*. But for a country with such a small population, we've become one of the world's main producers of films.

Aussie actors, known in Hollywood as the Gumleaf Mafia, are at last being recognised internationally by the industry. Peter Finch was the first Australian actor to win an Oscar, although he really wasn't born here, and Olivia Newton-John, who starred in the US movie *Grease*, was voted America's top female country vocalist in 1974.

Mel Gibson first attracted attention in the 1980s. He was born in America but trained in Sydney, and after kicking off his career in *Mad Max*, he graduated to the *Lethal Weapon* movies and *Braveheart*, for which he won an Oscar as best director.

By the 1990s Australians were regularly appearing in leading roles in Hollywood. Geoffrey Rush won an Oscar for his performance in *Shine* in 1996.

In 2000 Russell Crowe (actually born a Kiwi) also picked up an Oscar for his role in *Gladiator*, and followed it up with a Golden Globe award in 2002. Nine Australians were nominated for those awards that year, and they scooped the pool, with wins by Crowe, Nicole Kidman, Judy Davis, Rachel Griffiths and Baz Luhrmann.

Nicole Kidman found fame in Hollywood because of her own ability – her success had nothing to do with the fact that she married Tom Cruise (they are no longer together). She won the Oscar for best actress in 2003 for her role as Virginia Woolf in *The Hours*.

Hollywood knows enough about Australia now to come up with some ideas about why Aussies are now doing so well at the awards: Tom Hanks thinks the Australian diet has something to do with it, and reckons he is going to get stuck into a jar of Vegemite. And Steven Spielberg says that when Aussie actors take over Hollywood, the Americans are going to take over Australia. If you can't beat 'em, join 'em.

18   Fare go!

A bloke made friends with a ravishing lady at a pub, bought her a few drinks and at the end of the evening, offered to drive her home. On the way they stopped in a dark side street, hopped into the back seat and got down to some serious business.

'Hah,' says the lady. 'I'm really a working girl and this will cost you $100.'

'Yeah,' says the bloke. 'Well I'm really a taxi driver and the fare's $100, so we'll call it quits.'

Cabbies are a much maligned lot. A survey conducted in 2003 in NSW, Victoria, South Australia and Tasmania found that only 70 per cent of Sydney taxi users were happy with the service they get, compared with 92 per cent of Tasmanians.

Findings in the report included drivers falling asleep, talking too much or making comments about the way women dressed. One driver was accused of scratching himself in the wrong places.

In Melbourne, taxi drivers were investigated by police for alleged racist comments, after claims that some had applauded terrorist attacks and said that Australians were a legitimate target in the Bali bombings of October 2002. But while the Victorian Taxi Directorate had received a report about one driver's pro-terrorist stand, it could not verify the driver's name.

The taxi drivers turned the comments back on their passengers – the drivers said that they were more likely to be the victims of racist comments than the makers of them. One driver said that after hearing a clunk under the car, his passenger asked if he had a bomb under the seat.

Another driver called Mohammed said he had been told by his boss to cover his name badge to avoid getting nasty comments. He said other drivers with Middle Eastern names were doing the same.

A few years ago a NSW Government survey found many of the same complaints about Sydney drivers: they couldn't speak English, didn't know their way around the city and were rude and aggressive. One passenger complained about a driver who had to stop in the city to ask a pedestrian the way to the Harbour Bridge.

The survey also found that passengers thought taxi drivers were speedhogs, dressed shoddily, made unwanted advances to female passengers and often refused to stop when hailed. Many thought that they all took the longest possible route on every trip so that they could charge the highest possible fare, and that some asked too many personal questions.

The cabbies retaliated by saying that this was unfair criticism, and that they all copped it when it was only a minority of drivers who did the wrong thing. A Waterloo taxi manager commented that people seemed to assume that taxi drivers came out of the womb as taxi drivers.

A later AC Nielsen survey indicated that their image had improved somewhat. This time, passengers rated their services as good and praised the cleanliness of the cars.

However, there was still some concern, especially about the drivers' knowledge of Sydney, their proficiency in English and long waiting times. People also complained about the reckless way some of them drove – though in terms of the distance they cover, they're involved in fewer accidents than other motorists.

A group at Sydney University also did some research on taxi drivers. They found that long hours, poor diet and lack of public respect were common experiences. All that, together with being in heavy traffic all day, contributed to them being a pretty stressed out group of workers, much more so than most other occupations. Tearing around doing lots of illegal U-turns and running red lights definitely increases the risk of having a crash.

But despite the criticism in the 2003 survey, Sydney people still use taxis more than anyone else in Australia. The national survey showed that 25 per cent of passengers in Sydney's inner-city area caught a cab more than 21 times in six months.

More than half the trips were on Fridays and Saturdays, usually between 6 pm and midnight – that's when people go out on the town. But the trips were made by only one passenger half the time, and 80 per cent of the trips involved no more than two passengers.

People tell lots of tales about cabbies. In a survey run by a Fairfax newspaper, Brian Wilkin reckoned he travelled all over Australia and one thing he always made a note of was his experience in a taxi. He claimed Melbourne taxi drivers didn't speak English well and never knew where they were going. He was constantly amazed how they got a licence. Sydney drivers weren't as bad, he said, but they always took the longest way round and therefore fares in Sydney were always the highest. In his opinion, Brisbane drivers were the best.

'Sure, they are crusty old blokes, but Brisbane drivers are always polite, their taxis are always clean, plus they are funny and have a good sense of humour. I reckon the standard should be raised in terms of applying and passing an exam to get a job driving a taxi,' he said.

Several women complained about taxi drivers making sexual advances to them, and both men and women told of times when their driver had made them nervous. Melbourne man Norm Wilson said he and his girlfriend often called a taxi to get home early in the morning and often felt uncomfortable and intimidated by the drivers, particularly if they asked for the window to be closed on a freezing June night. 'My great-aunt of 96 relies on taxis, and while a few are wonderful, most are uncaring and some have driven her all over the place, not knowing where to go, until she exerts some authority and asks them to turn off the meter and work out where they are going, which is usually when she gives them directions. Not what I expect a senior citizen should have to do,' he said.

DK, of Melbourne, said the best free entertainment in the city central business district was watching taxi drivers scream at each other, gesticulate rudely at each other and not so occasionally punch each other at the taxi rank outside 101 Collins Street.

Another regular taxi user told of an experience in Brisbane. He and three friends going home after a night in town got about half way when the taxi broke down. 'The cabbie asked that we pay him and he didn't offer to get us another cab. I think in our naivety we did pay him. Grrr,' he said.

Roy Wilke drives a taxi in Brisbane on weekends and says some of his passengers probably think he is the best driver ever while others have got out of his cab thinking that neither of his parents knew one another. To deal with them all, he says, you need the patience of Job.

He offers some hints for getting the best out of a taxi driver. For a start, the word 'bank' is not spelt t-a-x-i. Try to hand the driver a bank note close to the fare – too many $50 notes will mean he has to spend half an hour looking for a 24-hour service station to replenish his stocks of small notes for change.

Don't drink in a taxi. If the driver has an accident while you're drinking from a stubbie, you're likely to swallow the bottle.

Smoking is another of Roy's pet hates. It's illegal in the workplace and a taxi is the driver's workplace, so don't do it.

Eating is also banned. Food scraps from Maccas hamburgers attract cockroaches, he says.

And don't change the station on the radio or pop a cassette or CD into the slot without asking. 'You don't go into a shop, leap over the counter and change the station, so don't do it in a taxi. If you want the radio on, off or the station changed, ask politely. I remove the fuse from the radio in my cab; it avoids a lot of arguments,' he says.

Sydney publicist Vikki Lord caught a taxi in Kings Cross to go to the city. It stopped at traffic lights and didn't move when they turned green, blocking drivers behind, who began honking. The cabbie was sound asleep at the wheel. He'd been working, he said, for 14 hours.

But that was nothing compared with another cabbie, who worked a shift from 6 am to 2 am, Monday to Thursday, and then drove from 6 am Friday through to Sunday afternoon, stopping only for showers and meals. He described himself as a workaholic.

First-day cabbie Reza Tahrani worked the shortest shift of the Sydney taxi fleet when he began his new job with a flourish. Driving towards the Harbour Bridge on his first call, the bloody thing caught fire. He abandoned ship and watched it burn from a safe distance while police closed three northbound lanes to the bridge for half an hour, banking up traffic for 4 km.

A Randwick man who caught a cruising taxi asked the driver why he hadn't picked up a woman who tried to flag him down back along the street. 'She had shopping, mate,' the cabbie said. 'I never pick 'em up when they've got shopping – they'll just want to go around the corner'. Although this is illegal, the drivers get away with it.

The 22,000 Sydney cabbies carry around 3.8 million passengers a week, roughly the population of the city, so it's little wonder they get complaints. But they also get some pats on the back.

RSL Cabs driver John Maroulis impressed three passengers on a trip to Petersham. They were talking about captive animals when John saw a fair-sized green frog hopping along the road just ahead. He screeched to a stop, jumped out of the cab and flagged down the traffic while he picked up the hapless amphibian, later taking it home and releasing it in a nearby creek.

A Point Piper man left his mobile phone in a Legion cab. The driver found it and returned it to the man's home. About six months later the man's wife left the same phone in a cab, and the next morning there was a knock at the door and the same driver brought it back, for the second time.

They're not all as honest as that, though, as British photographer Martyn Thompson and assistant Tara Darby, on assignment in Sydney for *marie claire* magazine, found out.

Tara hailed a cab in North Sydney to pick up her boss. She loaded his cameras, lenses and film into the cab's boot, and when the cab arrived at his hotel, left her wallet and bag on the back seat while she went inside to collect him. When they came out the cab was gone, along with all their gear – which was worth $50,000.

Then there was the embarrassing incident involving a senior Olympic official who was dropped at a suburban railway station and given directions by the taxi driver on how to get to his destination by train. The official had to catch a train to Central Station and then walk to the Sydney Olympics headquarters. The driver involved said he was changing shifts and couldn't complete the trip.

In a bid to brighten up the cabbies' image, the NSW Government brought in laws forcing them to wear uniforms, which were to be funded by an increased flagfall. But the heavy imported fabric of the shirts made some drivers sick – the shirts led to more cases of both heat exhaustion and skin irritations. The cabbies threatened to sue the Transport Department after around 120 drivers had been fined for not wearing the fancy new clobber.

One cabbie won a battle for compensation so the department agreed that drivers could wear a lighter weight shirt or all-cotton uniform, provided the colour and style were the same as the original ones. But the new fabric cost more, which the taxi operators weren't too happy about.

It's no surprise that taxi driving has one of the highest turnover rates of any industry. Figures show that only one in 20 people who get licences are still in the job after a year. So it's not everyone's cup of tea. The veteran cabbies call the new blokes 'firemen' – they say they jump in and out everywhere, and it usually takes two crashes before they wake up. Or get a different job.

Cabbies, who often liken their job to a prostitute – they too pick up their clients on the street and provide an anonymous and discreet service – are quick to point out that some of their passengers aren't exactly angels. Some can be so drunk that the trip becomes an exercise in settling down a troublemaker. Cabbies also accuse the public of being unreasonable in expecting them to know every street and building in the city.

There's lots of folklore associated with cabbies, especially stories about women passengers who reckon they haven't got the fare and want to pay with favours. One cabbie also mentioned the practice of reversing flat out into 'runners', passengers who leap from the cab without paying the fare.

But cabbies can easily get themselves into trouble. A driver who told a woman she had a good figure when she leant over the seat to pay the bill was fined $150 and ordered to pay $800 in legal costs. The court ruled he had made an offensive remark because it wasn't a social situation: if he had said the same thing in a pub, it wouldn't have been a problem.

On the other side of the coin, women taxi drivers have to deal with unwanted advances from male passengers.

The Olympic Games tested Sydney cabbies' resolve. Drivers were telling passengers that if they thought traffic jams were bad now, 'wait until the Games ...'. They were making such horror predictions about traffic chaos that Games officials began a campaign to get them thinking more positively. They wanted to change the attitude of cabbies and get them into the spirit of the Games, because cabbies were the best people, they said, the front-line of communications, to give information to overseas visitors and whip up enthusiasm. As it turned out, all the predictions were wrong – the period was quieter than normal.

Perth is the first city in the world to make having a camera in each taxi compulsory. A small camera mounted above the rear vision mirror and connected to a computer under the car, which is tamper-proof and waterproof, gives clear images of drivers and passengers, even at night.

The computer stores images for only about four trips and can be overridden at any time by the driver unless he presses an alarm button. The system is meant to be a deterrent for would-be robbers.

These cameras are on the agenda for taxis in South Australia and Tasmania as well. They cost around $1600.

There are about 5600 taxi drivers in Western Australia, half of whom work in Perth. Taxi companies there want to recruit more women into the job. A training manager for Swan Taxis said drivers often enjoy a chat with their passengers, and women have good interpersonal skills. Passengers often want to know which restaurant they should go to or what tourist attractions they should visit, he said, and women could answer those questions well.

Melbourne taxi drivers chalked up something of a first when they went on strike at Tullamarine Airport to protest against a $1.60 charge they had to pay to enter the airport. Hundreds of drivers switched off their engines and left passengers stranded.

The charge, which already applied at other airports (including Perth and Brisbane), was supposed to help fund a holding area for taxis. But the Melbourne cabbies reckoned they'd had enough of being tax collectors for the government. Harris Watson said drivers had reached the stage where enough was enough. 'Why bloody keep on our backs? Leave us alone, let us do our job. We just want to be left alone so we can generate income for our families,' he said.

Now a couple of tips. When the light on top of the taxi is on, it means the taxi is available – so if the driver doesn't stop, throw yourself in front of the cab. And if you want to make a complaint about a particular driver, the driver's taxi licence, with his or her licence number, must be clearly displayed inside the cab where it can be seen.

OK. Where to, mate?

19 | Our best friends

Aussies are a pet-loving lot. The RSPCA (Royal Society for the Prevention of Cruelty to Animals) says that when we go through tough economic times, people postpone their holidays or go without some other luxury rather than get rid of their pets.

One in three households has a pet, and while German shepherds, cats, bunnies, aquarium fish and guinea pigs top the popularity list, people have widened their interests to include pythons, ferrets, scorpions, rats, spiders, stick insects, land hermit crabs, beetles, roosters and cockatoos. And we love 'em all.

A Melbourne couple offered their Porsche to anyone who found their missing five-year-old Burmese cat, called Rusty. Don and Robin Pyke reckoned the cat was worth more to them than the car. He was just like their own son. He slept with them, ate with them and watched TV with them. 'We really can't live without him,' Mrs Pyke said. And getting him back in their lives was more important than owning the Porsche. The cat wasn't returned.

Ron Howard, a pensioner who lives on the NSW Central Coast, offered his 1984 'immaculate' Toyota Corona, worth $6000, plus $2000 cash, as a reward for getting his Maltese terrier–Sydney silky cross back. The five-year-old disappeared on a visit to Sydney and he was desperate to get her back. In the end, he too was left with his car.

Belle, a collie owned by NSW Government minister Carl Scully, really got the red carpet treatment. When she needed to be taken from the Scullys' Sydney home to a nearby friend's home, Mr Scully called a government pool car and chauffeur to pick her up.

The dog thought it was great sitting up in the back of the government limo. In fact she got so excited that she left a reminder on the leather seat, which failed to impress the driver. He cleaned up the mess, sprayed some air freshener around and hoped the next government minister using the car wouldn't notice.

Mr Scully, with the advantage of hindsight, admitted that he had done the wrong thing but said it wasn't a hanging offence. Normally he would have driven the dog himself, he said, but he was leaving on an overseas trip.

A smoke-shy parrot called Ricky returned the love he had been given by a Ballina family. He became the first bird to receive a bravery award from the NSW Fire Brigade – for saving his owners when their home filled with smoke from a burning electric blanket.

He escaped from his cage, latched onto a flyscreen door, banged it with his beak and squawked his head off until Roselyn Garland and her two young daughters woke.

Parrots are worth a few bob, too. Cornelis Bayens told the NSW District Court he bought two parrots and a chick for $10,000 each from a bird breeder and then discovered that the 'proven breeding pair' were both males. He sued the breeder for $250,000 – the cost of the parrots and the expected loss of revenue from their offspring.

Tango, a blue and gold parrot, was the star of a movie called *The Real Macaw*, filmed in Brisbane, and earned a fee of $10,000. Tango, like most actors worth their seed, had his own trailer (with air-conditioning, of course), his own dietician and a personal assistant.

He played a parrot who was kidnapped by pirates in 1870, learned of hidden treasure and later teamed up with a 12-year-old boy to try to find it. Tango was in good company. The film co-starred Academy Award winner Jason Robards from *All The President's Men*, Jamie Croft from *A Country Practice* and Deborah-Lee Furness from *Fire*.

The right cats can also be a bonanza for their owners. Breeder Nola Molloy sold Rowdy, one of her long-haired Abyssinians, for hundreds of dollars to an American trainer who wanted to use him for promotional work in Hollywood.

Rowdy was a star in the film *Babe II*, and caught the eye of two American talent scouts. Nola, who had a pet grooming salon, said Rowdy was made for showbiz, and though she would miss him like crazy, she didn't want to stand in the way of his career.

Talking about cats, the most popular name for pet cats in Australia is Puss. The name beat Cat by a whisker. This is a far cry from canaries called Pavarotti and pythons called Cleopatra! It seems most Aussies don't extend their imagination when it comes to naming their pusses. A Pet Care Information and Advisory Service survey found Smokey, Tiger and Tom were the next most popular names.

Dogs fared little better. The top five names were Jessie, Sam, Jack, Max and Ben. Dog was a disappointing sixth.

Those people who give their pets odd monickers come up with some beauties. A newspaper survey unearthed a female cat called Nonuts and another called Cooking Fat, dogs named Fish, Guess (as in 'What's your dog's name?') and a castrated goat called Adam (because he 'ad 'em once).

Dogs can also be fashion statements. Since the early 1960s, when corgis received a royal boost, the fads have included long-haired afghans, rottweilers (for the security-conscious) and dogs that resemble wolves, like the Siberian husky and the Alaskan malamute. Breeds such as the German shepherd are consistently popular.

The infamous cattle dog tops the list for causing the most blues – attacks on humans and other animals. It is followed by the German shepherd, the rottweiler, the bull terrier, the kelpie and the labrador.

Among the safest dogs are mastiffs, Gordon setters, Naranna sheepdogs, lowchens, English pointers, Welsh terriers and Jack Russells.

But pets aside, working dogs are an important part of Aussie life … There are floods in northern NSW. Paddocks are under water and the whole place resembles an inland sea. A city visitor held up in his car is amazed to see a dog's tail sticking out of the water like a periscope on a submarine.

He watches the tail move 60 metres to the right and stop. Then 30 metres to the left and stop. Then back to the right. The bemused city slicker asks an oldtimer watching near the fence: 'What's the matter with the dog? Is he drowning?'

'No way,' the oldtimer says. 'That's me best sheepdog. I told him to bring in a mob of sheep and come hell or high water, he's bloody well bringin' 'em in.'

There's been a long-running controversy over where the kelpie sheepdog originated, but the arguments were finally put to rest – well almost – when the small southern NSW town of Ardlethan unveiled a special monument claiming the honour. The town is now acknowledged as the home of the kelpie.

John (Jack) Gleeson went to Ardlethan in 1873 to work on Bolero Station, taking with him a black and tan female dog he called Kelpie. She'd been bred on Worrock Station in Victoria. Years later, Jack bred Kelpie II from Kelpie and a dog called Caesar, which had Scottish parents.

Kelpie II, a gift by Jack to Charles King, was entered in a sheepdog trial at Forbes Show in 1878 and won 20 guineas. It was the first show in Australia where a dog called Kelpie had won, and the breed has been called kelpie since then.

There's still a good working dog behind every good farmer, and in the pub at the end of the day, tales are rife about the wonderful deeds of man's best friend. Here's a true one.

A drover named Harrie Davis was taking a mob of sheep along Sydney's busy Parramatta Road to Flemington saleyards at 5 am one dark day back in 1932 and was hit by a car. He was badly injured, and was carted off to hospital.

Three hours after the accident the manager of the saleyards phoned Harrie's father to tell him a mob of sheep had turned up accompanied only by his son's sheepdog, which was called Ginger Meggs. The dog had driven the sheep there on his own.

Harrie Davis recovered from his injuries. His dog Meggsie, who after his working days were over became a beloved family pet – and a Western Sydney legend – died in 1940 and was buried on a hill called Devils Back, which is now part of the Western Sydney Regional Park. There is a historic walk past the spot, which is marked with a plaque.

Pip Hudson, tongue in cheek, tells the story of the city slicker who asked about one of his sheepdogs, which was happily sitting outside in the back of the ute.

The dog was a genius, Pip told him. He rounded up the sheep, caught rabbits, got the mail out of the box, chased the crows away and kept an eye on the homestead. The visitor asked whether he could buy the dog a drink. 'No way,' Pip said. 'He has to drive me home.'

Sheepdogs aren't quite that smart, but Pip Hudson believes Australia has the best in the world for its arid conditions. And he should know. He's been involved with kelpies and border collies for most of his life, winning a string of sheepdog trials (competitions) and representing Australia overseas. He was also narrator for a series on sheepdogs on ABC-TV, and was president of the Australian and NSW sheepdog associations.

Pip, who has a property between Cobar and Wilcannia, in western NSW, believes sheepdog trials should get more recognition as a sport. 'You go for relaxation and to meet people but you try to win,' he said. 'And win, lose or draw, you get great enjoyment, and so do the spectators. If it hadn't been for sheepdogs and the trials, I would probably still be out in the sticks without having been anywhere other than the RSL or the golf clubs at Cobar.'

Well-bred sheepdogs are easy to train, especially for a station job. The arena trials are more specialised, though. The dogs having to take three sheep around a set course and through three obstacles in 15 minutes.

But the same dogs still have to do the work on the property. They're used to muster wild goats, work cattle and do yard work, so they don't get things easy.

Australian kelpies are now being sold to people in Japan, Switzerland and Africa. Some collies are also being exported. They're specially bred to work sheep and don't need a lot of training. But they have to be tough as nails to work in heat and in countryside full of burrs, and unless they can do that, they don't make the grade.

Australia's native dog is, of course, the tawny-yellow dingo. It burst into the international spotlight in August 1980, when nine-week old Azaria Chamberlain disappeared from a campsite at Uluru in the Northern Territory.

Her mother Lindy said she was taken by a dingo, but few people believed her. The first inquest, in February 1981, ended with a live national TV broadcast from Alice

Springs, in which coroner Denis Barritt found that a dingo had indeed taken baby Azaria and that her body had been disposed of by 'a person or persons unknown'. He had heard evidence of a dingo growl, paw prints, drag marks and more, and had little difficulty reaching his verdict.

But the case was reopened in 1981. Barritt's finding was quashed, and the Chamberlains were committed for trial.

Lindy Chamberlain was found guilty of murder and sentenced to life. Her husband was found to have been an accessory but was released on a good behaviour bond. An appeal by Lindy Chamberlain was rejected in 1984, but the convictions against both of them were quashed by a royal commission in 1988. They were both exonerated and compensated.

A third inquest did not restore Mr Barritt's finding; coroner John Lowndes said that although there was considerable evidence supporting a dingo attack, he could not make a positive decision.

The case split the nation, and even today people still argue about the guilt or innocence of the parties involved, including the dingo. There was much debate about whether a dingo could have taken the baby – were its jaws strong enough? A pensioner named Frank Cole came forward in mid 2004 and claimed he shot the dingo that took the baby. He said his mates disposed of the body and told him 'he didn't need to know where'. His story couldn't be verified.

Back in April 1998, however, Alan Rowles told how a dingo bit and tried to drag his 14-month-old daughter into the bush from their campsite at Fraser Island, off the Queensland coast. He said he could see the dingo with its mouth on the baby's shoulder, shaking her and going into the darkness. He raced to his daughter and the dingo let go and ran off.

There have been numerous attacks by dingoes on people on Fraser Island since then, and one death: a nine-year-old boy was mauled to death. This prompted the Queensland Government to carry out a cull of the dingoes, but this was against the wishes of Aboriginal elders.

They believe tourists who go to the heritage-listed island should respect its wildlife – and they reminded everyone that the dingoes have been there for years. The government also approved a $1.75 million plan to upgrade facilities on the island; $1 million of this was for dingo management.

Dingo fanciers say the dogs make good pets, but they're classified as pests in some States and people who keep them can be fined. Despite this, the 3 Combat Engineers Regiment used to have a dingo as its mascot.

Called Sapper Wooleston Boorooma, he is also known as Bruiser – but he's just plain Woolie to his handler, Lance Corporal Simon Harvey. Woolie is an alpine dingo from Canberra and his parents are the only dingoes ever to have been taken inside Parliament House.

Woolie played with kids and chewed quite a few things over with other dogs while he was mascot. He went fishing with his handler and visited schools, where the children doted on him. He went walkabout a couple of times, too, once taking an Army explosives-detection dog along for company. And one day the entire regiment spent hours looking for his regimental coat, which he had slipped out of after becoming tired of standing around on a parade ground.

The dingo has added lots of colour to the Australian language. A person gets the name 'dingo' if they display characteristics popularly attributed to the dog, especially cowardice and treachery. If you 'dingo it', you're acting the coward or backing away. If you 'dingo' on a person, you're letting them down. A dingo's breakfast is a quick piss and a good look around. A dingo stiffener is someone employed to shoot the dogs.

Dingoes are smart animals, but they're not smart enough to outwit that mythical shearer, Crooked Mick of the Speewah. Mick was asked by the station boss to shoot the dingoes that were wreaking havoc on his sheep.

He waited at his campfire, where he was encircled by 200 pairs of dingo eyes. He aimed smack between the eyes and let fly with several hundred rounds of ammo. In the morning there wasn't one dead dingo to be found.

The next night he got his sharp-eyed friend to climb a tree and watch what happened. The dingoes came back and Mick again let fly with a barrage of bullets, again aiming straight between the glowing eyes, but the dingoes again disappeared.

His mate came down from the tree. 'You won't believe this, Mick,' he said. 'Them dingoes come along in pairs, and each has its outer eye closed, so that when you fired between their eyes, you were actually shooting between the two dogs. Ain't that clever?'

The next night Mick adjusted accordingly and cleaned them all up.

Moving on to a completely different kind of dog, here's a scheme that shows how dear to our hearts these four-footed friends are. A Sydney woman came up with a plan to put greyhounds which were too old to race into caring homes. Laboratory assistant Denise Wigney said the speedsters were intelligent, sensitive, gentle and sociable dogs and readily adapted to life as household pets.

Called Adopt-A-Greyhound, her scheme aimed at first finding foster carers who would help with the greyhounds' transition from the track to the loungeroom. She had kept pet greyhounds for years herself, and knew what good-natured dogs they were. She just needed to get the word out to other people – many seemed to have a bad opinion of the breed because they're required to wear muzzles. She said they were really couch potatoes and were well suited to being house dogs, although most never got the opportunity after their racing career ended, which was sad.

There are many things a greyhound has never been exposed to that an average pet dog would take for granted. Things like slippery floors, glass doors and windows, stairs – and other pets. Overseas experience has shown that there are no problems with having greyhounds as pets, but a particular dog's response to other breeds of dog, cats, and other animals (like chooks) has to be assessed before it can be placed permanently in a family's home. Her plan didn't get off the ground.

But keeping a pet has its problems. The NSW Government's Companion Animals Bill caused a public outcry, because part of it said that you would be allowed to kill a neighbour's dog or cat if you found it on your property and it had caused any damage at all. The then Local Government Minister, Ernie Page, had to scrap that section. He also slashed proposed fines for owners of 'nuisance' pets and removed plans to make it an offence to walk your dog past a restaurant that had chairs and tables on the footpath.

The Bill passed into law, and there is now an $11,000 fine for owners whose dogs attack people and cause serious injury. A barking dog attracts a fine of $1100, and cat owners can be fined $220 if their cat ventures within ten metres of a children's playground or onto school grounds.

20 Cricket, football and soccer

Sydney's 1970s harbour bridge painter and TV comedian Paul (throw another shrimp on the barbie) Hogan, who had a huge success with his first *Crocodile Dundee* film, knows how cricket, the summer pastime for thousands of Australians, really began. He claims it was actually invented in England in 1648 by the then reigning monarch, King Charles I, whom he describes as 'a hell of a good bloke …'

This is how Hogan explains cricket's origins: During Charles' reign there was no organised sport in England. No cricket. The nearest thing to it was public executions. Every Saturday they used to bundle all these wicked wretches into the square and lop their heads off. The crowd would roll up with an Esky full of coldies, a bit of zinc on the nose, and cheer for their favourite executioners.

Beheading as a sport had been going on for a long time in England, King Charles was getting worried, mainly because attendances were falling, gate takings were down and T-shirts weren't selling. Basically, it was a case of people getting bored with a sport where the scoreboard was always roughly the same: executioners 47, wretches 0.

Now Charles, to his credit, tried to brighten it up as a spectacle. He even brought in a Scottish entrepreneur, Kerron McPacker. He thought, well, we'll put the executions on at night. Night beheading, under lights. He even dressed the executioners up in brightly coloured uniforms instead of the traditional black, and hired half a dozen ex-axemen and put them up in the commentary box. You know, to sort of let people know what was happening. 'Lillee coming in off the short run', for example. He even tried using a white axe.

But it didn't really work. I think in the 17th century, floodlighting probably left a lot to be desired. So finally, in desperation, King Charles turned to his chief advisor – and here's the Australian connection – a gentleman by the name of Sir Walter Hogan. An ancestor. Now just as Queen Elizabeth sent Sir Walter Raleigh over to America and he came back with a ship full of tobacco, Charles had earlier sent Sir Walter Hogan to America. Unfortunately he landed in California, so he came back with a ship full of marijuana.

Anyway, Sir Walter, or Dopey Wal as he was known around the court, said to King Charles: 'Listen Chuck, baby, when I was coming back from the States, I called into India.' From America to England via India? Obviously Sir Walter's navigator had been sampling the cargo as well. But he said, 'Over there, they execute their bad eggs by bundling them into the town square and they invite all the townspeople to chuck bricks at them and they call it stoning. Very popular.'

Charles thought, that's the answer. Audience participation. So the following Saturday they bundled all these poor wretches into the city square and invited the mob to chuck bricks at them. It went over like a house on fire. Within minutes it looked just like The Hill at the Sydney Cricket Ground.

But suddenly, into the square strode a man of the cloth. A young chaplain from nearby Westminster Abbey. And he jumped out in front of the mob and he said, 'Stop, stop, stop. Hey, come on, fair suck of the sauce bottle. Hey, hey.'

And the mob said, 'Get out of the way. They're wicked wretches and they deserve to die.' And the chaplain said, 'I know they're wicked, but they're my flock. They're my wicked and I must defend them.'

With that he picked up a lump of four by two timber and started hitting the stones back. Just then another young man who had lodgings with this chaplain, at his boarding house, come running out of the crowd, picked up a lump of four by two and helped him. And the two of them stood there knocking the stones back.

Well the next day, there appeared in the paper – which, incidentally, was published by Sir Walter Hogan, under his nom-de-plume of Rupert – a portrait of this fantastic happening at the stoning. Beneath it was a caption, which was to become the world's first cricket headline. Nobody knew the name of this young chaplain, nor of the young man who lived at his boarding house. So the caption simply read 'Chaplain and boarder defending their wicked'.

King Charles, to his credit, was so disgusted with that dreadful pun that the next Saturday he had Sir Walter Hogan burned at the stake – and there he is, the original cricket ashes.

Cricket didn't quite start like that, of course. Neither did Kerry Packer's one-day series, which gave the game the punch it needed to regain national attention. But as a survivor from a bygone age, it could well have. It's a game described as a blend of ceremony and slapstick, tragedy and humour, greatness and insignificance.

The historian Jack Pollard wrote that when somebody told him a man once died from excitement at a cricket match, it was hardly a shock. It seemed to him a pleasing way to die.

Cricket was the dominant sport in the early days of the colony, with the first match being played in 1803 on a cleared paddock known as Phillip's Common (now part of Sydney's Hyde Park), between free settlers and officers of a supply ship – using makeshift equipment, naturally. The game became more formalised in the 1820s and cricket clubs were formed.

The first English team to come to Australia was captained by HH Stephenson. It came in 1862 and won 11 of its 13 matches. The first was played at the Melbourne Cricket Ground, in front of 15,000 people.

The first Australian team to go to England was a team of Aborigines from the western districts of Victoria, who also gave demonstrations of boomerang throwing while they were there. That was in 1868. The team was led by English professional Charles Lawrence; it won 14 matches, lost 14 and drew 19. That was the start of the cricket tradition between the two countries. The Ashes, the most coveted prize in Australia-England cricket, originated in 1882 when Australia beat England and the Sporting Times newspaper wrote that English cricket had died – it should be cremated and the ashes sent to Australia, the reporter mourned. The Ashes themselves are reputed to be a burnt bail in a wooden urn; this is so fragile that it stays in the museum at Lord's in London, but the two countries still play for them.

Cricket's biggest hitter was a bloke called George John Bonnor, who once belted a ball 160 km. In the NSW country town of Orange, his ball cleared the Wade Park ground and the adjacent street, and landed on a coal truck in the railway yards. The hit out of the ground has never been bettered, never mind the fact that the train and the ball ended up at Dubbo that night.

But probably Bonnor's most memorable hit was in the First Test between Australia and England at The Oval (in England) in 1880. The ball went so high that he was turning for his third run when he was caught by GF Grace, the England captain.

Bonnor the Basher, also known as the Colonial Hercules, went on to play 16 more Tests for Australia before retiring to play grade cricket at Orange, bringing the town considerable notoriety and frightening the flannels off many a visiting side. He knocked up a 100 or so every Saturday and finished his last season with a first-grade average of just over 200.

In one match for Bathurst against the Orientals of Sydney, he made 267 not out in less than two hours. In January 1884, playing for an Australian XI against NSW, he hit 64 in 28 minutes, which included five sixes and five fours.

The following season, in the Fourth Test against England in Sydney, Bonnor made 128, hitting the first 100 in 100 minutes. It was his only Test century, but it stayed in the record books as the fastest 100 scored in the first 28 years of Australia-England matches.

Our greatest cricketer was Don Bradman, who scored his first centuries for the Bowral team when he was 12. His Test average was 99.9 runs. He needed only four in his last innings in 1948 to bring him up to the 100 average but was bowled for a duck – he scored no runs at all.

Sir Don heads the list compiled in 2001 by Wisden, the world cricket authority, of the 100 greatest individual batting and bowling Test performances in a single innings. This winning innings occurred in the Third Test of the 1936-37 Ashes series. Bradman made 270 for Australia, which helped win the match, changing a 2-0 series deficit to a more healthy 2-1 – and Australia went on to win the series.

Sir Don died at his Kensington Park home in February 2001, aged 92. The nation went into mourning for weeks.

Football is Australia's biggest spectator sport. A Rafferty's Rules type of game was played by the colonial youth of early Sydney against soldiers from the barracks until a set of rules from the Rugby school in England was drawn up.

The Albert Cricket Club in Sydney put a set of the rules in its annual report in 1860, and a few years later students got a team going that was later to become the University of Sydney Rugby Club. They played sailors from visiting ships.

As more clubs were formed, the code attracted huge support and crowds around 20,000 were the norm at club games. A clash between NSW and New Zealand in 1907 attracted 52,000 people to Sydney Cricket Ground, but the same year saw a breakaway group form the professional game of rugby league – rugby had been struck a damaging blow.

Using much the same methods as modern-day super league, when Rupert Murdoch bought teams to run his own competition to feed pay TV, rugby league administrators in 1908 used their chequebooks to entice rugby's best to switch camps, beginning with Sydney's best player, HH 'Dally' Messenger.

In 1909, backers of the fledgling league put up £1500 to entice rugby's Wallabies to play a series against the league's national team, called the Kangaroos. Fourteen players accepted the offer – and were thrown out by the rugby union for 'turning professional'.

League was played mainly in NSW and Queensland until the 1990s, when media mogul Rupert Murdoch started his own pay TV competition. Half the teams in Sydney ratted on the league and joined Rupert, who also attracted new teams in New Zealand, Melbourne and Perth.

His competition caused a devastating split in the game and thousands of followers went elsewhere. This meant that a truce wasn't long in coming. But league probably has still not fully recovered, because clubs with a great tradition like South Sydney were forced out of the competition and others were made to amalgamate.

So the scars are still deep, although South Sydney beat the ARL (Australian Rugby League) in the courts in the end and were readmitted to the competition in 2002.

Manly, which had been forced to amalgamate with Norths, also went back to a stand-alone team in 2003.

The State of Origin series between NSW and Queensland is football's version of civil war, with both States whipped into a frenzy for days beforehand. The crowds at Brisbane are notorious for their one-sided antics and their can-throwing tantrums – they can't be subdued until the southern 'cockroaches' are vanquished, which of course does not always happen.

In a nice twist of irony, the super league war led to rugby union enjoying a new surge in popularity. The outstanding successes of the Australian team didn't hurt either. The Wallabies chalked up their most memorable win in the 2001 Test series, when they beat the British Lions 2-1 – for the first time in 102 years. Before that they won the World Cup.

In 2002 the Wallabies had a mixed year, with losses against the South African Springboks and the New Zealand All Blacks in the Tri-Nations series. But in the last seconds of the decider, Matt Burke kicked a penalty goal to beat the All Blacks 16–14 and retain the Bledisloe Cup.

But the All Blacks took it off a new-look Wallabies in 2003 after a poor start to a season in which they were also well beaten by England in the lead-up to the World Cup. The Wallabies came good, though, and won their way into the final after defying the odds and beating the All Blacks in a semi-final.

They met the Poms in the final and both teams hammered each other for the first 80 minutes, which ended in a draw, and then for almost 20 minutes of extra time, where the scores were still tied until 28 seconds before the whistle – when Jonny Wilkinson kicked a field goal and took the match for the Lions.

An estimated 4.2 billion people watched that game on TV around the world. In Australia it was the most watched program since the Olympics, pulling 4.34 million viewers. An estimated 125,000 people visited Australia from overseas for World Cup games.

Australian Rules, the third really popular football code in Australia, is referred to by many people as aerial ping pong. It was born in the 1850s in an effort to keep cricketers fit in winter. Thomas Wentworth Wills, who had played a Public school version of football when he was at the Rugby school in England, drew up the first rules.

In the same manner as with rugby and league, clubs were formed and a formal competition was started in Melbourne. After a few brawls between the rich and poor clubs, a group of teams in 1897 broke away from the Victorian Football Association to form the Victorian Football League, which in the 1980s changed its name to the Australian Football League and spread the game to Brisbane, Sydney, Adelaide and Perth.

AFL is a funny game. It is played only in Australia, but still attracts thousands of fanatical fans. NSW has a team with the poncey name of the Swans, and in the height of the super league war in the late 1990s, it picked up thousands of fans who wanted to be seen as trendsetters. But poor performances in 2002 lost many of them.

Few people in rugby league and rugby union can work out AFL. The beanpole players tear around in a mob, fumbling and knocking the ball until one of them actually picks it up and kicks it between some posts. And they have four posts instead of the traditional two, and different points are scored depending on which two you kick the ball between. The mystery is, why haven't other countries taken up the game?

Each year ex-players in their hundreds roll up to a lunch before an annual clash between Melbourne Grammar and Scotch College, who first played against each other on 7 August 1858. Some argue that that game, which was played in a paddock near the present Melbourne Cricket Ground, was the beginning of Aussie Rules.

There were 40 players a side, no behind posts (the outlying two posts the game now sports), and the ground was nearly a mile (1.6 km) long. The game started at noon and the players, who had to dodge gum trees in the paddock, kept going until dark. By then they had scored only one goal each so there was no winner.

They played again the following two Saturdays but neither side could score, so they abandoned the game. Now they have played a total of 262 times, with Scotch winning 76 games to Grammar's 74. There have been 112 draws.

Soccer, the only true international football code, was first played in Australia in 1870 by British coalminers. Organised soccer kicked off ten years later, when English school teacher WJ Fletcher formed the first club, the Wanderers. The first formal game was played against The King's School at Parramatta in August 1880, and 3 years later Australia was given affiliation to the Football Association.

In later years soccer was played mainly by migrants from Greece, Italy and Eastern Europe in clubs with foreign names like Prague, Marconi, Olympic and Apia-Leichhardt. Crowds increased at games and the code became a boom sport.

The national team, the Socceroos, reached the World Cup in 1965, but the vastly under-prepared players were well beaten by North Korea in two play-offs. The team again failed to make the finals in 1970, but made them in 1974 in West Germany.

In February 2003 the Socceroos excelled in front of chanting fans at Upton Park in London when they beat England 3-1 in a sport England thought Australia could never beat them at. A more hungry and dedicated Australian team punished England for their casual approach to the international friendly.

One of Australia's biggest losses in the history of international football came in June 1951, when the Socceroos were beaten 17-0 by a touring English FA XI at the Sydney Cricket Ground. It was one of seven one-sided matches between the two countries – Australia lost every one, conceding 55 goals and scoring only five.

Australia's goalie was Norman Conquest, who had conceded 30 goals in two matches in one week. He didn't play badly; there was just nothing he could do. Some players might have faked an injury to get off the field but he stuck it out, along with the crowd of 14,100 who had turned up to see England, the masters. The Socceroos were mere apprentices.

Probably the worst sporting team in Australia was the Robina Roos, an Aussie Rules outfit that won only one game out of 54 in three years. But the Gold Coast-based Roos maintained that they weren't in the competition for glory. They played for the love of the sport, friendship and hanging out together after their losses. Most of the blokes, who weren't paid and had names like Spooker, Tosser, Lappy and Lipper, just wanted to get out to have a kick.

A lot of the time they were short-handed, which didn't help their poor track record. Players often had to double up in the reserves, which had a slightly better record – they had two wins to their credit.

While the Roos were the perennial wooden spooners of their league, they made the most of their sole victory party: it lasted three days. Club secretary Glenda Brick, who started the club with her husband Les, believed the players had more heart than anyone else she had ever met. They lined up week after week for loss after loss without ever forfeiting, and that takes lots of guts.

Sports stars sometimes cash in their memorabilia when they need a bit of extra money, and they make thousands. In August 2001, Christies put up for auction a Sport in Australia collection of trophies and other treasures worth an estimated $2 million.

The collection included former Australian Test captain Greg Chappell's baggy green caps, bats, balls, stumps, personal correspondence, photographs and trophies, worth around $200,000.

The auction also offered a cricket bat autographed by both teams from the infamous Bodyline series of 1932–33 when England captain Douglas Jardine ordered his bowlers to aim at the batsmen's head or body to try to beat the Australians. One of the most sought after lots was a collection of trophies belonging to father and son racing drivers, Stan and Alan Jones. Alan won a Formula 1 world championship.

Auctioneer Michael Ludgrove believes there's a growing trend for sports stars to sell their stuff because 'they have to move on …' Shirley Strickland, the West Australian hurdler and sprinter who won more Olympic medals than any other woman athlete, competing in the 1948, 1952 and 1956 Olympics, sold her Olympic medals to raise money for her grandchildren. She died in early 2004.

Apparently Greg Chappell had no more room left in his house to keep his things. Ludgrove said Chappell travelled a lot and his memorabilia needed professional care, so he decided to sell everything off except a few portraits and things of personal significance. He even put up two personal letters from Don Bradman, which distressed Bradman's son John, who reckoned people should stop profiteering from his father's personal correspondence. The letters chastised Chappell for his comments to the press about World Series Cricket in 1977.

156

But sports-mad people, particularly those who yell abuse from the sidelines, could soon be banned under tough new guidelines set by the Australian Sports Commission, which is trying to make sport 'politically correct'. In another case of bureaucracy gone mad, sport police, or contact officers, could lay charges of harassment against supporters, coaches, administrators and players.

Players who back-answer referees or umpires, sledge in cricket or make any fired-up comments on the sporting field could find themselves fronting a tribunal. In extreme cases, the matter could be referred to the anti-discrimination boards or to police, with the matter ending up in court.

The commission's guidelines cover the legal and ethical obligations of sporting organisations with regard to harassment and racial, sexual and abusive behaviour. To be described as harassment, behaviour must be offensive, belittling or threatening; harassment can include jokes, parody and insults.

Most sportspeople say there's nothing wrong with a bit of yelling, and if it offends some spectators, they shouldn't go to games – particularly major events like State of Origin rugby league matches. Barracking for a team is a vital ingredient of sport, and a vocal crowd can often lift a team's performance, they say.

Coaches should also be on their guard. The guidelines suggest that they direct their comments at a player's performance rather than at the player, and that they should not use profane, insulting or otherwise naughty language. Derogatory or demeaning remarks about athletes must be avoided. And, according to the guidelines, coaches must always assume there are lesbian, gay and bisexual people in their teams and among coaching and support staff – even if they have not identified themselves.

21　Fore!

F our mates who played golf every Sunday morning asked a new member called Joe to fill in when one of them went on holidays. They arranged to hit off at 7.30 am. 'I'll be here, but I could be 15 minutes late,' Joe said. 'Wait for me.'

But Joe was there on time. He played right-handed, won the match with a fine 72, and agreed to fill in again at 7.30 am the following Sunday, but again added the proviso that he may be 15 minutes late. 'Wait for me if I am,' he said.

Sunday came and Joe was on the dot. This time he played left-handed, shot a 73 and won again.

'You OK for next Sunday?' one of them asked.

'Yes, but I could be 15 minutes late …'

'You keep saying you might be 15 minutes late but you've been on time every week and you still beat us, whether you play right or left-handed. What's the go?'

'Well,' Joe said. 'I'm superstitious. If I wake up and my wife is lying on her right side, I play right-handed. If she's on her left side, I play left-handed.'

'What if she's lying on her back?'

'Aah,' said Joe. 'That's when I'll be 15 minutes late.'

Let's face it. Golfers are a bloody funny lot and Australians are no exception. In the name of relaxation and wearing outlandish clothes, they wander around in small groups, belting the daylights out of little white balls with bent sticks, surrounded by hills, gum trees, grass, crows, sand, water, dozens of other players and millions of sticky bloody flies.

Mark Twain reckoned golf was a good walk spoiled. Winston Churchill said it was a game whose aim was to hit a very small ball into a very small hole, with weapons singularly ill-designed for the purpose. William Wordsworth believed that a day spent playing golf was a day spent in strenuous idleness.

Aussies reckon it's more like a love affair. If you don't take it too seriously, it can be fun. If you take it seriously, it can break your heart.

But the royal and ancient game still happens to be the most popular sport played by Australians. On average, around 385,000 people turn out in any two-week period, and 79 per cent of them are men. The Australian Golf Union estimates that members of our 1500 clubs play 36 million rounds every year.

And nothing, apparently, can stop them. Consultant surgeon Dr Frank Stening was playing in the 36 hole final of Bowral Golf Club's 1996 championship, on the south coast of NSW, when at the break he was called to the local hospital to perform an emergency appendectomy. After the patient was stitched up, he raced back to the course to hit off at 1.15 pm for the second 18 holes. He went on to win the championship two and one.

Then there was the player at The Lakes, in Sydney, who complained about the time it took him to finish 18 holes with his mate Fred. 'He had a heart attack and died on the 6th tee,' he said. 'And it was bloody tough going, I can tell you. Drag, hit, drag hit, drag hit …'

Golf has more than its share of hazards, too. Steven Shortens, a schoolboy, was playing a round with his friends at Grafton on the far north coast of NSW when he was attacked by a kangaroo. The teenager was searching for a ball when the big grey confronted him at the edge of the fairway, knocked him over, pinned him to the ground and gave him a few whacks across the face.

Golfing grannie Pauline Hunter was struck by lightning at the Tally Valley course at Tallebudgera on the Gold Coast – after telling a lightning joke against God. Approaching the 18th as a thunderstorm rolled in, Mrs Hunter asked her partners whether they had heard the joke about famous Mexican golfer Lee Trevino.

'He was going out to play in a thunderstorm and someone asked him if he was afraid of the lightning,' Mrs Hunter told them. '"Not really," Lee said. "If it gets too bad I'll just pull out a one iron and hold it up in the air. Not even God can hit a one iron properly."'

Minutes later there was a loud clap and Mrs Hunter, umbrella in one hand and an iron in the other, was knocked flying by a lightning bolt. 'The umbrella went up into the air like a balloon and I'm sure I saw the club glowing,' she said. 'I was terribly shaken.'

And there are all sorts of other hazards playing this silly game. A sign at Cairns Golf Club, in far north Queensland, says: 'Treat crocodiles as Ground Under Repair.' That means if your ball comes to rest near a crocodile, you drop it clear.

But the hazard to top them all comes from Maroochydore, on Queensland's

Sunshine Coast. A player was briefly stunned when a seagull dropped a 1 kg mullet on his head while he was playing in the Sunshine Open. To prove it wasn't another fish story, the club had the mullet stuffed and mounted.

Sometimes it's the golfers who are the hazards, as far as wildlife is concerned. Bruce Macfie reckons the odds must have been millions to one when he hit a mynah on the first hole at Pymble golf course in Sydney. And George Capsanis twice hit birds at Penrith, also in Sydney.

But Beryl Moore killed two ducks in one month on the Kambah course at Canberra. Her son David said she was traumatised by it. Especially when other club members nicknamed her 'Beryl the Duck Slayer'.

Generally, though, the most common injuries sustained in golf involve the hip pocket, rising blood pressure, losing a new ball while you've still got the crushed box in your pocket and falling off a bar stool at the 19th.

Understanding the rules also has more than its fair share of hazards. If there's a loose obstruction on the green, you can pick it up or brush it away with your hand or a club. But under no circumstances can you use your hat. And why can a golfer practise on the course before a matchplay competition but not before a stroke competition?

Playing at Sydney's Riverside Oaks course, David Richardson, of Strathfield, found that his Japanese partner, Mr Onohara, was perplexed at Rules of Play, No. 6: 'Staked or ornamental trees under two club lengths in height that interfere with the player's stance or swing must be lifted and dropped without penalty.' It seemed to him destructive – and besides, some of the trees would be hard to pull out!

Two West Australian players reckoned they had performed a golfing miracle with two holes-in-one with one shot. Brian Simpson had waited 50 years for his first ace, and it came in unique circumstances. His partner Bill Austin's shot on the 151 metre par 3 third at Busselton course, 200 km south of Perth, landed 10 centimetres from the cup. Brian, who commented that Bill had been slack to leave it short, hit his tee shot to the front edge of the green and it rolled into Bill's ball, knocking it in and then following it.

But Rule 18-5 says that if a ball in play and at rest is moved by another ball in motion after a stroke, the moved ball shall be replaced. Bill had to put his ball back where it was, 10 cm from the hole, and tap it in for a birdie. That's golf for you.

Australians are lucky because our courses are among the best – and worst – in the world, and they cater for all pockets, from the hackers who fork out $1 for a nine-hole round in a sheep paddock full of rabbit burrows and abandoned rusty cars to the multi-millionaires who consider $115 a bargain to play on the luxurious Mirage Country Club course at Port Douglas on the north coast of Queensland.

Port Douglas, designed by Australian golfer Peter Thomson, is a championship course and the original home of the Skins tournament in Australia. The six par 3s, six

4s and six 5s make up two distinctive nines: the journey out is known as the Reef Nine, because it is bordered by the Coral sea, and the trip home is known as the Mountain Nine.

Port Douglas now boasts the endorsement of former American President Bill Clinton, who had a couple of days there on a whirlwind visit to Australia. In his own words, he played 'some pretty good shots'. Earlier he had enjoyed 18 holes at the NSW Golf Club, at La Perouse in Sydney, with Greg Norman, another world-class Aussie golfer. The par 5 15th at NSW, which dog-legs through a dip between two hills, is one of Norman's favourite holes.

Australia's top courses include Royal Melbourne, Huntingdale, home of the Australian Masters, and Kingston Heath in Victoria. The natural elements – weather, vegetation and subsoil – combine to make the Melbourne sand belt great golfing country. In NSW, the New South Wales, the Australian, Royal Sydney and The Lakes are among the best, while in Queensland the top of the pick includes Kooralbyn Valley, Royal Queensland and Coolangatta Tweed.

But spare a thought for the enthusiastic golfers at Wyangala Dam, in central western NSW, who have a few extra hazards to contend with on their unique nine-hole course.

Privately built on Bruce and Robyn Anderson's Holsea property downstream from the irrigation dam wall, a round is made all the more difficult by rabbit burrows, washouts, millions of small white rocks that have a striking resemblance to golf balls, huge outcrops of boulders, long grass, grazing sheep, steep hills and the odd abandoned car. Yet on open days, up to 60 people brave the terrain to play the game of their lives.

Visiting golfers describe a game at Wyangala as an education, and say the members need a medal for their efforts and enthusiasm. A visitor one day said he heard two players arguing over the score. 'Down in five? I saw you take eight strokes,' one bloke said. 'Yeah,' his mate replied. 'But three were to kill the snake.'

The course was conceived at a barbecue on the property. Bruce Anderson, the inaugural club president, and his wife Robyn had invited a few friends over, including one regular golfer, Garry (Beau) Chapman. They were sitting around having a few cold tinnies when Beau pulled his clubs out of the car to belt a few balls.

They went out and used four rabbit dug-outs, about 60 or 80 metres apart, for holes. They played until dark, then they had a few more tinnies, got talking and reckoned they could put together a good course.

The next day Bruce and Beau walked around the paddock and drove eight pegs into the ground where they thought the greens should be. Beau borrowed a backhoe and they carted sand in from the nearby Lachlan River to make the greens. They scrounged old sump oil from every petrol station in the district to hold the sand together.

Originally there were eight holes and they played one twice to make up the nine, but on the opening day it was too confusing – players were coming and going everywhere – so they decided to put in the ninth hole.

Bruce believes the biggest hazard is the golf ball itself, but admits the rocks don't help. Players are meant to take a divot, but you can't do that at Wyangala because of the rocks. Beer is another hazard. And the old rabbit burrows and squats can also cause a few problems, but local rules allow you to lift your ball out provided you don't go closer to the hole.

Sheep are also a problem, but it's a sheep paddock, after all, and they keep the grass down on the fairways – the fairways can't be mown, of course, because that would destroy the feed for the sheep. Over a fence is out of bounds and dress regulations are simple: the local school teacher, who is also club captain, has to wear one long sock … and that's about it.

The par 33 course is 1800 metres long, but members reckon they walk double that distance in a round. There are no fees; the club just asks players to put a dollar in an honesty box on the first tee.

There are no tees for associates. The club believes in equal opportunities. Equal pay, equal tees, so women hit off from the same tee as the men.

And talking about tees, Bruce has perfected one of his own to stand up to the rigours of the Wyangala course. He got a plastic cork from a wine bottle and cut it off to the height he wanted. To stop the cork flying away, he tied a half-inch nut with about a foot (30 cm) of string on it. The tee has an added advantage: Bruce can put the nut in a position that gives him an angle to align his stance with.

The original open-fronted Wyangala clubhouse was about 3 metres by 7 metres, and made in true Aussie style – from stringybark posts and corrugated iron. Blue metal on the floor stopped the dust and a window at one end supplied extra light.

There was an outdoor barbecue for cooking the tucker, and an old fridge lying on its back and filled with ice kept the BYO beer cold. The toilets were donated by Meggsie Clements, another local larrikin. Who could ask for more?

Another top bush course is at Albert, a tiny speck on the map between Tullamore and Tottenham in western NSW. Few people other than golfers know how to get there, but when they descend on the 'Royal' Albert course for the annual Albert Open, the population of the village, usually around 30, more than trebles. Visitors say that words can't describe it. It's a golf day with the atmosphere of a picnic race meeting. They come and camp in tents across the road on the town common.

The par 70, 5772 metre, 18-hole course was built by voluntary labour inside the old Albert racetrack back in 1958. The only other course in the district – on Jumble Plains property – closed when the war started and was never reopened. The jockeys' rooms were used as the first clubhouse but they have since been replaced by a corrugated iron building with all modern comforts.

Members will tell you their sand greens are as good as grass, and professional golfer Rick L'Estrange once described them, tongue in cheek, as the best in the world. There are no hazards on the course other than a crow or two stealing balls and the likelihood of a ball landing in hoof marks or a rabbit burrow.

A group of crazy Gold Coast blokes hold an annual tournament in the front and back yards of their street – they call it the Jutland Classic. The 18-hole course takes in a tennis court, home driveways, a couple of gardens and a river. More than 30 golfers hack their way up and down the street before hitting across the river to a tennis court where they have to putt out under the net.

Organiser Neal King said the classic was an ideal excuse for old friends to get together. He also explained the very special rules: players have to drink a stubby of beer before teeing off from each hole. That's 18 beers for a round, and probably explains why some golfers never make it to the end.

One sliced a ball through a house window, leaving him with a difficult lie – on top of a double bed. He played it through the smashed window and back into the driveway. Thereafter he was nicknamed Crash.

There's yet another unique Aussie course, this time in outback South Australia. It has been carved out of the desert sands at Woomera, Australia's rocket town. Australia launched WRESAT (Weapons Research Establishment Satellite), a small scientific satellite, from Woomera in November 1967. This made Australia only the fourth country to launch its own satellite from its own territory, after the USSR, the US and France. The satellite, with its third-stage rocket motor still attached, was placed in a near-polar orbit by a US Redstone rocket.

Before that though, during World War II, the British had needed an area to test the rockets they planned to use to combat the German V2s and this chunk of outback desert northwest of Port Augusta fitted the bill. It was unpopulated and plenty big enough – perfect for a guided missile testing range. The population was as high as 7000 in those days.

The actual rocket range is 300 km wide and more than 2000 km long, extending all the way to the West Australian coast at Talgarno. Around 4000 rockets have been launched from Woomera, including the Redstone, the Spartan, Black Knights and Black Arrows, Seadarts and Skylarks, but almost all of this activity occurred between the war and the end of the 1960s. After that, the town almost died.

But recently there's been new interest in Woomera – from the Japanese, who want to use it for their $2 billion space shuttle program. Japan and Germany are already testing an Experimental Re-Entry Space System called EXPRESS there, and an American company, Kistler Aerospace, has launched its re-usable rockets there. The little town is looking to the future with glee.

About 1100 people live at Woomera now, about 40 per cent of them Americans. They have been allowed to bring in their own cars, on US Air Force cargo planes, and they get to watch their own satellite television. The town has excellent facilities, including squash and tennis courts, a 10-lane bowling alley, a 600-seat theatre, 14 active clubs, a 70-bed hospital, an RSL bowling club, a swimming pool, two ovals for football, cricket and baseball, netball and basketball courts, a youth centre built by the US Air Force, and the famous golf course!

Woomera Golf Club combines with nearby Roxby Downs to stage the annual Eldo Desert Classic, billed as the ultimate desert adventure. And that's pretty true. The course is set in the red sand among the saltbush, so most shots faced are fried eggs – balls buried in the sand. But that doesn't deter anyone, and big fields of players head to Woomera each year from all directions.

Another course where blades of grass are as scarce as hen's teeth is Bourke, in western NSW. Players can tee up if they want to, but the experts would rather take advantage of a 15 cm preferred lie (which means they can move their ball out of a hole), hoping there's a tuft of weeds or an ant hill close by to get their ball off the bare red dirt on the fairway.

Getting to the neighbouring Wanaaring golf course would test even the keenest hacker. It's a three-hour trip on a track that's only passable in dry weather. But along the way there are emus, kangaroos, goats, pigs, wedge-tailed eagles and cockatoos – which you won't see on your way to any other golf course in the world.

The club has good advice for visiting players: 'Stick to the fairways. The scrub is a shocker.' But like other bush courses, losing a ball is pretty hard to do. It stands out on the red dirt like a shag on a rock. Most of the time, it's snakes that you need to be on the lookout for!

And while most bush courses are like a magnet for golfers, it's a wonder anyone bothers to turn up for the annual club championship at Lyndhurst, in NSW's central west. They might as well give the trophy to Berry Lees and adjourn to the 19th hole for the day, because odds are he'll win it.

In fact, he's won the championship 47 consecutive times between 1956 and 2003 and 48 times in all, a feat nobody in the world has matched. The only other golfer to have come close is Richard Fewster, of Bandee Golf Club at Merredin, in Western Australia, with 36 consecutive titles between 1956 and 1992.

Berry has also won 27 club championships at the Sunny Ridge Golf Club at neighbouring Mandurama, where he works as manager, and son Tony has won it seven times. Keeping things in the family, Berry and daughter Anne take out more than their share of mixed foursomes championships. And he's partnered his wife Jan, who has won the associates' title, to win the mixed foursomes at Sunny Ridge.

Just to round things off, Berry has broken the course record at 11 NSW country clubs, including Hay, where he took it from Bruce Devlin, a highly successful pro golfer, with a three under par 69. He was also the first player to par the Oberon course. A left-hander who still plays off five but describing himself as a social golfer, he has an overall tally of more than 380 open events to his credit since he began playing in the early 1950s.

Berry always turns up for a major tournament in a collar and tie – because he says golf is a game for gentlemen – and believes a good bottle of overproof rum is the secret of his success. He seldom hits off without one in the bag, and then it's a tot at every tee; he says it helps soothe the nerves and keeps him straight down the middle. That's probably why he seems to play better as the day goes on.

Berry's problem is finding partners to play 18 holes with him. As soon as they hear the glasses clinking in the bag they make some feeble excuse … he thinks it's really because they can't handle their liquor. 'I don't really blame them, though, because it's usually a case of woe betide the silly bugger who comes with me. They're mostly a bit wobbly on their feet by the time we finish.'

In his younger days, Berry considered becoming a professional, but decided to stay on the family farm. He played a lot of golf in Sydney, with reasonable scores, but wasn't able to spend the time on golf that he would have needed to break into the big time.

Back on the course at Lyndhurst he'd practise on one hole all afternoon until he knew it backwards. Then he'd move to the next, where he'd do the same thing. It's easy to see why he's held the course record since 1959. The locals say he can go around with two irons and a putter and still finish under par. What's more amazing is the fact that they still turn up for the annual club championships, even though Berry winning it is a foregone conclusion.

Berry can hit a ball blindfolded. It's one of his tricks at charity golf days, when there's a registered bookmaker on the course, and always guarantees some easy money.

He can still put the ball on the green in one shot, and reckons all good golfers should be able to do the same. The secret, he says, is in the swing and comes from years of practice. He tells a story about a golfer who was having a terrible round. Then on the 18th he put his ball in the middle of a dam. Disgusted, he told his caddie to keep the clubs, because he was going to walk into the dam and drown himself. 'Bet you can't,' the caddie said. 'You'll never be able to keep your head down long enough …'

Patience plays a big part in golf. And one of the most patient people is solicitor Graham Billing, who spent ten years trying to convince the world's top players that a putter he developed in his backyard workshop could improve their game. But he's the first to admit now that he seems to have lost the battle. He went to America six times to visit pro-am tournaments, giving away dozens of the putters, and visited the Orlando Golf Show, but had little success convincing people of its worth.

American golfer Tom Watson used one in the 1991 Masters – but then sold it for US$575 at an auction in Kansas City to raise money for junior golfers. Watson putted well with the Ugly Duckling, as it was then called, but took a lot of flak from other golfers because of the putter's unusual T-shape design.

Graham, who has a legal practice at Orange, in central western NSW, has also given the putter to Greg Norman, who used it briefly in a Skins tournament, Jack Nicklaus, Seve Ballesteros and Bernhard Langer. He even gave one to Clint Eastwood, who he reckoned 'quite liked it …

'They all seemed happy with the putter, but they never used it long enough to form a proper opinion,' he said. 'And I can never talk to them afterwards. They all say, "Yeah, I'll let you know how it goes" but I can never find out.

'Langer was really keen but was always having putting problems and didn't really give it a fair go. Steve Conran, an Australian amateur champion, used one and won the Singapore Open with it. He's the best success I've had.'

Graham, who has put a lot of effort into promoting the putter, said it could well be one of those good ideas that is just not going to take off. 'I haven't given up, but I'm afraid I'm going to put it on the back burner for a while. The big manufacturers have copied some of the same principles – the balance and the shaft in the centre – and are making them with materials that are more up to date than the brass and aluminium I use. It's a disappointment, but then that's life.'

Many other people have tried to cash in on the huge golfing market by inventing all sorts of weird and wonderful things designed to add an extra 20 metres to their drive or take off a few valuable strokes.

And golfers who occasionally feel the need for divine intervention on the course might like to know that a Queensland priest has just the thing. Father John Hayes, of Blackall, in Queensland, made a set of rosary beads from golf balls that had been 'lost' on different courses. They were joined with a chain that went through holes drilled in the centres. But Father Hayes wasn't a golfer, so there was no need for players to worry about him having an unfair advantage on the course.

A Brisbane company used to sell a gadget called the Gopher, which found lost balls, saving strokes and money. It detected the molecular structure of the balls and was energised by static electricity generated while the golfer was walking. Just like a magnetic compass needle, which always points to the North Pole, the Gopher's direction-finding antenna always pointed in the direction of hidden golf balls.

When it's all boiled down, Aussies have done pretty well at golf. And they start young. Daniel Buczko was only three days from his seventh birthday when he holed in one on the 125 metre 4th at Gawler, in South Australia, in April 1989. He's the youngest player to do so in Australia.

The youngest champion was Harry Williams, who won the 1931 Australian Amateur title when he was 16. Country boy Brad McIntosh, from Dubbo in western NSW, became the youngest player to win an open junior event when he took out the Ross Law Memorial Cup at Armidale when he was 12. And Aaron Baddeley, when he was 15, was the youngest player to make the 36-hole cut in the history of the 1997 Victorian Open, an event that's been won by Greg Norman and Peter Thomson.

Encouraged by her grandfather, Karrie Webb started playing golf as an eight-year-old, and in her teens used to practise by hitting balls into a 1.5 metre circle of witches' hats on a makeshift practice fairway at the Ayr Golf Club in northern Queensland. She is now regarded as one of the best golfers in the world.

She was the first woman golfer to win US$1 million in a season and the first rookie to be the leading money winner in the US Ladies Professional Golfers Association Tour Championship. In 2001, at 26, she became the youngest LPGA player to win a grand slam, taking out the Australian Masters, US Open and Australian LPGA championship. Karrie fired a two under par 69 final round, a championship in Delaware in the US, and then made a mercy dash back to Australia to see her sick grandfather – unfortunately, she was several hours too late. She dedicated the win to him.

The oldest player to hole in one was Cyril Winser, on the 133 metre 8th at Barwon Heads, in Victoria, a week before his 91st birthday in 1975. The oldest women players to get aces were Kaye Kearney at North Adelaide in 1982 and Margaret Hart at Beaudesert, in Queensland, in January 1990. Both were 81.

The biggest winning margin in a major Australian event was recorded by Eric Cremin, when he won the 1946 Queensland Open at Brisbane Golf Club by 19 strokes, with a score of 282.

The world record fastest round was played by 70 Melbourne golfers: 18 holes at the Sunshine Golf Club in 10 minutes 52 seconds. When a ball was putted out, another was teed up and driven from the next tee. No score was kept, but the 35 professionals and 35 amateurs who set the record didn't lose a ball.

Well, that's golf and golfers. Huge parcels of perfectly good land have been taken over by these unpredictable people and their bags of high-tech sticks. And summer TV is wrecked by visions of ooohing and aaahing people with umbrellas following their every move.

Let's face it. Those bored shepherds hundreds of years ago who amused themselves belting around a few rocks with their crooks to fill in their day – or whoever else dreamt up this ridiculous game – have a lot to answer for. As comedian Jack Benny once said: 'Give me golf clubs, the fresh air and a beautiful partner and you can keep my golf clubs and the fresh air.'

22 Aussie kulture

The Sydney Symphony Orchestra planned a fundraising concert but the pianist took sick at the last minute and couldn't play. There was a big panic until the conductor phoned an old bloke who 35 years before had played with leading orchestras throughout the country. He was a bit the worse for wear – he'd fallen on hard times and now had a drinking problem – but he was their only hope.

He turned up on the night in his old tuxedo, plopped down on the piano stool and split the back seam of his trousers wide open, much to the horror of the people in the audience. 'Do you know your arse is bare?' the leader of the second violins whispered. 'No,' said the old bloke. 'But if you hum the tune, I'll soon pick it up.'

When Paul Keating was leading the country, he warned Australians about the dangers of moving from the cultural cringe to the cultural swagger. The cringe was the traditional belief that Australians came a poor second to everyone from overseas. That applied to people like musicians, singers, actors, artists and designers.

The cultural swagger was exactly the opposite. Australians in the 1990s began to think they were the best in the world at everything they did and had nothing to learn from anyone else. Neither the cringe nor the swagger is really appropriate, of course. But there are a few fields in which we can afford to skite. Cinema, as we saw earlier, is probably one of them.

Peter Allen, the singing pianist born at Tenterfield in northern NSW – and who was married for a while to Liza Minnelli – composed a sort of unofficial national anthem with his hit *I Still Call Australia Home*, while Kylie Minogue, dubbed the singing budgerigar, went on to bigger things in London after getting her start in the TV soap *Neighbours*.

Artists have also made names for themselves. A world record price of $2,312,500 was paid for an Australian painting by Frederick McCubbin called 'Bush Idyll'. Bidding for the painting at the Christie's auction started at $1.2 million! Other icons of Australian art include William Dobell, Sidney Nolan, Russell Drysdale and Norman Lindsay.

Lindsay waged a non-stop battle for 50 years with the wowsers who found his paintings of well-endowed women obscene. One painting, called 'Crucified Venus', caused such a stir when it went on exhibition in Sydney in 1912 that it was turned face to the wall.

Pro Hart is a modern-day artist whose talent developed while he worked in the mines in the NSW outback city of Broken Hill after leaving school. Pro, short for professor, is a nickname he picked up early in life because of his interest in everything mechanical. He loves to paint using cannons and old muskets – he puts all the colours in tiny balls and fires them onto the canvas.

There are lots of lesser artistic lights, and some of these are the real characters of Aussie kulture. Like Ron Clarke, who never quite made it in the painting world. He threw away his brushes for an oxyacetylene torch and began cutting pictures out of steel. Whatever he could create with a brush, he reckoned he could also do with the torch. But he didn't think people realised he could get a picture out of a lump of steel – a picture that would be functional, require little maintenance and last forever.

Ron, who lived in a closed motel on the Sturt Highway at Darlington Point, in southern NSW, used an old 44 gallon drum in the yard as a work bench when making his murals and signs. His parents ran out of money there while the family was on the way to Coober Pedy (in South Australia) in 1957 and they stayed put. There was nothing there then. Not even a tree. The family built a truckies' roadhouse, sold it later to the oil company and built a motel. But things changed. People wanted to stay in a town, so Ron closed the motel and moved in. It was a good base for his business.

Ron's biggest mural was a 3.6 metre Hereford bull for a stud farmer. He also made horses, busts of film star, trucks, Harley-Davidson motorcycles and company and farm signs. On average he received around $350 for his pieces. He reckoned he could probably make small things for tourists for around $30 or $40, but he said they wouldn't have any real value. 'I'm a bloody artist, mate. I don't want to flood the market with junk.'

A group of sculptors spent weeks hacking away at huge chunks of rock on a desert mountain top near Broken Hill, creating a sort of offbeat memorial to the late great eye surgeon Fred Hollows. They lined up their 4.2 metre monoliths with two peaks in the distant Pinnacle Mountains and Fred Hollows' grave at Bourke.

The sculptors, who came from all around the world – Georgia, Damascus, Syria, Mexico, Bathurst Island, Broken Hill, Katoomba and Gosford – spent eight weeks on the project. They reckon that besides being a fitting tribute to Fred, they resurrected the area's 30,000-year-old stone carving tradition. They carted the sandstone blocks, which weighed up to eight tonnes each, 195 km from Wilcannia.

Project boss Lawrence Beck said setting the blocks up on the mountain without cranes was an epic of skill and strength from the local people that was 'worthy of the ancient Egyptians ...' And Broken Hill, in his opinion, was a hero city for putting on a show like it.

The 12 sculptors, who camped on the site, were also heroes, he said, working away at their rock for 14 hours a day – and for the last two weeks they were living on nerves alone, because they were absolutely buggered.

A roadside sculpture made from slate, rock, mosaic tiles, glass and twisted steel girders from a collapsed bridge has travellers scratching their heads as they head into the NSW country town of Wellington on the Mitchell Highway.

The controversial sculpture, costing more than $80,000 and commissioned by Wellington Council, was intended to be an eye-catching gateway to the town. But townspeople argue that the money could have been better spent elsewhere. The council says the money, most of it from government grants, was designated for specific projects and if the sculpture was to be built, it had to be done properly.

Fran Ferguson, the artist who built it, looked at a few other ideas before coming up with the idea of using the steel girders from the Mitchell Highway bridge which collapsed into the Macquarie River in January 1989. Fran died in 2003.

Besides seven totems built from slate, the main structure is a tripod-shaped curve made from the girders to create the feeling of a cave. Massive wind chimes hang from the tripod – they are designed to look like stalactites from the nearby Wellington Caves. There's a windmill on top to pump water, and solid glass inserts in holes in the totems reflect light from the sun in the afternoon.

One of the main aims of the project was to involve the community, and Fran's design did that by giving three young Aborigines work for two days a week during its construction.

But there was heaps of controversy. A lot of people didn't like it and a cockatoo motif in the original design was taken out because it caused an outcry. However, people changed their tune when it was finished.

Ian Bartholomew, a creative arts graduate in woodworking, lives on a small timbered block at Hayes Gap, near Mudgee in central western NSW. When he first moved there, he didn't even own a hammer and chisel, so he used his chainsaw to carve out several chairs and a table from the ironbark logs on the block – and a new career was born.

People liked what he made, so he put some of the work in a shop in Mudgee and it sold well. He kept making things.

He had always made things out of wood, and he had intended to go into that after university; using a chainsaw instead of conventional tools just happened because it was all he had at the time. His only previous experience with a chainsaw had been cutting firewood.

Once he used up most of the dead trees on his block, he had to buy yellow box and ironbark logs from a neighbouring property owner, who also milled the fallen timber into slabs. Ironbark wood is very long-lasting and looks good – and there's lots of it around. Yellow box also suits his purpose and stands up to a beating from the weather. He also buys timber from old buildings and sheds.

When Glenn Morton sits at his easel to paint, he keeps the attention of his models by feeding them wheat. Glenn paints chooks. And the colourful oils attract so much interest that he's flat out keeping up with demand.

But it's a pastime the artist thoroughly enjoys. There's also the added advantage of not having to drive long distances to find landscapes. He just ducks out the back to his chook yard, where he has dozens of clucking and crowing models only too happy to co-operate. He paints them and the wire netting and orange trees … everything he sees in the yard.

He sits outside with a tin of wheat; he just keeps slinging some to them and they mill around. That way he always gets the chooks in a natural setting. But he can also paint them in his studio. They're so quiet they'll pose on a table beside him.

Capturing chooks on oils came about by accident for Glenn. Bad weather one day stopped him going out to work on a landscape – landscapes are still a major part of his work – so to fill in time, he painted one of his chooks. A Sydney woman liked it so much she bought it. That's how it began, and now he sells as many as he wants.

The Bald Archy Prize, a highlight of the Festival of Fun held at Coolac, a small village on the Hume Highway just out of Gundagai in southern NSW, is one of the most eccentric events on the Australian arts calendar. A less serious alternative to the better-known Archibald, the Bald Archy has only been around for a few years, but already attracts entries from all over the nation.

The rules say that portraits must be of Australians noted in the arts, science, politics, the media or sport. The inaugural Bald Archy had 14 Paul Keatings,11 Bronwyn Bishops and three Ros Kellys. The eventual winner was a portrait of the director of the NSW Art Gallery, Edmund Capon, and titled 'Yuk'.

The entries are put on show in the corrugated iron community hall, which for the duration of the exhibition becomes the National Gallery of Coolac. 'People going past on the highway stop and have a look and reckon the Bald Archy is better than the real thing,' says theatre director and playwright Peter Batey (the organiser).

'The entries, which come from a mixture of artists and cartoonists, are judged by a panel of five people who prefer to remain anonymous. But I take a selection of the paintings to Sydney for exhibition, just to cause a stir.'

Batey, who has been involved with the theatre in a whole range of activities since he completed Melbourne University's drama course, lives in an old school house at

Coolac. He did his national service training with Barry Humphries and later, as a foundation member of the Melbourne Theatre Company, helped create that glittery old exhibitionist, Dame Edna Everage.

It goes without saying that Dame Edna is a patron of the Coolac Festival of Fun, which has featured performances under the stars by a string of local celebrities, including Nancye Hayes, Elspeth Ballantyne and the late Leonard Teale. Batey for years directed the Reg Livermore shows, but eventually found his way to Coolac, where he opened a Devonshire tea café cum restaurant and a nursery called The Potted Dog to get a cash flow going.

'It's a good village. Had three pubs once and a general store. Henry Lawson and Banjo Paterson even stayed here a couple of times,' he says. 'But there wasn't much going on. The people in the district face droughts, bushfires, floods and famine and I thought they needed a bit of fun – that's why I got the festival going.'

And finally, a chapter on Aussie kulture would not be complete without Sir Les Patterson, aka Barry Humphries, who has made a career out of drinking, smoking and bludging. He doesn't have any problems handling fame. He likes it up there. It suits him, being recognised.

23 'Waltzing Matilda'

Once a jolly swagman camped by a billabong
Under the shade of a coolibah tree
And he sang as he watched and waited 'til his billy boiled
'You'll come a-waltzing Matilda with me.'

Chorus: *Waltzing Matilda, waltzing Matilda,*
You'll come a waltzing Matilda with me
And he sang as he watched and waited 'til his billy boiled
You'll come a-waltzing Matilda with me

Down came a jumbuck to drink at the billabong
Up jumped the swagman and grabbed him with glee
And he sang as he stuffed that jumbuck in his tucker-bag
'You'll come a-waltzing Matilda with me.'

Chorus

Up rode the squatter, mounted on his thoroughbred
Up rode the troopers, one, two, three
'Where's that jolly jumbuck you've got in your tucker-bag?
You'll come a-waltzing Matilda with me.'

Chorus

Up jumped the swagman and sprang into that billabong
'You'll never take me alive!' said he
And his ghost may be heard as you pass by that billabong
'You'll come a-waltzing Matilda with me.'

Chorus

In the gold rush days of the 1850s, men hoping to strike it rich wrapped a few belongings in a swag and walked to the diggings. When they failed to make their fortune, many 'waltzed Matilda', which simply meant taking to the road humping their swag in search of work.

A swag was usually made from a tent fly or strip of calico (which doubled as a shelter in bad weather), a couple of blue blankets, spare clothing and a few personal effects, rolled up in the core. The origin of the word Matilda is not clear, but it is believed to come from a German word.

It was Andrew Barton 'Banjo' Paterson who made the swagmen famous with the words of Australia's best-known song, 'Waltzing Matilda', which he wrote in 1895 (see Chapter 9, 'The Man from Snowy River').

The managers of the station, the Macpherson family, told him Robert Macpherson had come across an itinerant shearer named Samuel Hoffmeister camped under a coolabah tree beside nearby Combo waterhole on the Diamantina River. The story goes he had killed a sheep and put it in his tuckerbag for lunch.

Hoffmeister had apparently been implicated in a fire that destroyed a shearing shed on the property and was being hunted by three troopers and the property owner. When he saw them riding up and afraid of being shot, he jumped into the billabong and drowned. That's probably the most popular version.

Sitting on the verandah at Dagworth, Paterson listened to Christina Macpherson play an old Scottish song called the Craigielee March on an autoharp. She had picked up the tune from the town band at the Warrnambool races in Victoria in April, 1894.

Paterson liked it so much he scribbled down some words about the unfortunate shearer who he made a swaggie and after several rowdy sessions at the piano at the North Gregory Hotel at Winton, he and Miss Macpherson came up with 'Waltzing Matilda'. Militant shearers later adopted the song for their rallies but changed some of the words to 'you'll never take me alive, said he' to add defiance.

James Inglis, the distributor of Billy Tea, had the music and lyrics rewritten in 1903 to make the swagman 'jolly' so he could use the song as an advertising jingle. You can still pass by the billabong, which is now on Belfast Station, once a part of Dagworth, although you face a fair walk and millions of bloody flies.

But Richard Magoffin, of Kynuna, in central western Queensland, where Banjo Paterson wrote the poem, says the idea that the poem is about a swaggie is a lot of cock and bull. One of his versions is that 'Waltzing Matilda' is all about the rebellion in the wool industry.

A self-titled bush anarchist, he has made a lifetime study of the song, and he reckons it's an allegory, not the silly story it pretends to be. It isn't about a man who shoves a sheep in a sugar bag and then commits suicide in a shallow muddy pool while three policemen and a squatter just stand there and let the poor bugger drown.

It's a freedom song, he says, affirming the rights of an individual in a free society. And a reply by Paterson to Henry Lawson's 'Freedom on the Wallaby'.

Neither is the jumbuck one sheep. It represents bankers' and squatters' property which the union attacked; the tuckerbag is the living wage; and the swagman invites people to go waltzing with him in a journey to freedom, to fairness, to democracy, to the vote.

Even today, people see that three policemen and a squatter on one swagman is not fair. 'That's why I call it the ballad of a fair go,' Magoffin says.

He also disputes that the song was sung in public for the first time at the North Gregory Hotel in Winton, Queensland on 6 April 1895; he reckons it was the Post Office Hotel, further down the main street. He reckons they changed it because the Post Office Hotel was too far away from the shops to cash in on tourism!

There are also claims that the song was sung first at the Blue Heeler pub at Kynuna after Paterson had settled the shearers' strike. They say champagne was passed through a servery window and everyone got stuck into it.

But Winton has a $3.3 million Waltzing Matilda Centre to capitalise on the town's claim as the birthplace of the song. However, the Victorian town of Warrnambool has also staked a claim as 'Waltzing Matilda's birthplace.

There's a sign at the racecourse pointing out the fact that the band there was the first to play the old Scottish tune Christina Macpherson originally picked up and played to Paterson on her autoharp, but it's drawing a bit of a long bow. If that logic was followed, then Scotland might well be called 'Waltzing Matilda's birthplace.

'Waltzing Matilda' has long been regarded as Australia's unofficial national anthem, but it was always pretty low-key – until the 2003 Rugby World Cup. The International Rugby Board tried to put the knockers on fans singing the song at matches, but they failed.

Sydney's *Daily Telegraph* took up the challenge and promoted the song like never before. The newspaper's stand was backed by everyone from Prime Minister John Howard and NSW Premier Bob Carr down.

It urged fans to sing it after the national anthem, 'Advance Australia Fair', and every time the Wallabies scored or looked like scoring. In the Wallabies' semi-final against the New Zealand All Blacks, the huge crowd united for a haka-busting rendition of 'Waltzing Matilda' that was so loud the referee had to delay the start of the game until the song was over because the players couldn't hear him.

In the two days leading up to the final, between the Wallabies and England, there was a 'Waltzing Matilda' flood, with singers leading the way in public places like Sydney's Martin Place. Three hours before kick-off, radio stations and live TV sites across Australia had a national singalong of 'Matilda'.

Things came a little unstuck at the final, because half the 83,000 fans there were Poms, and their regular renditions of 'Swing Low, Sweet Chariot' almost did a job on 'Waltzing Matilda'. But the Aussies stuck to their guns and Australia's unofficial national anthem eventually won out – although the Wallabies lost the game.